A CLASSICAL AND BIBLICAL
REFERENCE BOOK

Greece and the Aegean.

A CLASSICAL AND BIBLICAL REFERENCE BOOK

H. A. TREBLE, M.A.

LONDON
JOHN MURRAY, ALBEMARLE STREET, W. 1

First Edition . . . 1948

Printed in Great Britain by
C. Tinling & Co., Ltd., Liverpool, London, and Prescot.

PREFACE

In his inaugural lecture delivered at Queen Mary College, University of London, Professor Sutherland describes how on one occasion he put to his students a number of questions designed to test their knowledge of (among other things) Classical Mythology and the Bible. " The results," he says, " were startling." There were twelve questions in the Classical section and the average score was three. The response to the ten questions on the Bible was much the same. From this he deduces that the general decay in classical education has left the student, whether undergraduate or schoolboy, with a real difficulty in the understanding and appreciation of English literature which is, at any rate up to the end of the eighteenth century, rich in Classical and Biblical allusions. Referring more especially to the Classics, Professor Sutherland concludes that a shift from the strong classical bias of the eighteenth-century school curriculum " has left the twentieth-century reader less well-equipped to respond to those literary associations on which our poets and prose writers were accustomed to play."

It is in recognition of this fact that the present book has been prepared. Few readers of to-day could take the opening scene of the fifth act of *The Merchant of Venice* in their stride : Troilus and Cressida, Thisbe and Dido, Medea and Aeson are names that have an immediate significance only to those who are familiar at first hand with Ovid's *Metamorphoses* and the *Aeneid* of Virgil. Fewer still could travel comfortably and confidently through *Lycidas*. The direct allusions as well as the indirect echoes of the Bible in which English literature abounds may well be lost on a generation which tends, for the most part, to forsake the reading of the Bible.

This book then has been designed as a friend and guide to those who, handicapped by that lack of cultural background which might have been their heritage two centuries ago, are anxious to appreciate their native literature to the full. If in addition it arouses in them a new interest in Classical Mythology and the Bible so much the better. For all such it will at least fulfil a need : I can only hope it will do more.

No excuse is needed for combining in one book associations scriptural and classical. Out of the wealth of his knowledge both of the Bible and of the classics of Greece and Rome, Milton saw fit to blend pagan and Christian ideas in his great poems.

The book is based largely on two standard works of reference : Smith's *Smaller Classical Dictionary* (revised by G. E. Marindin) and Murray's *Illustrated Bible Dictionary*. My thanks are due to Mr. Murray for permission to use these two works. I have consulted several other standard works, always with profit : *The Oxford Companions to English Literature* and to *Classical Literature*, both by Sir Paul Harvey ; Dr. Brewer's *Dictionary of Phrase and Fable;* Weekley's *Etymological Dictionary of Modern English;* the *Concise Oxford Dictionary*.

7

It remains for me to express my warmest thanks to Mr. H. E. Wilmott (indeed the book is born of a casual remark he dropped) and to Mr. J. N. Britton, both of whom have been greatly interested and most helpful at every stage in the preparation of the book. " At the eleventh hour " Mr. G. Irwin-Carruthers most kindly offered to read the manuscript. He corrected many errors of which I had been guilty and gave me much additional information and illustration— all of which I have incorporated with profit to the book. I offer him my most sincere thanks. Of course, for any errors that still remain I, and I alone, am responsible.

H.A.T.

CANTERBURY,
    June, 1948.

LIST OF MAPS

A CLASSICAL AND BIBLICAL REFERENCE BOOK

Aaron's Rod. Besides being the symbol of travel in the East, the rod is frequently an emblem of authority. Aaron's rod played an important part in the miraculous events that preceded the Exodus from Egypt (see *Ex.* 7$^{8-12}$). For " Aaron's rod that budded " see *Numb.* 17$^{2-11}$. Twelve rods, the name of a tribe inscribed on each (with the exception of *Aaron* for Levi), were deposited in the Tabernacle for a night. In the morning it was found that Aaron's rod had put forth buds, blossoms and ripe almonds. This sign was taken as a vindication of his pre-eminence over Korah, Dathan and Abiram who had rebelled against Aaron, and as proof of the right of his family to the priesthood. According to St. Paul Aaron's rod was afterwards kept *in* the ark.

Abigail, a lady's maid. Most likely the name came ultimately from that of the wife of Nabal, the churlish but wealthy owner of goats and sheep in Carmel. When David's messengers were slighted by Nabal, Abigail took the blame upon herself, supplied David and his men with provisions and thus appeased his anger. Ten days later Nabal died and David made Abigail his wife (1 *Sam.* 25).

More directly the name is derived from that of the waiting gentlewoman in Beaumont and Fletcher's play *The Scornful Lady* (1616). Readers will find Miss Dorothy

Margaret Stuart's light, but learned and exhaustive story of the Maids of Yesterday, *The English Abigail*, most acceptable reading.

Abraham's Bosom, the Heaven of the Christian. Lazarus was carried by the angels into Abraham's bosom (*Luke* 16^{22}), i.e. he died and was received among the blessed.

In classical times it was the custom to recline on a friend's bosom while dining. Hence ' bosom friend.' See *John* 13^{23} : " Now there was leaning on Jesus' bosom one of his disciples whom Jesus loved," i.e. St. John himself.

The Hostess (in *Henry V* ii, 3) protests that the dead Falstaff is " not in hell, he's in Arthur's bosom if ever man went to Arthur's bosom." She evidently knew the Arthur of Celtic romance better than the Abraham of the O.T.

Abraham's Supreme Test. We read : " God did tempt (i.e. test, prove) Abraham " who was commanded to take his only son Isaac, the son of his old age, and offer him on Mount Moriah for a burnt offering. The journey to the mountain took two days after which Abraham and his son ascended alone. Abraham took the wood of the burnt offering and laid it on Isaac : he took the fire in his hand, and a knife. Isaac naturally asked where the lamb for the sacrifice was and his father's reply was " God

will provide himself a lamb."
Then Abraham bound Isaac on the
altar and took the knife in his hand.
At that moment the angel of the
Lord intervened : Abraham's faith
had been proved. Abraham saw a
ram caught in a thicket by his
horns and this ram took the place
of Isaac as the sacrifice to God.
Such sacrifices were possible only
in a time and place where they were
regarded as the test of a father's
obedience to oracles of God. Abraham obeys, and by the result God's
character is more fully revealed
and the sacredness of human life is
affirmed.

Absalom, the third son of David,
a man of great personal beauty,
the darling of his father and the
idol of the people. He killed
Amnon at the sheepshearing at
Bethhazor, was exiled in consequence but recalled through the
intercession of Joab's instrument,
the wise woman of Tekoa. Restored after two years' seclusion,
Absalom used the popularity he
had never lost to foster sedition.
When all was ready, he rebelled.
David, whose influence had waned,
was forced to flee over the Jordan.
Ahitophel and most of David's
great men joined Absalom who
entered the capital and the death
struggle with his father began.
Absalom, having been crowned,
after some delay crossed the Jordan
and was decisively beaten in the
wood of Ephraim. As he turned
to flee, he was caught by the head
in a ' great oak ' and his mule went
off from under him. Learning that
he was hanging there Joab killed
him with his own hand, in spite of
David's prohibition. When the
news was brought to him by runner,
David forgot all and uttered the
familiar and pathetic lamentation :
" O my son Absalom, my son, my
son Absalom ! Would God I had

died for thee ! " Absalom's body
was cast into a pit and, perhaps a
mark of bitter contempt, was
covered with great stones by the
soldiers.
The full story of his rebellion and
tragic death is given in 2 *Sam.* 13-18.

Absy´rtus, son of Aeë´tes, king of
Colchis, and brother of Mēdēa. He
was taken by Jason and Medea on
their flight from Colchis, and was
murdered by Medea and his body
cut in pieces and thrown in the
path of her pursuing father to
delay him.

Abȳ´dos, a town of the Troad on
the Hellespont, the birthplace of
Leander. He swam nightly across
the mile-wide strait to visit Hero
in Sestos. He perished one stormy
night and next morning Hero
drowned herself.
See Byron's *Bride of Abydos.*
The late A. E. Housman's poignant
lines are apposite :

" By Sestos town, in Hero's
    tower,
On Hero's heart Leander lies ;
The signal torch has burned its
    hour
And sputters as it dies.

Beneath him, in the nighted firth,
Between two continents complain
The seas he swam from earth to
    earth
And he must swim again."
                    (*Last Poems,* xv.)

Acadē´mia, a grove near Athens,
originally belonging to the demi-
god Academus. Here Plato founded his school of philosophy and
hence he and his followers were
called the Academic philosophers.
' Academy ' is the name given to
learned assemblies for promoting
arts and sciences such as *The British
Academy* founded in 1899, *Académie
Française* founded in 1635 by

Richelieu, *The Royal Academy of Arts*, the headquarters of which is Burlington House.

We use the adjective ' academic ' to mean scholastic and (sometimes) pedantic.

Aceldama. When the traitor Judas threw the thirty pieces of silver, his reward for the betrayal of Christ, down in the temple, the priest could not put the money in the treasury as it was the price of blood. So with it the chief priests bought the potter's field " to bury strangers in." The name of this field, in the Jews' " proper tongue," is " Aceldama, that is to say, the field of blood."

See *St. Matthew's Gospel* 27³⁻⁸, and *The Acts* 1¹⁹.

Achae'ī, a brave warlike race, the first Hellenic invaders of Greece. Homer calls the Greeks in general Achaeans : similarly, the Peloponnesus (and sometimes the whole of Greece) is called Achaia. The Greeks called themselves ' Hellēnes,' i.e. descendants of Hellēn, son of Deucalion.

Achā'tēs, the trusty squire and friend of Aeneas. His fidelity has become proverbial as that of a true friend.

A'chĕron : the ' river of woe ' in the nether world.

In Homer's *Odyssey* it is the river into which the Phlegethon and the Cocytus (a tributary of the Styx) flow. In the *Iliad* the Styx is the only river of the lower world.

Achi'llēs, the chief hero of the *Iliad*, the handsomest and bravest of all the Greeks in the Trojan war. His mother, the Nereid Thetis, dipped him at birth into the waters of the Styx to render him invulnerable [See **Achilles' Heel**].

She foretold to him that his fate was either to gain glory and die early or to live a long but inglorious life. He chose an early death and so went willingly with Odysseus and Nestor to take part in the war against Troy, though he knew he was not to return. He led 50 ships against the Trojans and throughout was the bulwark of the Greeks and the favourite of the Goddesses Athene and Hera. In the tenth year of the war Agamemnon took from him the captive Briseïs. In consequence Achilles sulked in his tent and refused to take any further part in the war until the friend of his youth, Patroclus, was killed. Hephaestus now made new arms for him ; his voice alone put the Trojans to flight. He met Hector, leader of the Trojans, chased him thrice round the walls of Troy, slew him, tied the body to his chariot and dragged it to the ships of the Greeks ; but he gave up the body to Priam, Hector's aged father, who came to his tent to beg for it. Achilles was wounded in his one vulnerable spot by Paris, whose arrow was directed by Apollo, and he died of his wound. Achilles was affectionate towards his mother and his friends ; formidable in battle ; open-hearted and without fear. In a memorable line Horace summed up his character : " Impiger, iracundus, inexorabilis, acer," i.e. restless, passionate, relentless, keen of soul. His greatest passion was ambition and when his sense of honour was hurt he was unrelenting in his revenge and anger : yet he submitted obediently to the will of the Gods.

Dr. Rouse in *Achilles* (Murray) has told the story of the *Iliad*, i.e. of two months of the Ten Years' War, in delightfully simple English.

Achilles' Tendon (or Heel). Thetis, mother of Achilles, according to legend, sought to make her son invulnerable by dipping him in the river Styx, the waters of which rendered men invulnerable. She succeeded with the exception of the heel by which she held him. Achilles was wounded in the heel by Paris by an arrow directed by Apollo.

Anatomists call the great tendon which connects the heel with the calf of the leg 'The Tendon of Achilles.' Proverbially, ' the heel of Achilles ' is a vulnerable spot, a weak point.

See W. S. Landor's " Imaginary Conversation " between Achilles and Helen.''

Ăcrĭ′sĭŭs, father of Danaë. See Danaë.

Acro′pŏlis, i.e. the lofty or upper city, the name given by the Greeks to the fortified hill round which Athens (like many of their other towns) was built. Here are to be found the main architectural glories of Athens. The most important of them were the Parthĕnŏn, the Temple of Athene the Maiden, the chief glory of the Acropolis ; the Ĕrechthĕum ; the temple of Nīkē Aptĕros or Wingless Victory ; the Temple of Artemis. The approach to the Acropolis was through the magnificent Propylae′a, built of pure marble, like the Parthenon, at the time of Pericles. At the base of the Acropolis were numerous temples and the Theatre of Dionysus. The whole plateau measures about 300 by 150 yards.

See Shelley's *Ode to Liberty*, stanza v.

Actae′on, a huntsman, trained by the centaur Chiron. He was changed into a stag by Artemis, and torn to pieces by his fifty dogs on Mount Cithaeron, because he

The Acropolis from the West, shewing in the foreground the remains of the Propylae′a, the impressive porch of temples built under Pericles and partially destroyed by the Turks in the middle of the 17th century.

had seen the goddess bathing with her nymphs, or because he had boasted that he excelled her in hunting.

Adam. (a) the ' old Adam ' is man's worldly nature, original sin, what Canterbury in *Henry V* i. 1, 29 calls " the offending Adam."

(b) the ' penalty of Adam ' is the sufferings, e.g. " the seasons' difference", common to all men who live a natural life away from the artificialities of the town (*As You Like It* ii, 1, 5).

Admē'tus. The story of Admetus, king of Thessaly, is intertwined with that of Phoebus Apollo, the sun-god. Zeus had killed Aesculapius, Apollo's son, with thunderbolts made by the Cyclopes and in his rage Apollo killed the Cyclopes. For this offence he was banished from Olympus to become servant to a mortal, so he hired himself as a shepherd to Admetus whom he served nine years. As a return for the kindness shown to him all these years by Admetus, Apollo induced the Fates to spare the king's life if his father, mother or wife would die for him. His wife Alcestis voluntarily died instead of her husband and she was brought back by Heracles from the lower world :

" And lo, Alcestis was alive again,
And of Admetus' rapture who shall speak ? "

George Meredith's " Phoebus with Admetus," with its refrain hailing Apollo as the god of music, of song and of healing, tells the whole story.

Adō'nis, a beautiful youth in legendary story, beloved by Aphrodite. He was mortally wounded by a boar and on the spot where his blood fell the flower anemone or wind-flower was said to have sprung

up. Aphrodite's grief at his death was so great that Proserpina allowed him to spend six months of every year with her upon the earth. Thus was explained the death of nature in winter and its revival in spring.

The Syrian counterpart of Adonis is Thammuz. See *Paradise Lost,* i, 446-452. The notion that the blood of Thammuz, " yearly wounded," flowed again was the explanation of the reddening of the waters of the river Adonis due to red mud brought down by the river from the heights of Lebanon. See also the *Nativity Ode* 204, " In vain the Tyrian maids their wounded Thammuz mourn."

Aegae'on and his two brothers are described as huge monsters with a hundred arms and fifty heads who helped Zeus to defeat the Titans. Homer says that the gods called him Brĭā'rēūs. Milton is mistaken when he makes Briareus a Titan (*P.L.* i, 199).

Ae'gēūs, King of Athens and father of Theseus. Theseus went to Crete to deliver Athens from the tribute it had to pay to Minos. He promised his father that on his return he would hoist white sails as a signal of his safety. But he forgot his promise and when Aegeus saw the black-sailed ship approaching the Attic coast he thought his son had perished and threw himself into the sea. Tradition says that the sea was in consequence called the Aegean.

Aenē'ās, son of Anchīses and Aphrodītē, born on Mount Ida. His wife was Crĕū'sa, daughter of Priam and He'cŭba, and their son was Iū'lus or Ascănĭus. After the fall of Troy he carried his old father and his household goods in safety from the burning city and, after building a fleet, began his wanderings with Iulus. He came ashore at Carthage where he married Queen Dido ; but when he deserted her she committed suicide. Ultimately he reached Latium where he and the Italian Turnus fought for the hand of Lavi′nia, daughter of King Latinus. Turnus was killed and Aeneas married Lavinia. Aeneas became King of the Latins after the death of his father-in-law ; but he was soon killed in battle with the Etruscans.

Rŏ′mŭlus, founder of Rome, was directly descended from Aeneas, and the famous Julian family, one of the most ancient patrician houses at Rome, claimed descent from Iulus.

Ae′nĕid, the Latin national epic, definitely designed by Virgil to glorify the greatness of Rome and to flatter the Emperor Augustus and his family. The poem consists of twelve books, the first six of which are loosely based on the *Odyssey* and the second six, describing the wars Aeneas had to fight before he was able to found his kingdom in Latium, somewhat resemble the *Iliad*. Among notable actions in the epic are the story of the fall of Troy (told by Aeneas to Dido in Bks. 2 and 3) ; the episode of Aeneas and Dido Queen of Carthage (Bk. 4), the funeral games held by Aeneas in honour of his father (Bk. 5) ; the descent into the lower world where Aeneas was permitted not only to talk with the shade of his father Anchises but also to be shown the royal line of his descendants down to Romulus (Bk. 6). In the second portion of the poem we have the prowess of the friends Nisus and Euryalus (Bk. 9) ; the warrior-maiden Camilla and her exploits (Bk. 11), and the grim combat between Aeneas and his rival Turnus (Bk. 12).

The *Aeneid* has frequently been translated into both prose and verse. John Dryden's verse translation (1697) is very free and at times (like Pope's *Homer*) more Dryden than Virgil. The great Latin scholar John Conington translated the epic in English ballad style—a most successful piece of work. The blank verse translation by Frank Richards (Murray, 1928) will find favour, especially if episodes only, such as the stories of the Wooden Horse and of the various funeral games, and not the epic as a whole, are read at a sitting.

Ae′ŏlus, the god of the winds. When Odysseus was on his way home to Ithaca Aeolus gave him a bag in which all winds unfavourable to him were confined ; but Odysseus' comrades, thinking that Aeolus had given him a bag full of treasure, " undid the bag, the winds all rushed out, and in an instant the tempest was upon them " (Rieu's translation of the *Odyssey*).

Ae′schўlus (525-456 B.C.) the great Athenian tragic poet, the real founder of Greek tragedy. In his youth he fought at Marathon where his brother was killed in the attack in the ships. He himself describes

Aeschylus. The picture (from a gem) illustrates the well-known story of the dramatist's death.

the battle of Salamis in his play the *Persae*. We are told that he wrote seventy tragedies, only seven of which survive. There is a curious tradition about the manner of his death. An eagle, mistaking the poet's bald head for a stone, dropped a tortoise on it to break the shell. This was considered to fulfil an oracle by which Aeschylus was to die by a blow from heaven.

Ae′tna. A volcanic mountain in NE. Sicily. Under it Zeus buried Tўphōn (a fire-breathing monster of the primitive world) and Encĕlădus (a giant with 100 arms). In its caverns Hēphaestus and the Cyclōpes forged the thunderbolts of Zeus.

Ăgăme′mnon, son (or grandson) of Atreus, husband of Clytemne′stra and father of Orestes, Electra and Īphĭgĕnī′a. He became King of Mўcē′nae and thereby the most powerful prince in Greece. He was chosen commander-in-chief of the Greeks against the Trojans, and his army and fleet assembled in the port of Aulis. Here Agamemnon killed a stag, sacred to Artemis, who in return caused a calm which prevented the Greek fleet from sailing. To appease her wrath Agamemnon consented to sacrifice his daughter Iphigenia ; but at the moment she was to be sacrificed she was carried off by Artemis herself and another victim was substituted. The calm thereupon ceased and the fleet sailed. On his return home he was murdered by his wicked wife and his death was avenged by his son Orestes.

Though the chief commander of the Greeks throughout the ten years' war, Agamemnon is not the hero of the *Iliad:* in chivalrous spirit, bravery and character he is much inferior to Achilles. But he was a great king and warrior, wise and dignified in his bearing though of somewhat uncertain temper.

Agăni′ppē, a fountain of the Muses at the foot of Mt. Helicon.

Ā′jax (in the Greek Aias). (i) Ajax the Great is represented in the *Iliad* as second only to Achilles in bravery and as the hero most worthy, in the absence of Achilles, to contend with Hector. In the contest for Achilles' arms, which were to be given to the worthiest of the surviving Greeks, he was defeated by Odysseus. When Odysseus visited Hades and discoursed with the ghosts of the deceased heroes, the only soul " that stood aloof was that of Aias son of Telamon, still embittered by the defeat I had inflicted on him at the ships when defending my claim to the arms of Achilles " (*Odys.* xi, 545, Rieu's translation). Ajax went mad with rage and slaughtered a flock of sheep as though they were his Grecian foes : then he killed himself with the sword Hector had given him.

(ii) Ajax the Lesser, small of stature but brave, skilled in throwing the spear, and, next to Achilles, the most swift-footed among the Greeks. On his return from Troy his vessel was wrecked. He himself got safe upon a rock by the help of Poseidon ; but as he boasted that he could escape unaided, Poseidon split the rock with his trident and Ajax was drowned.

Alce′stis, a daughter of Pelias who promised her as wife to Admetus if he came to her in a chariot drawn by lions and boars. This Admetus performed by the aid of Apollo. [See **Admetus**]. Alcestis is the heroine of a play by Euripides in which her self-sacrifice on her husband's behalf is contrasted with the selfishness of his aged parents.

Older readers will probably enjoy Robert Browning's " Balaustion's Adventure " which is actually a very free translation of Euripides' *Alcestis*.

Alcī′des. The Greek termination —ides is a patronymic. Heracles was the grandson of Alcaeus.

Morocco, in *The Merchant of Venice* ii, 1, 32-5, refers to the story of Lichas, an attendant of Heracles, bringing his master the poisoned garment from Dē′ianī′ra. Heracles in anguish and wrath threw Lichas into the sea.

> " If Hercules and Lichas play at dice
> Which is the better (i.e. stronger) man, the greater throw
> May turn by fortune from the weaker hand :
> So is Alcides beaten by his page."

(H)alcy′ŏnē, daughter of Aeolus and wife of Cē′yx. Her husband perished in a shipwreck and in her grief she threw herself into the sea and was drowned. The gods out of compassion for the loving pair changed them into birds. (*Alkyōn* is the Greek word for kingfisher).

' Halcyon Days ' originally are the calm fourteen days supposed to exist at sea in midwinter during the time when kingfishers are nesting ; and so, days of peace and contentment.

Ale′cto. See **Eumenides.**
See Pistol's ranting line in 2 *Henry IV*, 5, 5, 37, " Rouse up revenge from ebon den with fell Alecto's snake."

Alexander the Great (356-323 B.C.) son of Philip II and Olympias. In his youth he was sent to Athens to study in the ' school ' of Aristotle : hence his life-long sympathy with Greek culture. At the age of sixteen he was entrusted by his father with the government of Macedonia, and on his father's murder he became king at the age of 20. The future ' Emathian conqueror ' began his reign by putting down rebellion in his own kingdom : then he compelled the submission of Thebes as soon as he appeared at its gates. The assembled Greeks at the isthmus of Corinth (with the sole exception of the Spartans) elected him to the command against Persia. He crossed the Hellespont and

> " Entering old Gordium cut the knot
> Which waited for the conqueror of Asia."

At Issus in Cilicia he defeated Darius whose wife, mother and children he captured, marched through Phoenicia into Egypt, where he was welcomed as the Egyptians had always hated the Persians, and founded the city of Alexandria. He then went north through Phoenicia and Syria to meet Darius a second time, crossed the Euphrates and the Tigris, and completely defeated the Persians at the battle of Arbela (331 B.C.). Alexander was now conqueror of Asia and began to affect Asiatic dress and manners. He marched on to India and extended his empire as far as the river Hydaspes (the Jhelum) on the banks of which he founded a city, Bucephala he called it in honour of his horse. This was the limit of Alexander's conquests : his men refused to march further.

> " His empire stretched from the Aegean Sea,
> O'er Asia Minor, Egypt and Iran :
> Alone he held the gorgeous East in fee
> From Europe to the verge of Hindustan." *

* Viscount Mersey's *Alexander of Macedon.*

On his return from the East he reached Babylon where he was attacked by a fever. He died after an illness of eleven days at the age of 32, leaving ' like Caesar and Napoleon only undistinguished sons who did not long survive him.' (Lord Mersey).

Lord Mersey has recently (1946) told the story of Alexander's exploits, in the heroic metre (*Alexander of Macedon*, John Murray), and it is from this narrative that we have twice quoted above. Naturally there are legends innumerable centred round an heroic figure of such stature. " Alexander's Feast," John Dryden's song in honour of St. Cecilia's Day, recalls some of these legends about the world's conqueror, " Philip's warlike son."

Alexander's name still survives in a corrupted form (" Iskander ") in Kandahar and Secunderabad. For an orientalized version of the legends built round him and the Greeks read J. E. Flecker's " The Ballad of Iskander."

Alpha and Ŏ′mega, i.e. the first and the last. *Alpha* is the first letter of the Greek alphabet and, therefore, typically a beginning, and *omega* the last, an end. " I am Alpha and Omega, the beginning and the ending, saith the Lord " (*Rev.* $1^{8, 11}$). cp. *Isaiah* 41^4.

A′māzons, a mythical race of warrior-women who came from Asia and, according to various local traditions, engaged in battle with different Greek heroes. Towards the end of the Trojan war their queen Penthesilea allied herself with Priam ; but she was slain by Achilles. Plutarch says that Theseus defeated the Amazons when they invaded Attica, and then married their queen Hippolyta. This is the story followed by Shakespeare in *A Midsummer Night's Dream*.

The adjective *Amazonian* is used in *Coriolanus* meaning ' beardless ' :
" . . . with his Amazonian chin
   he drove
The bristled lips before him."
" The river *Amazon* was so named by Spanish travellers from female warriors encountered there " (Weekley).

Amphi′on, son of Zeus and Antī′opē, and twin-brother of Zēthus.

Wounded Amazons. *The Amazons are a favourite subject both in great sculptures and on vases.*

The brothers took Thebes and fortified it with a wall. When Amphion
played his lyre, given to him by
Hermes, the stones moved of their
own accord and formed the wall.
This story has been explained by
supposing that Amphion by his
eloquence persuaded a wild and
uncivilized people to unite and build
a town to protect themselves against
the attacks of their enemies.

Cf. the story of the building of
Troy by Lāo′medon assisted by
Neptune and Apollo, at the sound of
whose lute the stones are said to have
moved into their appointed places.

Tennyson's somewhat rollicking
" Amphion " and his much more
stately " Tithonus " make allusion
to these legends.

Amphitrī′tē, a Nereid or an
Oceanid, wife of Neptune and
mother of Trīton.

Anak, Sons of, the giant race of
men, the Anakim, dwelling in and
around Hebron. They seem to
have been a formidable race of
fighters, although somewhat dull
of intellect. It was the war-like
appearance of the tribe that so
terrified the Israelite spies : " And
there we saw the giants, the sons
of Anak . . . and we were in our own
sight as grasshoppers, and so we
were in their sight " (*Numb.* 13³³).
The Cyclopean walls of the Cana-
anitish strongholds, 30 or 40 feet
broad and many feet high, seem to
be partly responsible for belief in
a race of giants who built and
inhabited them.

Samson claimed for himself
                            " some proof
Of acts indeed heroic, far beyond
The sons of Anak."
(*Samson Agonistes* 527-9).

Anani′as. The story of Ananias
and Sapphira his wife is told in *Acts*

5¹⁻¹⁰. They were guilty of attempted
fraud against the common fund of
the Christians of Jerusalem. On
St. Peter's denunciation of the sin
Ananias (probably to Peter's aston-
ishment) fell dead. The offence of
Sapphira was more serious : hers
was an attempt to deceive the
Holy Ghost, and consequently the
sentence of death passed on her by
Peter was more explicitly pronounced.

Ana′thĕma. The Greek ' anathema ' is literally " a thing hung
up " in a temple and so dedicated
to the god. Any object so devoted
to the Lord was irredeemable.
Occasionally the vow involved the
death of the innocent, as with
Jephthah's daughter (*Judges* 11³¹)
and Jonathan (1 *Sam.* 14²⁴) who
was saved only by the interposition
of the people. In N.T. ' anathema '
is frequently used to mean ' anything devoted to evil ' or ' accursed.'
St. Paul concludes 1 *Cor.* with these
words : " If any man love not the
Lord Jesus Christ let him be
Anathema Maran-atha." *Maran-
atha* is two Hebrew words meaning
' the Lord cometh.' The words are
used to strengthen the Greek, in
much the same way as ' Amen '
strengthens the prayer to which it is
appended. Lord Macaulay follows
St. Paul's example when he says
" The principles of liberty were . . .
the Anathema Maran-atha of every
fawning dean."

Ancae′us, helmsman of the
Argo. A well-known proverb is said
to have had its origin with him.
He had been told by a seer that he
would not live to taste the wine of
his own vineyard. Afterwards, when
he was on the point of drinking
a cup of wine, the produce of his
own vineyard, he laughed at the
seer, who, however, replied :
" There is many a slip between the

cup and the lip." At that moment Ancaeus was told that a wild boar was near. He put down his cup, went out against the boar and was killed by it.

Anchī′sēs, a Trojan prince so handsome that Aphrodite came down from heaven to Mount Ida to enjoy his company. Their son was Aenēas. When Troy was taken Anchises had become so infirm that Aeneas, whom the Greeks allowed to take away whatever he esteemed most, carried him through the flames upon his shoulders and thus saved his life. He went with Aeneas in his voyage towards Italy and died in Sicily at the age of 80.

Cassius (*Julius Cæsar* i, 2, 112) refers to this rescue :

" I, as Aeneas, our great ancestor,
    Did from the flames of Troy
       upon his shoulder
    The old Anchises bear, so from
       the waves of Tiber
    Did I the tired Cæsar."

So, too, in 2 *Henry VI*, v, 2, 62 Young Clifford, taking up his father's body from the battle-field :

" As did Aeneas old Anchises
       bear,
    So bear I thee upon my manly
       shoulders ;
    But then Aeneas bare a living
       load,
    Nothing so heavy as these
       woes of mine."

Andro′clus (or Androcles), the slave of a Roman noble, was sentenced to be exposed to the wild beasts in the circus ; but a lion which was let loose on him greeted him with affection. It appeared that Androclus, while he was in Africa, had run away from his master and had taken refuge in a cave from the heat of the sun. A lion entered, apparently in great pain, went up to him and held out

his paw. Androclus found that a thorn had pierced it, which he drew out. They lived together for some time in the cave, the lion catering for his benefactor. But at last Androclus left the cave, was apprehended by soldiers, brought to Rome and condemned to the wild beasts. He was pardoned and presented with the lion, which he used to lead about the city.

Mr. G. B. Shaw's two-act fable play, *Androcles and the Lion*, may in parts interest young readers, for it is intensely comic. Indeed it may turn out to be Shaw's masterpiece, though he is said to have regarded it as a mere " pot-boiler."

Andro′machē, wife of Hector and mother of Astyănax (whom his father called Skamandrios). Her father and her seven brothers were slain by Achilles at the taking of Thebes. Her parting from her husband, who was going to the battle in which he was killed, has been regarded as the most tender and pathetic of all passages in the *Iliad*. On the taking of Troy her son was hurled from the walls of the city and she herself, in the division of the spoils, fell to the share of Neoptŏ′lĕmus, Achilles' son, who treated her well. She afterwards married Hĕ′lĕnus, a brother of Hector.

Andrŏ′mĕda, daughter of the King of Ethiopia and of Cassiopēa. Her mother boasted that her daughter's beauty surpassed that of the Nereids who prevailed on Poseidon to send a sea monster to ravage the country. The oracle of Jupiter Ammōn promised deliverance if Andromeda were given up to the monster. So Andromeda was chained to a rock where she was found and rescued by Perseus who turned the monster into a rock (by showing him Medusa's head).

Read the story of *Perseus* in Kingsley's beautiful prose. The same writer has the story of *Andromeda* in hexameters which are more difficult but which well repay careful study. Hexameter verse is used by Homer and by Virgil in their great epics but it is not a comfortable metre in English.

Animals, Clean and Unclean. Animals which chew the cud and part the hoof were clean and might be eaten by Jews. Hares and rabbits could not be eaten because (although they chew the cud) they do not part the hoof. Pigs and camels were unclean because (although they part the hoof) they do not chew the cud. (Brewer).

This law regarding Meat that might and that might not be eaten is most important in the Law of Moses. In the Gospel story Our Lord distinguished (as the Scribes did not) bodily and spiritual cleanness, and laid it down that what goes into a man cannot defile him. "This he said, making all meats clean" (*Mark* 7¹⁹ R.V.). In *Acts* 10 Peter's vision at Joppa was most significant and it took him some time to grasp its full import. "What God hath cleansed, that call not thou common or unclean." Just as uncleanness among animals was no more, so the Gentiles were henceforth to be admitted to the Church, and Cornelius of the Italian cohort at Cæsarea was the first to be baptised.

Antæ′us, son of Poseidon and Gē (the Earth), a mighty giant and wrestler in Libya. According to some accounts he was invincible as long as he remained in contact with his mother earth. Therefore Heracles lifted him from the ground and strangled him in the air.

Cf. the story of Prince Arthur and Maleger, told by Spenser in *Faerie Queene* ii, xi. Prince Arthur, recognizing the source of Maleger's repeatedly renewed strength,
> " carried him perforce
> Above three furlongs, taking his full course,
> Until he came unto a standing lake ;
> Him thereinto he threw without remorse,
> Ne stird, till hope of life did him forsake."

Antē′nor, one of the wisest among the elders at Troy. He received Menelaus and Odysseus into his house when they came to Troy as ambassadors, and advised his fellow-citizens to restore Helen to Menelaus and so conclude the war. Post-Homeric stories say he was a traitor to his country who concerted a plan of delivering the city into the hands of the Greeks. Hence, on the capture of Troy he was spared by the Greeks.

Anthropo′phagi, a legendary people of Scythia who fed on human flesh.

Othello uses this resounding title for amazing people he had met with in his ' travel's history ' :
> " And of the Cannibals that each other eat,
> The Anthropophagi, and men whose heads
> Do grow beneath their shoulders." (*Othello* i, 3, 143).

Anti′gŏnē, daughter of Oedĭpus and his mother Jocasta, sister of Ĕtĕocles and Polynīces. In the tragic story of Oedipus Antigone appears as a noble maiden, attached to her father and brothers. When Oedipus had blinded himself and was obliged to quit Thebes, he was accompanied by Antigone who remained with him till he died in Colōnus, and then returned to

Thebes. After her two brothers had killed each other in battle, and Crĕon, king of Thebes, would not allow Polynices to be buried, Antigone alone defied the tyrant and buried her brother's body. Creon thereupon ordered her to be shut up in an underground cave where she took her own life.

Anti′sthenēs, an Athenian, pupil of Socrates and founder of the Cynic school of philosophy. He taught in the Cȳnŏsa′rgēs, a gymnasium outside the walls of Athens sacred to Heracles, whence probably his followers were called ' Cynics.' Others derive their name from their contentiousness and ' dog-like ' roughness of manner (Greek kyōn = dog). They paid little attention to art or learning. He taught that virtue is the sole thing necessary, and that virtue consisted in avoiding evil and having no needs. He showed his contempt of all the luxuries and outward comforts of life by his mean clothing and hard fare.

' Cynic ' sometimes merely means an unmannerly, currish fellow, as when Cassius says of the poet in the quarrel scene with Brutus, " How vilely doth this cynic rhyme ! " See **Diogenes.**

Antony. From Shakespeare's *Julius Cæsar* and *Antony and Cleopatra* we can learn almost all we need know about this great Roman. He was an early supporter of Julius Cæsar : the two became the consuls in 44 B.C. As surviving consul he pronounced the funeral oration over Cæsar's body and read his will to the people, thereby inflaming them against the assassins. But he found a rival in the young Octavianus, Cæsar's adopted son, who hastened to Rome, assumed the name of ' Cæsar ' and joined the Senatorial party (led

by Cicero) against Antony. The Senate, encouraged by Cicero's *Philippics*, declared Antony a public enemy. He was defeated at Mutina and then joined Lepidus and Octavianus to form the Second Triumvirate. In the proscriptions which followed Cicero lost his life. The triumvirs then defeated Cæsar's assassins at Philippi. Antony now went to Asia, where he met Cleopatra and followed her to Egypt. He gradually gained power in the East, married Cleopatra, laid aside the character of a Roman citizen and assumed the pomp and ceremony of an Eastern despot. Many of his supporters were alienated and Octavianus thought the time was ripe for crushing his rival. The contest was decided by the memorable sea-fight off Actium in September, 31, in which Antony's fleet was utterly defeated. Accompanied by Cleopatra he fled to Alexandria where, on a false report of Cleopatra's death, he put an end to his life in 30 B.C. Cleopatra was now in danger of falling into the power of Octavianus, so she poisoned herself by the bite of an asp.

Ape′llēs, one of the most celebrated of Greek painters, of the time of Alexander the Great. Throughout his life he laboured to improve himself and is said never to have allowed a day to pass without practising. Hence the proverb *Nulla dies sine linea* (no day without a line, i.e. without doing a little writing or drawing or painting). His most celebrated portrait was that of Alexander wielding a thunderbolt, his most admired picture that of Aphrodite rising out of the sea.

Aphrodī′tē, the Greek Goddess of beauty and love, worshipped by the Romans as Venus. Legend represents her as sprung from the foam of the sea (Greek *aphros* = foam). Zeus ironically gave her in marriage to Hephaestus, the lame

Aphrodite, from Melos. The original statue found at Melos and now in the Louvre.

ugly blacksmith-god of Olympus; but she was really in love with Ares the god of war. She was the mother of Aenēas. Of her statues the most celebrated are those made by Praxiteles and the "Venus of Milo," found in 1820 in the island of Mēlos and now in the Louvre. See **Venus; Apelles.**

Apo'crypha, the collection of fourteen books reckoned non-canonical by the English Church, (but not by the Roman Catholic Church) which "the church doth read for example of life and instruction of manners; but yet it doth not apply them to establish any doctrine." The primary meaning of *Apocrypha* is " (the writings) hidden away," i.e. excluded from the Bible at the Reformation; but much later the word came to mean "of doubtful authority." Weekley quotes from the *Great Bible* of 1539: "The other followynge, which are called *apocripha* (because they were wont to be reade, not openly and in common, but as it were in secrete and aparte) are neyther founde in the Hebrue nor in the Chalde."

So we have the adjective *apo'cryphal* = ' of doubtful authority,' and therefore ' sham.'

Apo'llo, one of the great divinities of Greece. He was son of Zeus and Leto, born with his twin-sister Artemis on the island of Delos. He was identified with the sun, and hence he is

(1) The god who brings back sunshine and light in spring.
(2) The god who sends plagues, but also the god of healing who averts plagues. Sunstroke sometimes kills directly and all sudden deaths were ascribed to Apollo's arrows. His arrows slay men as those of Artemis slay women. See **Niobe.**
(3) The god of oracles. He is represented as the mouthpiece of Zeus. His chief oracular temple was at Delphi.
(4) The god of prophecy. He was the leader of the Muses, the god of poetry and of music.

(5) The ideal of manly youth and beauty, and hence a patron of athletes.

In statues Apollo is generally represented as a handsome beardless youth. As the god of music he is clothed in his long tunic and holds a lyre. The so-called ' Belvedere ' Apollo is a beautiful marble copy of an original in bronze : the left hand held the ægis ; the right was empty. It is in the Vatican.

See **Admetus** for a legend of his tending the flocks of certain kings.

The ' Belvedere ' Apollo (in the Vatican), a beautiful marble copy of an original in bronze. The God is wearing the ' chlamys ' of a hunter, fastened by a brooch over the right shoulder.

Shelley's " Hymn of Apollo," if not too difficult, deserves attention :

" I am the eye with which the Universe
Beholds itself and knows itself divine ;
All harmony of instrument or verse,

All prophecy, all medicine is mine,
All light of art or nature ; — to my song
Victory and praise in its own right belong."

Apostle, i.e. envoy, one sent on a special mission. But the ordinary N.T. application is to the twelve disciples and to those subsequently added to their body—Paul, Barnabas, Silas. Though the name was conferred on the Twelve by Christ Himself (*Luke* 6[13]), it seldom occurs in the Synoptists and never in the Fourth Gospel where they are always called " the disciples." The one essential qualification for apostleship was to have been a witness of the Resurrection (*Acts* 1[21]), and this evidently means to have seen the Lord after He had risen. The function of apostles was first of all that of witnesses (*Luke* 24[48] and repeatedly in *Acts*), and in this qualification of first-hand witnesses the Apostles could have no successors. Further, an apostle had the power to communicate the gift of the spirit (*Acts* 8[17], 19[6]), to perform miracles and to found churches.

A'ppian Way (so called from Appius Claudius who planned it in 312 B.C.), the most celebrated of the Roman roads, the great line of communication between Rome and southern Italy. Leaving Rome, it passed through The Three Taverns and Appii Forum (see *Acts* 28[15]) to Capua (131 Roman miles). Later it was extended through Beneventum and Tarentum to Brundisium (modern Brindisi), a total distance of 363 miles.

Apple (i) The Apple of Discord. In Greek mythology the apple was the symbol of discord (among other

Judgment of Paris. (*From a vase*). *Hermes is leading up the three goddesses, who offer respectively Eros* (*love*), *a helmet* (*warlike fame*), *and a lion* (*sovereignty*).

things). All the gods, with the exception of Eris (or Discord), had been invited to the marriage of Pēleus and Thetis on Mt. Pēlion. The goddess, angry, like the malignant fairy in a fairy tale, because she alone was not invited, threw among the guests a golden apple with the inscription ' to the fairest.' Thereupon Hera, Aphrodite and Athena each claimed the apple. Zeus ordered Hermes to take the goddesses to Mt. Ida and to entrust the decision of the dispute to the beautiful shepherd Paris. Each of the goddesses offered him a bribe to decide in her favour—Hera, the sovereignty of Asia and great riches, Athena, renown in war, and Aphrodite, the fairest of women for his wife. Paris decided in favour of Aphrodite and gave her the apple. He then sailed away to Greece, and succeeded in carrying off Helen, wife of Menelaus and the most beautiful woman in the world. This gave rise to the Trojan war.

See Tennyson's *Œnone.*

(ii) **The Golden Apples of the Hesperides.** The eleventh ' labour ' imposed by Eurystheus on Heracles was fetching the apples of the Hesperides. Heracles sent Atlas to bring the apples and in the meantime bore the weight of heaven for him. Atlas returned with the apples, but refused to take the burden of heaven on his shoulders again. Heracles, however, contrived by a stratagem to get the apples and hastened away. On his return Eurystheus made him a present of the apples ; but Heracles dedicated them to Athene who restored them to their former place. Another tradition gives the story that Heracles killed the dragon Lādōn which guarded the apples.

Milton in *Comus* (393-6) refers to the apples in beautiful language :

" Beauty, like the fair Hesperian tree

    Laden with blooming gold, had need the guard

    Of dragon-watch with unenchanted eye

    To save her blossoms and defend her fruit.''

Ara′chnē, a Lydian maiden famous as a dyer in purple (cf. *Acts* xvi[14]). She challenged Athene, the goddess of the art, to compete with her in weaving. Athene's work showed the Olympian gods in all their dignity. Arachne produced a piece of cloth in which the amours of the gods were woven. Indignant at the taunt and jealous of Arachne's skilful work, Athene tore it to pieces. Arachne in despair hanged herself ; but the goddess loosened the rope and saved her life. The rope was changed into a cobweb and Arachne herself into a spider. (Greek arachnē = spider).

Eden Philpotts has written a partly rationalized (but not unnecessarily so) version of the legend in his " Arachne."

Arcă′dĭa, a mountainous country in the middle of the Peloponnesus, the Switzerland of Greece. The Arcadians were simple in their habits : they were a primitive people engaged chiefly in hunting and the tending of cattle, and their rustic simplicity and contentment have always been proverbial. In later times they became equally celebrated as mercenary soldiers.

Archimē′dēs of Syracuse (c.287-212 B.C.), the greatest mathematician of antiquity and one of the foremost inventors in the realm of physical and mathematical science. Among his mechanical inventions was what is known as ' the screw of Archimedes,' a sort of pump first used in Egypt for raising water from a lower to a higher level, e.g. from the hold of a vessel. He is said to have exclaimed " Eurēka " (I've found it!) when he had discovered a method of testing whether base metal had been introduced into gold. The test was one of specific gravity, the result of his observing the amount of water displaced by his body when he was in his bath. When the Romans were besieging Syracuse, their general gave orders that Archimedes should not be harmed ; but a Roman soldier

killed him while he was intent on a mathematical problem and refused to obey orders.

Ā′rēs, the Greek god of war, identified by the Romans with Mars. He was an unpleasant character, hated by gods and men alike. Homer describes him as rejoicing in tumult and bloodshed, fickle, for he helped the Trojans though he

Ares (from a statue in Rome). From the time of Pheidias Ares is represented in art as a handsome beardless youth, naked or nearly so, with a spear and sometimes a helmet.

promised aid to the Greeks. His love for Aphrodite, wife of his brother Hephaestus, made him an object of ridicule in Olympus. Probably his worship was of Thracian (i.e., to the Greeks uncivilized and foreign) origin and this would account for its unpopularity with the Greeks.

Arethū′sa, nymph of the famous fountain of Arethusa in the island of Ortў′gĭa near Syracuse. The legend was that the nymph was pursued by the river-god Alphēus, that both were changed to streams passing under the sea and finally united at Ortygia.

A'rgonauts, i.e. the sailors of the *Argo,* the heroes who sailed to Colchis to fetch the golden fleece. Among the fifty heroes who accompanied Jason were **Theseus, Nestor, Heracles** and the singer **Orpheus.** As the barest outline of this great epic story we quote two-thirds of Wm. Morris's ' Argument ' to his *Life and Death of Jason:* " Jason, the son of Aeson, King of Iolchos, having come to man's estate, demanded of Pelias his father's kingdom, which he held wrongfully. But Pelias answered, that if he would bring from Colchis the golden fleece of the ram that had carried Phryxus thither, he would yield him his right. Whereupon Jason sailed to Colchis in the ship Argo, with other heroes, and by means of Medea, the king's daughter, won the fleece ; and carried off Medea also ; and so, after many troubles, came back to Iolchos again." Their voyage, which takes them up a river into Scythia, then, after a portage to another river, into the Baltic, round past Britain and homeward through the Pillars of Hercules, is probably a patchwork of travellers' tales which has put together into one voyage a number of the ancient trade routes.

For a complete version of the epic in delightful prose we recommend English readers to study Story II in Kingsley's *The Heroes* and to select according to individual taste portions of Morris's very long poem.

A'rgos, the name of more than one town or district in ancient Greece. The inhabitants, the Argives, worshipped Hera whose temple, the Heraeum, lay between Argos and Mycenae. These two towns were the capitals of Agamemnon's kingdom. Later, Mycenae declined in importance and Argos

Athene superintending the Building of the Argo (from a terra-cotta panel in British Museum).

Central Greece and the **Plain of Argos.**

became the leading city. These events belong to mythology.

A′rgus, surnamed *Panoptes,* ' the all-seeing,' because he had a hundred eyes. Hera appointed him guardian of the cow into which Io had been changed ; but Hermes, at the command of Zeus, put Argus to death after lulling him to sleep by the sweet notes of his lyre. Hera transplanted his eyes to the tail of the peacock, her favourite bird.

Odysseus' dog was called Argus. " As for Argus, he had no sooner set eyes on Odysseus after those nineteen years than he succumbed to the black hand of Death "

(*Odyssey,* Rieu's trans.). We use ' argus-eyed '=watchful.

Aria′dnē, daughter of Minos and Pāsi′phăē. She fell in love with Theseus when he was sent by his father to convey the tribute of the Athenians to Mi′notaurus, and gave him the clue of thread by means of which he found his way out of the Labyrinth. Theseus in return promised to marry her and she accordingly left Crete with him ; but on their arrival in the island of Naxos she was killed by Artemis.

According to another version Theseus abandoned Ariadne on Naxos where she was found and consoled by Bacchus.

Arī'ŏn, a lyric poet and a celebrated player on the cithara (a sort of guitar). A beautiful fable is told of his escape from the sailors with whom he sailed from Sicily to Corinth. He went to Sicily to take part in a musical contest. He won the prize and, laden with presents, embarked for Corinth. The sailors, who coveted his wealth, were about to kill him when he asked leave once more to play on the cithara. Standing on the prow he invoked the gods in inspired strains and then threw himself into the sea. But many song-loving dolphins had assembled round the vessel and one of them took the bard on its back and carried him to Taenărus whence he returned to Corinth in safety.

Byron has 'some rude Arion,' i.e. some unskilled minstrel.

Aristŏ'phănēs, the great comic poet of Athens (*c*.444-*c*.380 B.C.). His comedies are of the highest historical interest, containing as they do an admirable series of caricatures of the leading men of the day. Among the eleven surviving comedies special mention may be made of *The Frogs* in which Aeschylus and Euripides contend in the lower world for supremacy in Tragedy, and Dionysus, called upon by Pluto to decide the matter, chooses Aeschylus. The title of the play is taken from a chorus of frogs who sing while Charon is ferrying Dionysus over the marsh.

A'ristotle, the philosopher of Sta'gĭra (384-322 B.C.). He became a pupil of Plato who called him the 'intellect of his school.' Later he undertook the instruction of Philip of Macedonia's thirteen-year-old son. On returning to Athens he delivered lectures in the 'shady walks,' walking up and down (whence, from the Greek, our

'peripatetic') and not sitting. This work continued for thirteen years during which time he composed the greater part of his writings. Perhaps his most interesting work to students of English is his *Poetics* in which he outlined three general principles of dramatic art, called the 'dramatic unities'—that of *action*, that of *time* and that of *place*. Aristotle insisted on the unity of action—that is to say, a play should consist of one main action to the carrying on of which everything in the play must be subservient—but the unities of time and place are not regarded as important. *The Tempest* observes all three unities.

Ark of the Covenant. The Ark was a chest 2½ cubits long by 1½ broad and deep, made of acacia wood overlaid inside and out with pure gold. Four gold rings, one at each corner, through which were passed two staves of acacia wood overlaid with gold, were used in carrying it. On top of it was a plate of gold, called " the mercy-seat," and on this golden slab were fixed two cherubim of solid gold, facing each other, their wings meeting above. St. Paul (*Hebrews* 9⁴) says the Ark contained, besides the two " tables of the covenant," " the golden pot that had manna and Aaron's rod that budded." Its ultimate fate is not known, but it probably perished when the Temple was destroyed by Nebuchadnezzar (2 *Kings* 25⁹). There was no ark in the second Temple.

1 *Samuel* has much to say about the Ark. It was taken into the battle with the Philistines at Ebenezer (4⁵) ; it was captured and set up in the house of Dagon, the Philistine god, at Ashdod (5²). It was sent to Gath and to Ekron and remained altogether seven months in Philistia. It was then returned

to Israel on a new cart, with a coffer containing golden mice and tumours, emblems of the plagues which God had inflicted on the Philistines. The men of Bethshemesh were smitten for " looking into the ark " (6[19]). It remained twenty years in the house of Abinadab at Kirjath-jearim (7[1,2]). Later, David had the ark removed from Gibeah, and Uzzah was smitten for touching it (2 *Sam.* 6[6,7]). It remained three months in the house of Obededom. David would not permit it to be carried with him when he fled before Absalom (15[24-29]). Solomon had it placed in the Holy of Holies in the Temple (1 *Kings* 6[19]).

A′rtemis, identified by the Romans with Diana, was the daughter of Zeus and Leto and twin sister of Apollo. She was, like her brother, armed with a bow, quiver and arrows, and sent plagues and sudden death among women and animals. Delighting in wild beasts,

Artemis. (*Louvre, in Paris*), the *huntress of wild animals.*

she was the virgin Huntress. As the counterpart of Apollo, she was the Moon Goddess (Phoebe). She was attended by a band of maidens and any man who intruded on her privacy was punished, e.g. **Actaeon.**

Ascǎ′nius or Iū′lus, son of Aeneas and Creusa. The great patrician family of Rome, the gens Julia (to which Julius Cæsar belonged), was traditionally descended from him.

Medieval legend gave him a son Brutus, who, after accidentally killing his father, set out with a band of adventurers and conquered Britain to which he gave his name. See Geoffrey of Monmouth's " Histories of the Kings of Britain " (or at any rate " Tales of Old Britain " by E. P. Roberts, Macmillan E.L.S. series) which is the basis of many of the legends about King Arthur.

Asclē′pius, called Aescŭlā′pius by the Romans, the god of the medical art, son of Apollo. He was instructed in the art of healing by Chīron the Centaur. He not only cured the sick but called the dead back to life. Zeus killed him by lightning as he feared lest men might contrive to escape death altogether. His chief temple was at Epidaurus. In art his distinctive attribute is a staff with a serpent twisted round it.

Ash-Wednesday, the first day of Lent. It is said to derive its name from penitents sprinkling ashes on their heads. Brewer says the ashes were those of the palms burnt on Palm Sunday. The French have a similar name for the day—*Jour des cendres.*

Astȳ′anax, son of Hector and Andrŏmāchē. After the taking of Troy the Greeks hurled him from the walls that he might not restore the kingdom of Troy.

Ătăla′nta, an Arcadian princess. Her father, who had wished for a son, was disappointed at her birth and exposed the infant on a hill where she was brought up by a she-bear. After she had grown up, she slew the centaurs who pursued her, and took part in the Calydonian hunt. Her father subsequently recognized her as his daughter ; and when he desired her to marry, she required every suitor to contend with her in the foot-race. If he won, she would marry him : if not, he was to be put to death. She was at length overcome by Mīlăn′iōn with the help of Aphrodite. The goddess had given him three golden apples and during the race he dropped them one after the other. Their beauty charmed Atalanta so much that she could not abstain from gathering them, and Milanion thus reached the goal before her. She accordingly became his wife.

Read Swinburne's Chorus from ' Atalanta ' :

" Bind on thy sandals, O thou most fleet,
Over the splendour and speed of thy feet."

Morris's " Atalanta's Race " from *The Earthly Paradise* will interest many readers. On her marriage Atalanta

" in token of her service new
Shall give to Venus offerings rich enow,
Her maiden zone, her arrows and her bow."

Ā′tē, the Greek goddess of mischief. Homer says she was the cause of such strife that Zeus " straitway seized Ate by her bright-haired head and swore a mighty oath that never again to Olympus should she come. He said, and whirling her in his hand flung her down from the starry heaven, and quickly came she down among the works of men." On earth and in hell she led men into hasty actions, as she had done the gods in Olympus. Later accounts, especially tragic poets, represent her as a goddess who punished offenders (and their posterity) for their rash deeds rather than caused them herself. Thus her character is almost the same as that of Nĕ′mĕsis (Vengeance) and Erī′nys (the Fury).

Shakespeare several times refers to Ate. In *Much Ado* he labels her " the infernal." Mark Antony's great speech in *Julius Cæsar* was intended to invoke the spirit of mischief among the citizens of Rome. So, he says,

" Cæsar's spirit, ranging for revenge,
With Ate by his side, come hot from hell,
Shall, in these confines with a monarch's voice,
Cry ' havoc ' and let slip the dogs of war,"

i.e. no quarter given when famine, sword and fire are unleashed in civil war.

Athē′nē, or -a, one of the great deities of the Greek race, identified by the Romans with Minerva. Early tradition says she sprang, fully armed, from the head of Zeus. She was the goddess of wisdom, of industry and of the strategy of war ; she was the champion of the Greeks, and especially of the wise Odysseus, in the Trojan war. Her greatest gift to Athens was the olive. The story ran that Poseidon and Athene contended for control of the city. The gods decreed that whichever produced the gift most useful to mortals should possess the city. Poseidon struck the ground with his trident and a horse (or, according to another account, a well of salt water) sprang up. Athene produced the olive and was adjudged the giver of the better gift. She called the city Athenae, after herself. The owl and the serpent were sacred to her.

See **Acropolis, Pheidias, Arachne.**

Atla′ntis, according to ancient tradition, a great island somewhere west of the Pillars of Hercules, i.e. in the Atlantic Ocean. It fought successfully against a combination of Mediterranean powers ; but its inhabitants became wicked and impious and the island was swallowed in the Atlantic in a day and a night. The Canary Islands or the Azores, which perhaps were visited by the Phoenicians, may have given rise to the legend ; but some more modern writers think that it shows a vague belief in the existence of the Western hemisphere.

Bacon called his political romance *A New Atlantis.* Actually it is a Utopia as seen by the author.

A′tlas, brother of Prome′theūs and of Epime′theūs. He made war with the other Titans on Zeus and being conquered was condemned to bear heaven on his head and hands. The myth probably came from the idea that lofty mountains support the heavens. Later tradition makes Atlas a man who was changed into a mountain. Perseus asked him for shelter and was refused, whereupon by means of Medusa's head he changed him into Mount Atlas on which rested heaven with all its stars.

" The application to a map-book is said to be due to Mercator (end of the xvi century) who used a figure of *Atlas* supporting the globe as a frontispiece " (Weekley).

Atlas, condemned to bear heaven on his head and hands.

A′treūs, son of Pelops and father (or grandfather) of Agamemnon and Menelaus who are thus known as the ' Atridae.' The dreadful calamities of his family form the subject-matter of the greatest Greek tragedies, especially the grim triology of Aeschylus known as the ' Orestei′a.'

A′tropos, the Fate with ' th' abhorréd shears ' who cuts the thread at the time appointed for a man's life to end.

See **Fates.**

Attic. (*a*) the basic meaning is 'of Athens,' ' of Attica.' ' Attic ' is the dialect of Greek spoken by the Athenians. ' Attic faith ' signifies inviolability, the opposite of ' Punic faith.'

(*b*) architecturally, the top storey of a large building ; originally " a small decorative order placed above a greater (usually Attic) order. An attic is upright, a garret is in a sloping roof " (Weekley).

(c) as an epithet, applied, e.g. to *taste*, *wit*=delicate and refined, elegantly simple, such as was characteristic of the ancient Athenians. In Latin *sal Atticum* means ' delicate wit.' *Sal*=both ' salt ' and ' wit.'

Attïla, King of the Huns from A.D. 434 to 453. He is said to have ruled Europe from the Caspian Sea to the Rhine and to have called himself the ' Scourge of God '—a measure of the fear he inspired. In 451 he marched on Gaul with an army of upwards of three-quarters of a million men, and was defeated by a mixed army of Romans, Goths, Franks and others at the decisive battle of Châlons. The temporary allies, however, did not follow up their victory, and Attila crossed the Alps and went on to attack northern Italy, capturing Aquilëia (on the site of modern Venice) after a siege of three months ; but he was induced by Pope Leo the Great not to attack Rome.

See Gibbon's *Decline and Fall*, c. 35.

Augē'an Stables. Eurystheus King of Argos imposed upon Heracles the labour (his fifth) of cleansing in one day the stables of Augē'as, King of Elis. Augeas had a herd of 3,000 oxen whose stalls had not been cleansed for 30 years. By turning the rivers Alphē'us and Pēnē'us through the stalls Heracles cleansed them in a single day.

The adjective *Augean* thus means ' filthy ' or ' difficult.'

Autŏ'lÿcus, son of Hermes and maternal grandfather of Odysseus. He was renowned for his cunning and robberies, and was able to defy detection by changing the colour

and the shape of stolen property. Sisyphus, however, was as crafty as he. He was able to recognize his own oxen, stolen by Autolycus, by a mark which he had made under their feet.

Shakespeare calls his pedlar-pickpocket, the ' snapper-up of unconsidered trifles ' in *The Winter's Tale*, Autolycus. Read the amusing scene (iv, 2) in which he robs the old shepherd's son :

> *Autolycus* : Softly, dear sir ; [*Picks his pocket*] good sir, softly. You ha' done me a charitable office.

Babel. The inhabitants of the great alluvial tract through which the Tigris and the Euphrates pass before entering the sea—the tract known in later times as Chaldea or Babylonia—were the Sumerians. Naturally as clay was the only building material available to them they used bricks and not stone, and slime (i.e. bitumen) from the asphalt springs of Hit for mortar, in the building of their cities (*Gen.* 11².·). Babel (Babylon) was one of their chief cities which were constantly at war with each other. Tall towers were built by each of them as a safeguard against attack from their neighbours.

The Tower of Babel was probably that known as " the Tower of Babylon," called by Herodotus the " Temple of Belus." The historian says the stages of the pyramid tower were seven in number and an ascent going round the structure gave access to the top. Here was a shrine regarded by the Babylonians as the god's dwelling-place. There was probably no idea of " scaling heaven " in the minds of those who raised these stage towers : the expression " Let us build us a city and a tower, whose top may reach unto heaven " (*Gen.* 11⁴) is a mere exaggeration for a great height.

These lofty temple towers, solid and imposing pieces of architecture called Ziggurats (or Zikkurats), may have been built partly because the Sumerians felt that, when sacrificing or worshipping, those on the summit were nearer to the deity than those on the plain below.

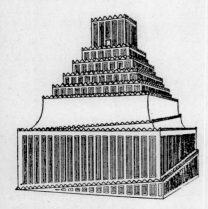

Temple of Tower of Babel. Probable form of the "Tower of Babylon," based on Mr. G. Smith's account, the description of Herodotus, and the remains of similar structures in Babylonia and Assyria.

Baleāres, three islands in the Mediterranean off the coast of Spain, distinguished by the names *Major* and *Minor*, and Epusa, whence their modern names Majorca, Minorca and Iviça. Their inhabitants were celebrated as slingers.

Balm in Gilead. Gilead is a rocky district east of the Jordan. It was famous for its balm, a rare aromatic vegetable juice with medicinal properties. See *Genesis* 37²⁵ : " Behold, a company of Ishmeelites came from Gilead with their camels bearing spicery and balm and myrrh, going to carry it down to

Egypt," and *Jeremiah* 8²² : " Is there no balm in Gilead ? "

Behemoth. See Leviathan.

Belial. ' Belial ' literally means ' worthlessness.' In the O.T. the word is always used as a common noun, denoting an extreme degree of depravity, e.g. the sons of Eli were " sons of Belial," for they profaned the priestly office (1 *Sam.* 2¹²) ; Hannah, clearing herself of the charge of drunkenness, begged Eli : " Count not thine handmaid for a daughter of Belial " (*1 Sam.* 1¹⁶). In the N.T. the word became a proper name, a title of Satan (2 *Cor.* 6¹⁵).

In Milton, the name is identified with one of the fallen angels :

" Belial came last, than whom a
    spirit more lewd
Fell not from Heaven."

Similarly Macaulay personifies Belial (and Mammon) :

" Down, down, for ever down
    with the mitre and the crown,
With the Belial of the Court and
    the Mammon of the Pope."
        (*Battle of Naseby*).

Belle'rŏphon, son of the Corinthian King Glaucus. Being banished for murder, he fled to Argos where he was guilty of an offence against King Proetus' honour. Proetus could not himself kill his guest, so he sent him to Iŏ'bătēs, his father-in-law, with a request that the messenger should be put to death. Accordingly, Iobates sent him to kill the monster Chimaera, but obtaining possession of the winged horse Pegasus, Bellerophon rose with him in the air and killed the Chimaera. After further similar successful exploits, Bellerophon married the daughter of Iobates and succeeded to the throne. Later traditions assert that Bellerophon attempted to fly to heaven on

Bellerophon, Pegasus, and Chimaera. (*From a vase*).   *Mounted on the winged horse Pegasus, clad in chlamys and petasus, Bellerophon slays the Chimaera.*

Pegasus, but that Zeus sent a gadfly to sting the horse which threw off the rider.

'Bellerophon' is used in R.N. as a ship's name; e.g. it was the Bellerophon (corrupted by sailors into 'Billy Ruffian') which took Napoleon to St. Helena.

See **Pegasus**.

Bellō′na, the Roman goddess of war, wife of Mars.

Shakespeare poetically calls Macbeth 'Bellona's bridegroom.' In *I Henry IV* 4, 1, 114 Hotspur describes Bellona as "the fire-eyed maid of smoky war." See, too, *Paradise Lost* ii, 922,

> "Bellona storms,
> With all her battering engines bent to rase
> Some capital city."

Benjamin, Jacob's youngest son and only full brother of Joseph.

His mother Rachel died in giving him birth. She called him "Benoni"=the 'son of my sorrow,' but his father called him "Benjamin"=the 'son of the right hand.' The only indication we have of Benjamin's personal character is found in the blessing of Jacob (*Gen.* 49^{27}) where he is compared to a wolf. Jacob loved Benjamin best of all his sons and he would not send him with his brothers to Egypt in quest of corn "lest peradventure mischief befall him" (*Gen.* 42^4). On the second visit of Jacob's sons to Egypt Joseph, now overlord of the country, made them a feast and Benjamin's "mess" was five times as much as any of theirs (*Gen.* 43^{34}).

A 'Benjamin' is, therefore, the pet son of a family, and a 'Benjamin's mess' is the largest share.

Bethel. The name in Hebrew means 'House of God' (*Gen.* 28^{17}).

In the nineteenth century some Nonconformist bodies gave the name to their place of worship. Weekley says ' Bethesda ' (=House of Mercy, *John* 5²) was similarly used, especially in Wales.

Bible, The English. (a) Authorized Version, based largely on the text of the Bishops' Bible, the work of a group of 54 revisers convened by James I, published in 1611. Its scholarship is not exact, but the beauty of its prose and diction is superb. The Revisers of the N.T. say of it : " The longer we have been engaged on it, the more we have learnt to admire its simplicity, its dignity, its happy turns of expression . . . the music of its cadences and the felicity of its rhythm." No book has had greater influence on the formation of English prose style.

(b) Revised Version, published 1885, was made by 25 scholars, the most prominent of whom were Dr. Hort, Dr. Scrivener and Bishop Westcott.

Older versions were :

(i) Wm. Tindale's faithful version of the N.T. which, he said, would cause the lads at the plough to become more familiar with the Bible than were the clergy of his own day, was printed in Antwerp in 1524-6.

(ii) Cranmer's, or the Great Bible (so called from its size) was first printed in 1539. It was ordered to be set up in all the churches throughout the kingdom under a penalty of 40/- a month.

(iii) The Bishops' Bible (referred to above) was promoted by Archbishop Parker and published in 1568.

Various Bibles containing errors which have given them their names are known as The Vinegar Bible, the Treacle Bible, The Bug Bible, and the Breeches Bible.

Boa'dicĕa, more correctly **Bou'dicca,** queen of the Icĕni who occupied the present-day counties of Norfolk and Suffolk. She incited the Britons to rebel, but was finally defeated by Suetonius Paulinus, and put an end to her own life, A.D. 61.

Scenes from John Fletcher's *Bonduca* are worth reading and acting. William Cowper's ballad is magnificently conceived and written :

" Rome shall perish—write that word
In the blood that she has spilt."

Boane'rges, the surname Christ gave to James the son of Zebedee, and John the brother of James. The word means ' Sons of Thunder ' and is well applied to men of impetuous character such as these two apostles were (see, for example, *Luke* 9⁵¹⁻⁵⁶).

Figuratively, the word is used of a loud-mouthed orator, a tub-thumper.

Boeō'tia, a district in ancient Greece nearly surrounded by mountains, but containing fertile plains. The atmosphere was damp and thick, and its inhabitants were proverbially dull-witted. The two Thebans, Pindar in literature and Epaminondas in war, were however brilliant exceptions.

Bŏ'rĕas, the N. (or more correctly the NNE.) wind, brother of the other winds—Zĕphўrus (W. wind) and Nŏtus (S. wind). It is probably the same as the furious NE. wind (called ' Euraquilo ' in R.V.) which drove Paul's ship off its course (*Acts* 27¹⁴).

Boreas. (*From the monument at Athens*). *He is blowing on a Triton's horn, to signify his power of raising storms at sea.*

Bread upon the Waters. " Cast thy bread upon the waters : for thou shalt find it after many days " (*Ecclesiastes* 11¹) ; i.e. do good without looking for gratitude or immediate or definite return (C.O.D.). There is reference to the inundation of the White Nile, the current of which is weak. It carries a considerable amount of very fertile mud which is deposited on the land and gives it its marvellous productiveness. As soon as the fields are free from water agricultural labours begin. The rice-seed is sown in the alluvial deposit and " after many days " it produces a rich crop.

With this, contrast Hosea's " They have sown the wind and they shall reap the whirlwind " (8⁷), where severe retribution is the promised harvest for those who sow the seed of iniquity. " He that soweth iniquity shall reap vanity " (*Prov.* 22⁸).

Briă'rēūs, see **Aegaeon.**

Bricks are mentioned in the Bible as early as the days of the Tower of Babel (*Gen.* 11³). Egyptian bricks were not generally dried in kilns but in the sun ; and even without straw they are as firm as when first put up. When made of Nile mud they required straw to prevent their cracking. The Hebrews, in common with other captives, practised brick-making in Egypt, and the brick-kiln was common in David's time (2 *Sam.* 12³¹).

Pharaoh compelled the Hebrews to "make bricks without straw", i.e. without materials essential for their manufacture.

Brīsē'is. See **Chrȳsē'is.**

Būce'phălus, the horse of Alexander the Great, which his father Philip purchased for 13 talents and which no one was able to break in except Alexander. This horse carried the conqueror throughout his Asiatic campaigns and died in India. It was so named because its head resembled that of a bull.

See **Alexander the Great.**

Burning Bush. Moses had spent forty years tending the flocks of his father-in-law, the shepherd-priest Jethro, while waiting for a call from God. When it came, the revelation was made by the appearance of a burning bush (probably the bramble or blackberry) which was not consumed—a sight which was bound to attract the attention of Moses in the midst of the surrounding granite mountains. Then came God's own voice: " Put off thy shoes from off thy feet, for the place whereon thou standest is holy ground," followed by instructions to Moses to return to Egypt and to lead thence the chosen people unto " a good land and a large, unto a land flowing with milk and honey."

The full story is given in *Exodus* 3 and is referred to by Our Lord in *Luke* 20³⁷.

Bushel. No doubt a bushel was a cylindrical wooden box used for measuring dry goods such as corn and fruit (*Matt.* 5¹⁵ and elsewhere in the Gospels), i.e. it was a measure of capacity. Just as a lamp (or candle) must not be placed under a bushel when it is required to show light, so by his open conduct the Christian must bear witness to his profession : " Even so let your light shine before men that they may see your good works."

Bus'kin, the cothurnus, the closed boot worn by Roman tragedians. Its special characteristic was the

Cothurnus, the tragic boot worn in Roman times by tragedians, cf. *Soccus.*

great height of its sole, the object being to give the principal characters a grandiose and superhuman stature.

In *The Bard* Gray refers to tragedies, and especially those of Shakespeare, as ' buskin'd measures.'

See **Sock.**

Ca'dmus, son of Agē'nŏr, King of Phoenicia and brother of Europa. When Europa was carried off by Zeus to Crete, Agenor sent Cadmus in search of her. Unable to find her Cadmus settled in Thrace ; but having consulted the oracle of Apollo at Delphi he was commanded to follow *the white cow* and to build a town on the spot where the cow should lie down. Immediately on leaving the temple he saw a spotless white cow and followed her into Boeotia where she lay down on the spot on which Cadmus built the Cadmea, afterwards the citadel of Thebes. Intending to sacrifice the cow to Athena he sent men to the neighbouring well of Ares to fetch water. The well was guarded by a dragon (a son of Ares) who devoured the men Cadmus had sent. Cadmus slew the dragon and, on the advice of Athena, sowed the teeth of the monster. The crop was armed men, called *Sparti,* i.e. *the Sown Men.* Cadmus stirred up these armed men to fight each other and only five of them survived. These five helped him to build the Cadmea and they were the reputed ancestors of the Thebans. The gods loved Cadmus and gave him a beautiful wife, Harmŏ'nia, daughter of Ares and Aphrodite. In the end, owing to the misfortunes of their children, Cadmus and Harmonia left Thebes. They were changed into serpents and Zeus removed them to Elysium. See **Harmonia.**

The ancient Greeks believed they learnt the art of writing from the Phoenicians. Cadmus is reputed to have introduced the alphabet of 16 letters into Greece from Phoenicia.

A ' Cadmean victory ' (from the fight among the *Sparti*) is one involving the ruin of the victor. Cf. Pyrrhic Victory.

Cadū'cĕus, the staff or mace

carried by Greek heralds and ambassadors in time of war. Hermes was the messenger of the gods, so

Caduceus of Bronze, 16 in. in length. (British Museum). It was the mace carried by Greek heralds and ambassadors in time of peace. Hermes (Mercury) is usually represented carrying this staff (see Charon and Hermes p. 44).

he is represented with a caduceus in his hand. With it he conducted the souls of the dead to the infernal regions ; by its touch he could lull to sleep or even raise a dead person to life.

Cae′sar, Julius (100 or 102-44 B.C.). Julius Caesar was perhaps the greatest man of antiquity. He was at one and the same time a general, a statesman, a law-giver, an orator and an historian. His main work as a statesman was to reorganise the government of the state, which had been fitted for the control of Italy but not for the rule of an empire. During the whole of his busy life he found time for literary pursuits. The purity of his

Latin and the clearness of his style were celebrated by the ancients themselves. Only his *Commentaries* have come down to us. They relate the history of the first seven years of the Gallic War and the history of part of the Civil War. What he has to tell us of his two invasions of Britain in 55 and 54 B.C. and of the character and occupations of the native Britons is of especial interest to us.

Cain, The Curse of. See *Genesis* 4¹⁰⁻¹⁶ and v. 15 in particular. This does not mean, as Longfellow seems to believe, that God put any actual mark on Cain's body : rather, He gave Cain some unrevealed token (very much as *signs* were afterwards given to Moses, Elijah and Hezekiah) that he might still repent.

" . . . every nation that should lift again
Its hand against a brother, on its forehead
Would wear for evermore the curse of Cain."
        The Arsenal at Springfield.

The ' curse of Cain ' in general is the wrongdoer's conscience which tortures him and makes him restless. " A fugitive and a vagabond shalt thou be in the earth " was the sentence God passed on the fratricide.

Ca′lchas, the wisest soothsayer among the Greeks at Troy. He foretold the length of the Trojan war, explained the cause of the pestilence which reigned in the Greek army, and advised the Greeks to build the wooden horse.
See **Mo′psus.**

Calends, the first day of the Roman month. Literally ' proclamation ' day (old Latin *calo* = to proclaim), because on that day the pontiffs or high-priests ' proclaimed ' the beginning of the month.

Greek Calends: never.

Calf, The Fatted. Read the parable of the " Prodigal Son." (*Luke* 15[11-32]).

" To kill the fatted calf " is to welcome with open arms the returning reckless spendthrift of the family, the ' Prodigal Son.'

Căli'gŭla, Gaius Caesar, Roman emperor, A.D. 37-41. *Caligula* was a surname given him by the soldiers from his wearing in his boyhood small *Caligae* or soldiers' boots. To express it mildly, he was most eccentric and cruel. He even considered himself a god and built a temple to himself. He raised his horse ' Incitā'tus ' to the consulship. With his troops he advanced to the ocean as if intending to cross over into Britain : he drew them up in battle array and then gave them the signal—to collect shells, which he called the spoils of conquered ocean. Not unnaturally, he was murdered. Without doubt his vices, peculiarities and eccentricities were partly due to madness.

Calli'măchus, a native of Cyrene in Africa and a celebrated poet who lived at Alexandria in the 3rd century B.C. He was said to be chief librarian of the famous library of Alexandria. His most famous poem, a six-lined epigram on his friend Hēraclī'tus of Halicarnassus in Asia Minor, was translated by Cory, an Eton master (374 in the World's Classics edition of the Golden Treasury). This is regarded by many scholars as the most perfect piece of translation ever done :

" They told me, Heraclitus, they told me you were dead,
They brought me bitter news to hear and bitter tears to shed.

I wept, as I remembered, how often you and I
Had tired the sun with talking and sent him down the sky.

And now that thou art lying, my dear old Carian guest,
A handful of grey ashes, long, long ago at rest,
Still are thy pleasant voices, thy nightingales, awake ;
For Death, he taketh all away, but them he cannot take."

Calli'opē, the Muse of Epic Poetry. See **Muses.**

Cal'pē, the Rock of Gibraltar, a mountain in S. of Spain on the Straits between the Atlantic and the Mediterranean. This and Mt. A'bўla opposite to it on the African coast were called the *Pillars of Hercules,* from the fable that they were originally one mountain which was torn asunder by Heracles.

" Through Calpe's straits survey the steepy shore ;
Europe and Afric on each other gaze ! "
(*Childe Harold* ii, xxii.).

W. S. Blunt's sonnet ' Gibraltar ' will interest.

Căly'psō, a nymph inhabiting the island of Ogy'gĭa on which Odysseus was shipwrecked. Calypso loved him and promised him immortality if he would remain with her. Odysseus refused, and after she had detained him seven years, the gods compelled her to allow him to continue his journey homewards. Possibly Ogygia is to be identified with Gozo in the Maltese group.

Modern Negro topical doggerel songs are said to be called Calypso's, but no satisfactory explanation is available.

Cami'lla, one of the swift-footed servants of Diana, accustomed to the chase and to war. She was so swift that she could run over a field of corn without bending the blades, and make her way over the sea without wetting her feet. She helped Turnus against Aeneas.

In his *Essay on Criticism*, Pope says that most critics judge a poem by its versification. The poet's acute ear chooses words in which there is correspondence of the *sound* with the *meaning*. As an example of ' sound echoing sense ' he gives :

"Not so when swift Camilla scours the plain,
Flies o'er th'unbending corn, and skims along the main."

Capernaum, our Lord's ' own city' (*Matt.* 9¹), on the coast of the Sea of Galilee, in the fertile plain of Gennesaret (*Matt.* 14³⁴). It was chosen as His base of operations after His expulsion from Nazareth (*Luke* 4¹⁴⁻³⁰). It had a synagogue built by a Roman centurion (*Luke* 7⁵) and was a military station. It was on the important trade-route between Egypt, Jerusalem and Damascus, and hence taxes were levied there on all goods in transit through the lake-port by the ' publicans ' (i.e. the small local tax-collectors) who had their " receipt of custom " (A.V.), " place of toll " (R.V.) on the shores of the lake. But Capernaum shared in Christ's severe condemnation of the Galilean cities, unrepentant despite His miracles and teaching : " And thou, Capernaum, shalt thou be exalted unto heaven ? thou shalt go down unto Hades : for if the mighty works had been done in Sodom which were done in thee, it would have remained until this day . . . It shall be more tolerable for the land of Sodom in

The Porch of the Maidens (*the Erectheum*). *The Caryatids are used instead of columns to support the Entablature.*

the day of judgment, than for thee " (*Matt.* 11²³,²⁴ R.V.).

Carā'tăcus (or wrongly, for the name is a Latinization of the Welsh 'Caradoc,' Cara'ctăcus), King of the Silures (in modern South Wales), defended his country against the Romans. He was at length defeated and fled to the Queen of the Brigantes (who dwelt in the N. of Britain from the Humber to the Roman Wall) ; but she betrayed him and he was carried captive to Rome. When brought before Claudius, he addressed the emperor in so noble a manner as to secure his pardon.

In Fletcher's *Bonduca* he appears as Caratach, Boadicea's brother-in-law and most able warrior :
" a Caratach,
A Roman-hater, a scourge sent from heaven
To whip these proud thieves from our Kingdom."

Carthage, one of the most famous cities of the ancient world. It was long the rival of Rome and the mistress of Spain, Sicily and Sardinia. The three Punic wars saw its destruction (146 B.C.). The Carthaginians bore the character of a faithless and treacherous people.
See **Punic Faith ; Cato the Censor.**

Carthāgo Nŏva, New Carthage, founded by Hasdrubal in 243 B.C., is the modern Cartagena.

Caryă'tids are female figures sometimes fancifully used in place of columns in the architecture of Greek temples. The name has been commonly given to the figures supporting the portico of the Erechtheum on the Acropolis. Originally the Caryatides were figures of maidens, the 'Caryatides' or priestesses of Artemis at Caryae in Laconia, executing the ritual dance in

honour of their goddess. See the accompanying figure. Cf. **Telamon.**

Caryatid from the Erechtheum at Athens. A figure of a maiden fancifully used as a supporting column.

Cassa'ndra, daughter of Priam and Hecuba. When she grew up her beauty won the love of Apollo who gave her the gift of prophecy ; but she afterwards refused to listen to his guile. Thereupon the god wetted her lips with his tongue and so brought it about that no credit should ever be put upon her predictions, however true or faithful they might be. She predicted to the Trojans the ruin that threatened them. On the capture of Troy she fell to the lot of Agamemnon who took her with him to Greece. She repeatedly foretold to him the sudden calamities that

awaited his return ; but he gave
no credence to her and was assassinated by Clytemnestra. Cassandra
shared his fate.

Ca′stor. See **Dioscuri.**

Căto, Marcus Porcius, surnamed
Censorius (i.e. Censor). He was
distinguished for the simplicity of
his life, and was violently opposed
to the luxury of the Roman nobles,
the great family of the Scipios in
particular. Towards the end of his
life he was sent to Africa to arbitrate
between the Numidians and the
Carthaginians ; and he returned
home convinced by the strength of
Carthage that Rome would never
be safe so long as Carthage remained
in existence. So, from that time
on, whenever he was called upon
for his vote in the Senate, even
though the debate had had no
relation to Carthage, he would
preface his remarks by the words
Delenda est Carthago (Carthage must be blotted out).
Compare the Dickensian
story in *David Copperfield*
of the harmless lunatic Mr.
Dick, who found it im-
possible to keep King
Charles's Head out of his
thoughts. Cato, like Mr.
Dick, was rather a man of
one idea, though he was
certainly not a lunatic.

Cē′crops, said to have
been the first King of Attica
and to have founded Athens,
the citadel of which was
called ' Cecropia ' after him.

Cen′chrĕae, the E. harbour of Corinth. Here
Paul with Priscilla and
Aquila embarked for Syria
on his return from his
second missionary journey
(*Acts* 18¹⁸). Paul must

have escaped from some personal
danger during his long stay at
Corinth and, in gratitude, he took a
vow upon himself, as Jews frequently did in similar circumstances.
He would let his hair grow until
the end of the time for which he
had taken the vow [*see* **Nazarite**].
Then the hair would be shaved off
and burnt, with accompanying
rites, in the temple. But Paul was
far away from the temple, so at
Cenchreae he redeemed his vow
by *polling* his hair and keeping it
until such time as it could be burnt
and he could have his head shaved,
to bring his vow to an end, at the
temple in Jerusalem.

Centaurs, a mythical race inhabiting the mountains of Thessaly,
represented as half men and half
horses. The ancient Thessalians,
having tamed horses and appeared
to their neighbours mounted on
horseback—a most uncommon sight

Centaur. (*Metope from the Parthenon*).
*Contests between Gods and Giants or the
Lapithae and Centaurs are the subjects most
commonly treated in metopes.*

at the time—easily gave the impression that horse and rider were but one creature. Chīrōn alone among the Centaurs is represented as possessing wisdom, learning and culture.

Cĕ′phălus, husband of Procris. Though neither husband nor wife was a pattern of fidelity, they ultimately became reconciled. But Procris still had some suspicion of her husband, and Cephalus, hearing her rustling among the leaves of a bush, mistook her for a wild beast and killed her with his unerring spear.

> *Pyramus* : Not Shafalus to Procrus was so true.
> *Thisbe* : As Shafalus to Procrus, I to you.

Thus, in the Interlude (*A Midsummer Night's Dream*, v, 1) Pyramus and Thisbe clownishly blunder over the classical names.

Ce′rberus, the dog guarding the entrance to Hades. Some poets represent him with 50 or even 100 heads, but later writers describe him as a monster with three heads, the tail of a serpent and serpents round his neck. His den is placed on the further side of the river Styx at the spot where Charon landed the shades of the dead. Here he prevented the living from entering the realms of Pluto and the dead from leaving them. The last (and most difficult) of the twelve labours of Heracles was bringing Cerberus from the lower world. He was not allowed the use of any weapons, but he seized the monster with his hands and carried him to the upper world. After he had shown him to his master Eurystheus he carried him back again to Hades.

A sop to Cerberus. When a living person (e.g. the Sibyl in *Aeneid* vi :

" The Sibyl, as the snakes reared on his neck,
Flung him a sop made drowsy with drugged meal
And honey, which the three throats gaping caught
With ravenous hunger.")

visited Hades, he threw a medicated cake (a ' sop ') to Cerberus who ate it and promptly fell asleep, thus allowing the visitor to pass. So ' a sop to Cerberus ' is a bribe offered to a formidable opponent, an attempt to persuade an official to overlook an offence, or the like.

Cē′rēs. See **Demeter.**

Chărĭtēs, called **Gratiae** by the Romans, the three Graces, constant attendants of Aphrodite, were daughters of Zeus or Bacchus. Their names were Euphrŏs′ўnē or ' cheerfulness ', Aglă′ĭa or ' brightness ' and Thalī′a or ' bloom '.

In *L'Allegro* Milton invokes the Graces :

" But come, thou Goddess fair and free,
In heaven yclep'd Euphrosyne,
And by men, heart-easing Mirth,
Whom lovely Venus at a birth
With two sister Graces more
To ivy-crownéd Bacchus bore."

Chă′rōn, son of Erebus, the surly ferryman who rowed the shades of the dead across the rivers of the lower world. An obol was placed under the tongue of every corpse previous to its burial in order that Charon might receive his fee.

" These floods and rivers a dread ferryman,
Grim squalid Charon, guards ; matted grey hair
Covers his chin ; his eyes are glaring flame :
Foul on his shoulders hangs a knotted plaid.
His own hand punts the boat, he tends the sails,

Charon, Hermes and Soul. (*From a Roman lamp*). *Charon is represented as a bearded man clothed in the sailor's exōmis, his right arm bare so as to permit freedom of movement.*

Towing the corpses on his rust-
   red craft.
Old now, yet a god's age is
   fresh and green."
         Virgil : *Aeneid* vi,
         tr. Frank Richards.

   Endymion refers to Charon's ' penny pelf ', and Troilus, in his quest for Cressida, says :
   " O, be thou my Charon,
And give me swift transportance
   to those fields
Where I may wallow in the lily-
   beds
Proposed for the deserver."

   Chimae′ra, a fabulous fire-breathing monster of composite form. The fore part of the body was that of a lion, the hind part that of a dragon and the middle that of a goat. The origin of the notion of this monster is probably in the volcano of the name of Chimaera in Lycia. It vomited flames from its summit, lions dwelt in the upper forests, goats in the pasture slopes and snakes in the marshes at its foot.

We call any wild idle fancy a ' chimera '. The adjective chimeric (-al) = fanciful.
   Greek khimaira = she-goat.
Virgil links
   " . . . the awful hiss
Of Lerna's brute, Chimaera
   armed with fire,
The Gorgons . . ."
among the dwellers in the entrance of the gate of hell. Milton follows him in *Paradise Lost* :
   " . . . all prodigious things,
Abominable, inutterable, . . .
Gorgons and Hydras and Chim-
   aeras dire."

   Chi′ron, the wisest and justest of all the Centaurs. He lived on Mount Pelion. He was instructed by Apollo and Artemis, and was renowned for his skill in hunting, medicine, music, gymnastics and the art of prophecy. All the most distinguished heroes of Grecian story, as Peleus, Achilles, Diomedes, Jason, are described as the pupils of Chiron in these arts. Heracles was his friend ; but when he was fighting with the other Centaurs, one of his poisoned arrows accidentally struck Chiron who, although immortal, would not live any longer and gave his immortality to Prometheus.

   Chrysē′is. There was trouble in the Greek camp over a captive maid, Chryseis, daughter of a priest of Apollo. Achilles had taken her prisoner and in the distribution of booty she fell to the lot of Agamemnon who refused to allow her father to ransom her. In consequence Apollo sent a plague into the Greek camp. To stay the plague Agamemnon was obliged to relinquish Chryseis. He then took in her place Brisē′is, a slave-girl belonging to Achilles. Naturally Achilles was angry and he vowed he would take no further part in the fighting. " See how Agamemnon has dishonoured me and stolen my prize," he lamented to Thetis his mother as he sat in grief by the sea. He continued to nurse his grievance until his friend Patroclus was killed.

Ci'cero, Marcus Tullius, the Roman orator (106–43 B.C.). He exposed the conspiracy of Catiline in 63 and became consul. After Caesar's assassination he vehemently attacked Antony in his Philippic orations and was proscribed and put to death by the Triumvirate in 43. His true fame rests upon his writings. 56 of his Orations are extant as well as upwards of 800 personal letters, most of them addressed to his friend Atticus and to his brother Quintus.

Shakespeare gives us some glimpses of Cicero. Brutus says :
" Cicero
Looks with such ferret and such fiery eyes
As we have seen him in the Capitol,
Being cross'd in conference by some senators " ;
and Brutus again :
" He will never follow any thing That other men begin ",
i.e. he was a conceited man who would never pursue to the end a policy laid down by someone else.

From the orator's name we have the word ' cicerone '=a guide who escorts visitors round museums.

Cimme'rians : (i) a mythical people fabled to live in the furthest west on the " deep-flowing River of Ocean and the frontiers of the world, where the fog-bound Cimmerians live in the City of Perpetual Mist " (E. V. Rieu's trans. of the *Odyssey*).
(ii) The historical Cimmerii, according to Herodotus, dwelt to the north of the Euxine. Their name

is retained in the modern ' Crimea.'

Cincinnā'tus, a favourite hero of the old Roman republic and a model of old-fashioned frugality and integrity. He lived on his farm, cultivating the land with his own hand. He was called from the plough to the dictatorship in order to deliver the army from a perilous military position. He saved the army, defeated the enemy and, after holding the dictatorship only sixteen days, returned to his farm.

A great man in retirement might be referred to as a Cincinnatus. In his " Ode to Napoleon Bonaparte " Byron called Washington the ' Cincinnatus of the West '. Washington lived several years in retirement after he had compelled Britain to acknowledge the Independence of the Americans.

Cir'cē, a sorceress, daughter of Hēlios, who lived in the island of Aeāē'a upon which Odysseus was cast. His companions tasted of the magic cup which Circe offered them and were changed into swine. Having received from Hermes the root *moly* which fortified him against enchantment, Odysseus drank the magic cup without

Circe and Odysseus, and his Companions changed into swine. (From an ancient bas-relief).

injury, and then compelled Circe to restore his companions to their former shape. After this he tarried a whole year with her.

See the attendant Spirit's opening speech in *Comus* :

"Who knows not Circe,
The daughter of the Sun, whose
    charmed cup
Whoever tasted lost his upright
    shape,
And downward fell into a
    grovelling swine ? "

Samson compares Dalila with Circe :

"Thy fair enchanted cup, and
    warbling charms,
No more on me have power,
    their force is nulled."
        (*Sam. Agon.* 934, 5).

Clay in the potter's hand.
See *Jeremiah* 8 where, under the type of a potter, God's power in disposing of nations is shown. The potter first of all trod down the clay to soften it and prepare it for his wheels. These consisted of a lower and an upper disc which revolved in opposite directions on the same vertical axle. The lower disc was driven by the potter's foot while the clay was placed on the upper wheel and formed by the hand (*Ecclesiasticus* 38$^{29-31}$). The vessels were then baked in an oven.

A person is " clay in the potter's hand " when his disposition is malleable, pliable, capable of being influenced by a more masterful disposition.

Clĕŏpa′tra. See **Antony.**

Cli′o, the Muse of History.
See **Muses.**

Cli′tus, a Macedonian general who saved the life of his foster-brother Alexander the Great at the battle of Granĭcus. Some years later Clitus provoked Alexander's jealousy :

"in anger each saw red,
And Alexander's dart struck
    Clitus dead,"—

a crime for which Alexander never forgave himself.

Clō′thō, the Fate who spins the thread of life.
See **Fates.**

Cloud. Among both Hebrews and Arabs the clouds were closely studied with a view to forecasting much desired rain, so naturally clouds enter largely into Oriental imagery. With both peoples a ' cloud without rain ' is a figure for ' promise without performance ', e.g. in *Prov.* 16^{15} : [the King's] " favour is as a cloud of the latter rain." After his victory over the Gods of Baal on Mount Carmel Elijah sent his servant seven times

The Potter. *Hath not the potter power over the clay?* (Romans 9-^{21}).

to look towards the sea to watch for signs of rain. After the seventh visit the servant reported : " There ariseth a little cloud out of the sea, like a man's hand." Presently " the heaven was black with clouds and wind and there was a great rain " (1 *Kings* 18$^{43\text{-}5}$).

Cloud by Day, Pillar of Fire by Night.

In their journey from Egypt to Canaan the Israelites were preceded by a pillar of cloud by day and of fire by night. See *Ex.* 13 ^{21,2}.

In general the expression means ' divine (and therefore infallible) guidance.'

Clytaemne′stra,

wife of Agamemnon. During her husband's absence at Troy she lived with Aegisthus and on Agamemnon's return to Mycenae she murdered him with the help of Aegisthus. She was afterwards put to death by her son Orestes.

Coals of Fire.

" If thine enemy be hungry, give him bread to eat ; and if he be thirsty, give him water to drink : for thou shalt heap coals of fire upon his head (*Prov.* 25 ^{21,2}, repeated by Paul in *Rom.* 12^{20}). In these passages " coals of fire " metaphorically expresses the burning shame men must feel when their evil is requited by good.

Coat of Many Colours.

" Now Israel (i.e. Jacob) loved Joseph more than all his children because he was the son of his old age ; and he made him a coat of many colours " (*Gen.* 37^3). This may have been a " coat of divers colours," or it may have been a coat with bright-coloured patches such as Arabs still wear. We do not know when the art of dyeing became known to the Hebrews. The Hebrew probably means " coat with long sleeves." In either case it is not a coat in which hard work could be done, and so could be worn only by the spoilt favourite of the family.

Co′cles,

Horātius—that is, Horatius the ' one-eyed '—a hero of the old Roman lays who is said to have defended the Sublician bridge with Spurius Lartius and Titus Herminius against the whole Etruscan army under Porsena, while the Romans broke down the bridge behind them. When the work was nearly finished Horatius sent back his two companions. As soon as the bridge was destroyed, he plunged into the stream and swam across to the city. As a reward

" They gave him of the corn-land,
   That was of public right,
As much as two strong oxen
   Could plough from morn to night;
And they made a molten image,
   And set it up on high,
And there it stands unto this day
   To witness if I lie."

See Macaulay's " Horatius " from *Lays of Ancient Rome.*

Cocȳ′tus,

the river of ' wailing ', in the lower world.

Cognomen,

a third name indicating the family to which a Roman belonged. It was literally a ' nickname ' (i.e. an additional name) and indicated sometimes (i) some physical characteristic, e.g. Barbātus (bearded) ; Cocles (one-eyed) ; Nāso (big-nosed) ; Caecus (blind) ; sometimes (ii) disposition, e.g. Sevērus, Serēnus, Superbus ; sometimes (iii) origin, e.g. Gallus, Tuscus.

A special application of the cognomen, a fourth name, properly called an *agnomen*, was often given to great statesmen or generals or other persons for work of national merit. See **Scipio** [Africānus] ; **Coriolānus** ; **Manlius** [Capitolīnus ; Torquātus] ; **Fabius** [Cunctātor].

In the same way titles are conferred on our statesmen, generals and admirals for work of outstanding national importance, and these titles are generally taken from the scenes of their most memorable actions : thus Lord Montgomery *of Alamein.* Lord Louis Mountbatten *of Burma* and Admiral Lord Frazer *of North Cape.* But by the early days of the Empire, or even in the later days of the Republic, this system of names came to be misapplied or even disregarded altogether.

Coins, mentioned in the Gospels. (i) *Silver.* (*a*) the *stater,* the Hebrew *shekel,* worth about half-a-crown of our money. This was the coin (called ' a piece of money ' in A.V., ' a shekel ' in R.V.) found in the fish's mouth and used to pay the Temple Tax for Peter and our Lord (*Matt.* 17²⁷).

Every adult Jew paid a *half-shekel* annually toward the upkeep of the Temple. " They that received the tribute money [R.V. the half-shekel] came to Peter and said, Doth not your master pay

(*1*) **Silver Tetradrachm of Antioch :** " *Piece of Money* " (*Stater, Mt.* 17²⁷).
(*2*) **Copper " Farthing " of Pontius Pilate.** (*Mk.* 12⁴²).
(*3*) **Copper Assarion** (*Mt.* 10²⁹ ; *Lu.* 12⁶). The " *farthing* " of the New Testament.
(*4*) **Silver Half Shekel.** *Didrachma, i.e. Double Drachma.*
(*5*) **Silver Denarius** (" *Penny* " ; *Mt.* 20.²) of Tiberius.

tribute [R.V. the half-shekel] ? "
(*Matt.* 17²⁴).

(*b*) the *Denarius* or Roman penny,
bearing the image of the Roman
Emperor, and a superscription.
Jews from 14 to 65 years of age
paid to Rome a poll-tax, called in
N.T. ' tribute '. " Shew me the
tribute money " said Christ to the
tempting Pharisees and Herodians.
" And they brought him a penny."
(*Matt.* 22¹⁵⁻²²).

(ii) *Copper*. The *farthing*, and its
half, the ' *mite* ', formed the chief
native currency. The farthing was
the smallest Roman coin, worth
about ⅛ penny. The poor widow
cast into the treasury chest ' two
mites which make a farthing ',
(*Mark* 12⁴²). " Are not two
sparrows sold for a farthing ? "
(*Matt.* 10²⁹) ; " Are not five sparrows sold for two farthings ? "
(*Luke* 12⁶).

It may be of interest to note that
the South African farthing has two
sparrows on the reverse, i.e. its
Biblical commodity value (*Matt.*
10²⁹).

Colosse′um or **Colise′um**, so called
on account of its gigantic size or
from the colossal statue of Nero
which stood close by, was built for
staging the gladiatorial combats,
the ' *venationes* ' or exhibitions of
wild beasts fighting with one
another and with men, and the
' *naumachiae* ' or naval battles
fought in the flooded arena. These
exhibitions were as dear to the
average Roman as professional football matches are to-day to their supporters. The amphitheatre was
begun by Vespasian, dedicated in
80 by his son Titus and added to
by Domitian. It was built on
marshy ground which had pre-

*Amphitheatrum Flavium, or Colosseum, begun by Vespasian and completed
by Titus in 80 A.D.*

D

viously been the lake of Nero's palace. For a general description of the building see Gibbon, ch. xii.

" Arches on arches ! as it were
    that Rome,
Collecting the chief trophies of
    her line,
Would build up all her
    triumphs in one dome,
Her Coliseum stands."
        (*Childe Harold*, iv, st. 128.)

Colo'ssus. Astride the entrance to the harbour of Rhodes tradition says there was a huge bronze statue of Apollo, one of the reputed Seven Wonders of the Ancient World. It was high enough for the tallest ships to sail under its legs into harbour. The word came to be used by both Greeks and Romans to mean any statue larger than life.

Cassius, speaking to Brutus, compares the mighty Cæsar with such a statue. Cæsar is the super-man, others are furtive creatures, petty men who " peep about " for some means of breathing the same air as he :

" Why, man, he doth bestride
    the narrow world
Like a Colossus, and we petty
    men
Walk under his huge legs."
So, too, in I *Henry IV*, 5, 1, 123, the Prince tells Falstaff that " Nothing but a Colossus " can defend him when he has fallen in battle.

Cŏrĭŏlā'nus, the hero of one of the most beautiful of the early Roman legends. His original name was Caius Marcius and he received the surname Coriolanus for his bravery at the capture of Corioli. His haughty bearing towards the commons made him unpopular and he was rejected in the consular elections. After this, when there

was a famine in the city and a Greek prince sent corn from Sicily, Coriolanus advised that it should not be distributed to the commons unless they gave up their tribunes. For this he was impeached and condemned to exile. He now took refuge among the Volscians and promised to help them in war against the Romans. He was appointed general of the Volscian army. He advanced close up to Rome where he encamped, and the Romans in alarm sent to him embassy after embassy of the most distinguished men of the state. But he would listen to none of them. At length the noblest matrons of Rome, headed by Veturia, the mother of Coriolanus and Volumnia his wife, with his two little children, came to his tent. His mother's reproaches and his wife's tears bent his purpose. He led back his army and lived in exile among the Volscians till his death. Other traditions (followed by Shakespeare) relate that he was killed by the Volscians on his return to their country.

Shakespeare's play is not one of his greatest or most popular ; but it has some magnificent passages e.g. Coriolanus' pride struggling against affection as he sees the matrons of Rome approaching (V, 3, 22–33).

Cre'ssida, daughter of the Trojan priest Calchas. In a post-classical story, popular in medieval times and used by Chaucer and Shakespeare, she loved Trŏ'ilus, a son of King Priam and a prince of chivalry. They vowed to be faithful to each other for ever. When prisoners were exchanged between the Greeks and the Trojans she was brought to the Greek camp by Diomede to whom she transferred her affections. She is regarded as a horrid example of a faithless woman.

In the exchange of Classical stories between Lorenzo and Jessica at the opening of the last act of *The Merchant of Venice*, Lorenzo begins with this story :

" In such a night
Troilus methinks mounted the
   Trojan walls,
And sigh'd his soul toward the
   Grecian tents,
Where Cressid lay that night."

Shakespeare's ironical *Troilus and Cressida* is of little interest. See Charles Williams's short poem " Cressida " in *Windows of Night*.
See **Thersites**.

Crĕŭ'sa, daughter of Priam and Hecuba, wife of Aeneas and mother of Ascanius. She perished on the night of the capture of Troy after being separated from her husband in the confusion.

Croe'sus, last King of Lydia, noted for his wealth. The fame of his power and wealth drew to his court at Sardis all the wise men of Greece, and among them Solon. To the question who was the happiest man he had ever seen, Solon replied that no man should be deemed happy till he had finished his life in a happy way. When the Persians captured Sardis Croesus was condemned to be burnt to death. As he stood before the pyre the warning of Solon came to his mind, and he thrice uttered the name of Solon. Cyrus enquired who it was that he called on ; and upon hearing the story not only spared the life of Croesus, but made him his friend. Croesus survived Cyrus.

Crŏ'nus, the youngest of the Titans and father of Demeter, Hera, Poseidon and Zeus. When the Cyclōpes were delivered from Tartarus, the government of the world was given to Cronus, but he was later dethroned by Zeus. The Romans identified their Saturn with Cronus.

Cunctā'tōr. See **Fābius.**

Cy'clădes, a group of islands in the Ægean Sea, so called because they lay in a " circle " round Delos, the most important of them as being the birthplace of Apollo. They were the chief source of marble (from Păros and Naxos), as well as of various metals.

Cyclōpes, i.e. creatures with circular eyes. Homer speaks of them as a gigantic and lawless race of shepherds in Sicily. The chief of them was Polyphēmus. According to another account they were Titans and were thrown into Tartarus by Cronus but were released by Zeus. A still later tradition regarded them as assistants of Hephaestus. Volcanoes were the workshops of that god and Mount Aetna was considered their abode.
Wordsworth speaks of the daisy as

" A little Cyclops, with one eye
   Staring to threaten and defy."

Cynic. See **Diogenes** and **Antisthenes.**

Dae'dălus, a mythical workman of great skill who built the famous labyrinth at Cnōsus in Crete in which King Minos kept his monster

Coin of Cnosus, representing the labyrinth built by Daedalus near Cnosus in Crete.

Minotaur. For some reason he fell into royal disfavour and was imprisoned in the labyrinth. As Minos had seized all the ships on the coast of Crete to prevent his leaving the island, Daedalus made wings for himself and his son I'cărus. The father crossed the sea safely, but, as Icarus flew too near the sun, the wax by which his

Daedalus and Icarus. *Daedalus is making wings for himself and his son so that they may escape from Crete.*

wings were fastened on his shoulders was melted and he dropped into that part of the Ægean which was called after him the Icarian Sea. Daedalus took refuge in Sicily. He is said to have been the inventor of such tools as the saw and the auger. The story of the labyrinth is probably based on the elaborate ground-plan of the palace at Cnosus.

Damas'cus, the capital of Syria, on the river Barada (the Abana of 2 *Kings*, 5¹²). It is one of the oldest cities in the world : in fact there is a Jewish tradition that Abraham had a house there of which Eliezer was steward (*Gen.* 15²). David captured the city, taking shields of

gold, chariots and chariot-horses as booty (2 *Sam.* 8⁵,⁶). Later it passed into the hands of the Romans, being conquered by one of Pompey's commanders in 65 B.C. For St. Paul's connexion with Damascus see *Acts* 9²⁻²⁵, 22⁵⁻¹¹. The ' Street called Straight ' still runs from E. to W. right through the city. It is now a beautiful city of well over 200,000 inhabitants, lying amid gardens and poplars surrounded by tilled lands.

The peculiarly Oriental art known as ' damascening ', i.e. decorating sword-blades with threads of gold or silver hammered into the metal to make ' Damascus blades ', was first established at Damascus. Damascene plums are known to us as damsons. Damask, i.e. linen, cotton or silk material with flowered patterns in gold or silver thread, takes its name from the city of its origin.

Da'moclēs, companion and flatterer of the elder Dionysius of Syracuse (4th century B.C.). Damocles having called Dionysius happy because of his wealth and power, the tyrant invited him to test what his happiness really was. He seated him at a banquet in the midst of which Damocles saw a naked sword, "the Sicilian's hair-suspended sword " as Shelley calls it, suspended over his head by a single horse-hair.

Allegorically, the ' sword of Damocles ' implies imminent dangers that threaten the apparently prosperous and prove to them that human happiness is ever insecure.

Dā'mon and Phin'tias, two Syracusan youths whose devotion and friendship are proverbial.
See **David and Jonathan.**

Dan to Beersheba. An O.T. term (*Judges* 20¹ and elsewhere) signifying the whole length of Palestine, from N. to S., a distance of about 150 miles. Cf. our " John o' Groats to Land's End " and the Greek " Olympus to Malea."

Dǎ'nǎē, daughter of Acrǐ'sǐus. An oracle had declared that she would become the mother of a son who was destined to kill his grandfather. So her father kept her shut up in a brazen tower. Zeus, however, visited her in a shower of gold and Perseus was her son.

Daniel, type of eminent judge, though there is no mention of him as such in the Book of Daniel ; but he does appear as a judge in *The Apocrypha.*

In the trial scene (*Merchant of Venice,* IV, i, 221, 2) Shylock hails Portia as " A Daniel come to judgement ! Yea, a Daniel ! " and later in the same scene Gratiano echoes Shylock with " A second Daniel, a Daniel, Jew ! "

Da'phnē, daughter of a river-god. She was loved by Apollo and as she was on the point of being overtaken by him, she prayed for aid and was changed into a laurel-tree. (Greek daphnē = laurel-tree).

Da'rdǎnus, son of Zeus and Electra, mythical ancestor of the Trojans.

Dār'ǐus, King of Persia (521– 485 B.C.). His reign saw the beginning of the great war between the Persians and the Greeks. He was defeated at Marathon in 490 by the Athenians under Miltiades and spent the next three years preparing his whole force for the conquest of Greece. He died, however, in 485 and left the execution of his plans to his son Xerxes.

David and Jonathan, the Biblical pair of inseparables. " It came to

pass that the soul of Jonathan was knit with the soul of David, and Jonathan loved him as his own soul " (1 *Sam.* 18¹). The news of Jonathan's death on the battlefield of Gilboa occasioned David's celebrated lament for him. (2 *Sam.* 1¹⁷⁻²⁷).

Cf. the classical story of Damon and Phintias. In *Woodstock* (c. 5) Scott quotes proverbial instances of friendship between men :

" You hold me, I am sure, for your friend ? "

" True as steel—chums at College and at Lincoln's Inn—we have been Nisus and Euryalus, Theseus and Pirithous, Orestes and Pylades ; and, to sum up the whole with a puritanic touch, David and Jonathan, all in one breath."

Dē'ǐǎnī'ra, wife of Heracles. She was the unwilling cause of her husband's death by presenting him with the poisoned robe which the centaur Nessus gave her. In despair she put an end to her own life.

Dēǐ'phǒbus, a son of Priam and Hecuba, and so brother of Paris. Next to Hector he was the bravest of the Trojans. He married Helen after the death of Paris. Accordingly, on the fall of Troy, the vengeance of the Greeks was directed chiefly against him. His house was one of the first committed to the flames, and he himself was slain and mutilated by Menelāus.

Delilah, the woman—probably a Philistine—loved by Samson, Judge of Israel. She teased him until he told her the secret of his strength, and then betrayed him. Her nerve and forethought were remarkable. She thrice failed without Samson's guessing her intent. Finally he told her that he had been a Nazarite from birth : " If I be shaven then my strength will go from me." She extorted an enormous sum of money from the Philistine lords for the betrayal (*Judges* 16⁴⁻²⁰).

In ordinary language a ' Delilah ' is a temptress. Milton calls her Dalila, and naturally this callous, heartless juggler is a prominent character in his *Samson Agonistes*. Handel's oratorio " Samson " and Saint-Saëns three-act opera " Samson et Dalila " will probably be known, at least in parts, to many readers.

Dē′los, the smallest (but the chief) of the Cy′clădes, a group of islands in the Ægean which lay in a circle around it. According to a legend (founded perhaps on some tradition of its volcanic origin), it was called out of the deep by the trident of Poseidon, but was a floating island until Zeus fastened it by adamantine chains to the bottom of the sea that it might be a secure resting-place to Leto for the birth of Apollo and Artemis. It contained the temple of Apollo with its great oracle.

Keats has a wonderful description of Delos :

" Chief isle of the embowered Cyclades,
  Rejoice, O Delos, with thine olives green
And poplars and lawn-shading palms, and beech,
In which the Zephyr breathes the loudest song,
And hazels thick, dark-stemm'd beneath the shade."

(*Hyperion*, Bk. 3, 23–7).

De′lphi, a small town on the S. slope of Mount Parnassus, regarded as the central point of the whole earth. It was the principal seat of the worship of Apollo. Here, too, every four years the Pythian games were celebrated. The temple of Apollo at Delphi was immensely wealthy, for rich offerings were presented to it by those who had received favourable replies from his celebrated oracle. Apollo's priestess, called Py′thia, took her seat over an opening in the ground from which from time to time a vapour arose. After inhaling the vapour she uttered what were regarded as the revelations of Apollo. These revelations were carefully written down by the priests and were afterwards communicated in hexameter verse to the person(s) who had come to consult the oracle.

Dēmē′tēr, called Cĕrēs by the Romans, was the goddess of the corn-bearing earth, of agriculture and of settled family life. Her daughter Perse′phonē was carried off to the lower world by Pluto and, as Demeter could get no help from Zeus, she left Olympus and dwelt in anger upon earth at Eleusis : so the earth produced no crops. Zeus sent first Iris and then all the gods to persuade her to return, but she refused. Zeus then sent Hermes to Hades to bring Persephone back. Pluto consented to her return, but gave her the seed of a pomegranate to eat. Demeter returned to Olympus with her daughter, but as Persephone had eaten in the lower world she was obliged to spend one-third of the year with Pluto. The earth now brought forth fruit again. In this myth, Persephone, who is carried off to the lower world, is the seed-corn which remains concealed in the ground part of the year. Persephone, who returns to her mother, is the corn which rises from the ground and nourishes men and animals.

Dēmo′sthenēs, the most famous of Athenian orators (383–322 B.C.).

He had to struggle against the greatest physical disadvantages. His voice was weak and he stammered. He is said to have spoken with pebbles in his mouth to cure himself of stammering ; to have repeated verses of the poets as he ran uphill, to strengthen his voice ; to have declaimed on the seashore to accustom himself to the noise of the popular assembly. Among his sixty orations that have survived, the most famous are the three ' Philippics ' in which he defended Athenian independence against Philip of Macedon. He took poison in a temple of Poseidon rather than fall alive into the hands of the Macedonians.

Deucǎ′lǐon, son of Prometheus. He married Pyrrha, daughter of Epimetheus. When Zeus had resolved to destroy the degenerate race of men of the Bronze Age, Deucalion and Pyrrha were on account of their piety the only mortals saved. On the advice of his father, Deucalion built a ship in which he and his wife floated in safety during the nine days' flood which destroyed all the other inhabitants of Hellas. At last the ship rested on Mt. Parnassus. He and Pyrrha then consulted the sanctuary of Themis as to how the race of man might be restored. The goddess bade them cover their heads and throw the bones of their mother behind them. They interpreted ' the bones of their mother ' to mean the stones of the earth. From the stones thrown by Deucalion there sprang up men, from those thrown by Pyrrha women. That is why, says Apollodorus, in Greek people are called *lāoi*, from *lāas*, a stone.

deus ex māchinā : (literally, a god out of a machine) a god lowered on to the stage by means of some theatrical apparatus to solve a dramatist's trouble. Hence, an unusual turn of events, unexpected intervention to save a difficult situation, especially an obvious device used by an author to help him to resolve difficulties in his plot.

This device was used by Euripides to solve the dramatic problem in half his extant plays.

Devil. The word means ' slanderer ', ' traducer '. Cf. **Satan.**

Dǐǎ′na, an ancient Italian divinity whom the Romans identified with the Greek Artemis.

At Ephesus, the chief city of the Roman Province of ' Asia ', was the famous temple (the ' Artemesium ') of an early deity to whom the Greek settlers ascribed not only the name, but some of the characteristics of their own Artemis. She was the nature-goddess of fertility and animal wild-life. Inside the temple was a crude wooden image of the goddess which was believed by these Ephesians to have ' fallen from heaven '.

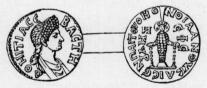

Greek imperial copper coin of Ephesus and Smyrna Allied ; Obv. : Domitia. Bust facing right. Rev.: Ephesian Diana (cf. Acts 19-¹⁹).

Replicas of this image were made and sold, possibly as votive offerings, by the silversmiths of the city. Paul's preaching was likely to interfere with the sale of these replicas—hence the uproar raised in the city by Demetrius. (See *Acts* 19²⁴···).

See **Artemis.**

See " Hymn to Diana ", sung by Hesperus in Ben Jonson's *Cynthia's Revels* (Golden Treasury Bk. II) :
" Queen and Huntress, chaste
and fair."

Dĭ'do, also called Eli'ssa, the reputed founder of Carthage. She was a Tyrian, married to her uncle, a man of vast wealth. When he was murdered, Dido sailed secretly from Tyre with the treasures and reached Africa. Here she purchased as much land as might be covered with the hide of a bull ; but she ordered the hide to be cut up into the thinnest possible strips. With them she surrounded a spot on which she built a citadel called Byrsa (a Greek word meaning " bull's hide.") She later erected a funeral pile on which she stabbed herself in the presence of her people rather than marry the neighbouring King Iarbas who was jealous of the new city's prosperity.

Virgil has wiped out an interval of more than 300 years to make Dido a contemporary of Aeneas, with whom she falls in love on his arrival in Africa. When Aeneas hastened to seek the new home which the gods had promised him, Dido in despair put an end to her life on a funeral pile.

Dĭŏ'gĕnes, Greek philosopher and pupil of Antisthenes, founder of the Cynic school of philosophy, was born about 412 B.C. His youth is said to have been spent in extravagance ; but at Athens he attached himself to Antisthenes and began to practise the greatest austerity of life. Finally, according to the common story, he took up his residence in a huge earthenware jar. He was captured by pirates and sold to Xeniades of Corinth. Here his interview with Alexander the Great is said to have taken place. We are told that Alexander admired Diogenes so much that he said : " If I were not Alexander,

Diogenes in his tub. (*From fragment of lamp in British Museum*). *The ' tub ' was a large earthenware jar.*

I should wish to be Diogenes." He died at the age of ninety.

See the speech of Comus to the Lady (*Comus* 706–55) in which he castigates the philosophy of the " bridge doctors of the Stoic fur
Who fetch their precepts from
the Cynic tub."

Diomē'dēs, next to Achilles the bravest hero in the Greek Army. He led eighty ships against Troy. He was helped by Athene against Hector and even against the gods who aided the Trojans. He thus wounded both Aphrodite and Ares. In the *Odyssey* we are told that he reached his home in Argos on his return from Troy in three days.

Dionȳ'sius, the name of two ' tyrants ' i.e. Kings, father and son, of Syracuse. The elder tyrant is said to have built a prison in a subterranean cave, a sort of ' whispering gallery ', in which he placed a guard who could hear the slightest whisper of those imprisoned. To preserve the secret of his terrible prison Dionysius put to death all who had helped to build it. The Gestapo must have learnt some lessons from the tyrant.

In *The Fortunes of Nigel* King James refers to this prison as " a lurking-place called the King's *lugg*, or *ear*, where he could sit undescried and hear the converse of his prisoners."

Diony̅'sus, also called Bacchus both by the Greeks and the Romans, the god of wine. He was the son of Zeus and Se'mele̅. Zeus loved Semele and appeared to her in thunder and lightning. She was terrified by the sight and, being seized by the flames, she gave premature birth to a son. Zeus saved the child from the flames, sewed him up in his thigh and thus preserved him till he came to maturity. When he grew up he was driven mad by Hera (who was jealous of his mother) and wandered over the earth as far as India. Zeus provided him with a company of followers called Bacchantes. Wherever he went he introduced the vine and the sweet drink he had created out of water and sunshine. He was driven in a golden chariot drawn by tigers and panthers, the Bacchantes dancing round him with wands twined round with ivy in their hands and ivy wreaths on their heads. In art he is represented as a youth with a languid expression, clad only with a fawn-skin and crowned with ivy or vine-leaves.

Dio'scūri, i.e. sons of Zeus, Castor and Pollux. Castor was famous for his skill in managing horses, and Pollux for boxing. They took part in the expedition of the Argonauts, during which Pollux in a boxing match defeated and slew Ă'my̆cus,

the giant son of Poseidon. There are many legends connected with " the Great Twin Brethren." They are said to have come to the aid of the Romans at the battle of

The Dioscuri. (*From a coin of Bruttium, of 3rd cent. B.C.*). *The ' great twin-brethren ' are represented as wearing hunters' dress and conical cap.*

Lake Regillus, clad in white armour and riding snow-white horses. They
   " washed their horses in the well
      That springs by Vesta's
        fane . . .
   Then, like a blast, away they
      passed,
   And no man saw them
      more."
    (Macaulay's " Lake Regillus.")
They were worshipped as the protectors of travellers by sea and their stars appeared above the ship as a sure sign of help—a myth which is probably derived from the phenomenon ' St. Elmo's Fire '.

Di'rae, a Roman name for the Greek Erīnyes or Eume'nides.

Disciple is a learner who follows and imitates his master, a pupil. The word is used
   (i) of the followers or pupils of others than Christ, e.g. John the Baptist (*Matt.* 9[14]) and Pharisees (*Mark* 2[18]). When used of the personal followers of our Lord it is often
   (ii) equivalent to " apostles." Thus the Twelve are often called the disciples, or the twelve (or

eleven) disciples. After the Ascension the word is used constantly in *Acts* as

(iii) equivalent to Christian, where the disciple was not a personal follower of Jesus in His lifetime, e.g. Timothy (*Acts* 16¹).

Dives and Lazarus. See our Lord's parable of the rich glutton and the beggar (*Luke* 16¹⁹⁻³¹). The rich man, Dives, " was clothed in purple and fine linen and fared sumptuously every day " ; Lazarus " was laid at his gate, full of sores, and desiring to be fed with crumbs which fell from the rich man's table." This is the only instance where a proper name occurs in a gospel-parable.

The name ' Lazarus ' has always had special association in the Christian Church with lepers and work among them. ' Lazar-house ' and ' Lazaretto ' are common Continental names for hospitals for the treatment of people with loathsome diseases, lepers in particular.

Readers will find the old ballad " Dives and Lazarus " (No. 109 in Quiller-Couch's *Oxford Book of Ballads*) quaint and interesting.

Dōdō′na, the most ancient oracle in Greece, dedicated to Zeus. The will of the god was declared by the wind rustling through the lofty oaks or beech trees ; and in order to render the sounds more distinct, brazen vessels were suspended on the branches, which were set in motion by the wind and so come in contact with one another. These sounds were interpreted in early times by men, but afterwards by prophetic priestesses.

Dorcas. " Now there was at Joppa a certain disciple named Tabitha, which by interpretation is called Dorcas " (*Acts* 9³⁶). She was full of good works, among

which that of making clothes for " the widows " is specifically mentioned. She must have been a person of some means. St. Peter restored her to life when she was already laid out for burial, in circumstances which bear a close resemblance to the raising of Jairus's daughter (*Matt.* 9²⁵⁻·). The Aramaic ' Tabitha ' and the Greek ' Dorcas ' mean ' roebuck ' or ' gazelle '—fairly common as a woman's name.

A society of well-to-do ladies, connected with a church, which meets regularly for the purpose of making and providing garments for the poor, is called a Dorcas Society.

Dō′ric, a dialect of Greek spoken in the small and mountainous country of Dōris. It is characterized by the use of broad vowel sounds and, compared with Attic, is unrefined and uncouth. So, any rustic dialect (and especially the Scottish) is often labelled ' Doric '.

Milton's " uncouth swain " in *Lycidas*

" Touched the tender stops of various quills,
    With eager thought warbling his Doric lay."

By ' Doric lay ' Milton implied pastoral song. The *Idylls* of Theocritus which give many pictures of the ordinary life of the peasants in Sicily (i.e. they are pastoral poems) are written in the Doric dialect.

Drăcō(n), author of the first written code of laws at Athens, in which the penalty of death was affixed to almost all crimes, however petty. Hence it was said that his laws were written not in ink but in blood.

We use the adjective ' Draconian ' = severe.

Drўǎdes. See **Nymphs**.

Eborā'cum, York. It was the headquarters of the sixth legion and the residence of the Roman emperors when they visited Britain. Part of the ancient Roman walls still exist. The Archbishop of York signs ' —— Ebor.'

Echi'dna, a monster half-woman, half-serpent, the mother of such classical horrors as the Chimaera, the dragon of the Hesperides, the Colchian dragon, the Sphinx, Cerberus and Scylla.

Milton based his figure of Sin on a classical description of Echidna :

> " . . . [Sin] seemed woman to
> the waist, and fair,
> But ended foul in many a scaly
> fold
> Voluminous and vast, a serpent
> armed
> With mortal sting."
> (P.L. ii, 650-3).

Ēchō, a mountain-nymph punished by Juno because she had enabled Jupiter to deceive her. The nymph was changed into an Echo—that is, a being with no control over its tongue, able neither to speak before anyone else has spoken, nor to be silent when somebody else has spoken. Shelley says she

> " pined away
> Into a shadow of all sounds."

Echo in this state fell desperately in love with Narcissus ; but as her love was not returned, she pined away in grief, so that in the end there remained of her nothing but her voice.

See the Invocation to Echo,

> " Sweet Echo, sweetest nymph,
> that liv'st unseen "

in Milton's *Comus*, ll. 230-43.

See **Narcissus**.

Pan and the Nymph Echo. (*From a lamp at Athens*). *The god is represented as a sensual being, with horns and goat's feet.*

Eden. The place where lay a garden which was the first abode of Man (*Gen.* 2⁸⁻¹⁴). In Hebrew the word means ' pleasure ', ' delight ', and so a paradise.

In a glorious outburst of Elizabethan patriotism the dying Gaunt calls England, among many felicitous things, " This other Eden, demi-paradise " (*Richard* ii 2, 1, 42). Milton probably had this noble speech in mind when he wrote *Comus* 18-28.

Egypt. (*a*) *To spoil the Egyptians* i.e. to strip them of their goods. God's message to His people in bondage was : " It shall come to pass that, when ye go, ye shall not go empty . . . Ye shall spoil the Egyptians." (*Ex.* 3²¹⁻²²).

(*b*) *The flesh-pots of Egypt,* i.e. emblems of physical well-being, abundance of good food. The Children of Israel murmured against their hardships in the Wilderness of Sin and longed to return to their state of slavery in Egypt when they " sat by the flesh-pots and did eat bread to the full." (*Ex.* 16³).

(*c*) *Egyptian darkness.* The plague of darkness inflicted by God on the stubborn Egyptians, " even darkness which may be felt ", lasted three days during which " all the Children of Israel had light in their dwellings " (*Ex.* 10²¹⁻²³).

(*d*) *Corn in Egypt,* i.e. food in plenty. " Now when Jacob saw that there was corn in Egypt . . ." (*Gen.* 42¹).

Ēle′ctra, daughter of Agamemnon and Clytaemnestra, sister of Orestes. When Orestes, whose life she had saved in his boyhood, had grown to manhood, she incited him to avenge their father's death by murdering Clytaemnestra. Orestes gave her in marriage to Pȳ′ladēs with whom he had been educated.

Eleu′sis, a town in Attica about 12 miles N.W. of Athens. It was approached from Athens by the ' Sacred Way '. It gave its name to the great festival and mysteries of the ' Eleusinia ' celebrated in honour of Demeter and Persephone.

Elgin Marbles, The.
See **Parthenon.**

Ēly′sium, the paradise of Greek mythology, a happy land where there is neither snow, nor cold nor rain. Hither favoured heroes pass without dying and live, under the rule of Rhadamanthus, in flowery meadows, delighting themselves with games and music.

Tennyson has more than one echo of the Homeric Elysium ; e.g.
" . . . the island valley of Avilion,
Where falls not hail, or rain, or any snow,

Nor ever wind blows loudly ;
    but it lies
Deep-meadow'd, happy, fair with orchard lawns
And bowery hollows crown'd with summer sea."
(*The Passing of Arthur,* 427–31).

Emmaeus, the village a few miles from Jerusalem to which the two disciples were on their way when our Lord appeared to them on the day of His resurrection (*Luke* 24¹³⁻³⁵). He made Himself known to them when " He took bread and blessed it and brake and gave to them."

Empe′doclēs, a learned and eloquent philosopher of Sicily. One tradition says that he threw himself into the flames of Mount Ætna, that by his sudden disappearance he might be believed to be a god ; but it was added that the volcano threw up one of his sandals and thus revealed the manner of his death.

Milton refers to him :
" he who to be deem'd
A god, leap'd fondly into Ætna flames,
Empedocles."
(P.L. iii, 469–71).
Lamb had this passage in mind when he wrote " All Fool's Day." " Good master Empedocles, you are welcome. It is long since you went a salamander-gathering down Ætna. 'Tis a mercy your worship did not singe your mustachios." Matthew Arnold used his story for his *Empedocles on Etna.*

Encĕ′lădus, son of Tartarus and Gē (Earth), and one of the hundred-armed giants who made war on the gods. He was killed, by a flash of lightning, by Zeus who buried him under Mt. Ætna.

Endȳ′miŏn, a youth distinguished by his beauty. As he slept on

Mt. Latmus his surprising beauty warmed the cold heart of Selēnē (the moon) who came down to him and kissed him. She caused him to sleep for ever that she might be able to kiss him without his knowledge.

The legend would be well-known to Elizabethans through John Lyly's *Endimion, The Man in the Moone.* Portia refers to it :

" Peace, ho ! the moon sleeps
    with Endymion
And would not be awaked."

John Keats retold the legend in a long narrative poem of 4,000 lines which was fiercely attacked by the critics of the day.

E′ōs, in Latin Aurō′ra, the goddess of the dawn. Homer gives her the stock epithets " early-rising, rosy-fingered." At the close of every night she rose from her couch and ascended to heaven to herald the coming light of the sun.

A. W. Kinglake called his Travel-book in the Near East *Eothen,* i.e. ' From the East '.

E′phesus. See Diana.

Epicū′rus, the founder of a school of philosophy that bears his name. Among the principles taught by him was that man should rely for his welfare on the evidence of the senses. Accordingly he discouraged the degrading fear of death and belief in the supernatural.

In *Julius Caesar* (v. 1.) Cassius said that he had been a stout Epicurean ; but when he saw ravens, crows and kites replace the two mighty eagles which had accompanied the army to Philippi, he changed his mind and was inclined to believe in portents.

Epidau′rus, in Argolis, was the chief seat of the worship of Asclepius whose temple was situated a few miles from the city. Not far away is the theatre, the best preserved example of a Greek theatre.

Epimē′theūs.
See **Prometheus ; Pandora.**

E′rătō, the Muse of Love Songs. See **Muses.**

E′rĕbus, son of Chaos. The name signifies darkness and is therefore used by poets as the personification of Hell.

So Brutus :
" If thou (i.e. conspiracy) path,
    thy native semblance on,
Not Erebus itself were dim
    enough
To hide thee from prevention."
        (*Julius Cæsar,* ii, 1, 84) :
and Lorenzo speaks of " The man that hath no music in him " :
" The motions of his spirit are
    dull as night,
And his affections dark as
    Erebus."
    (*Merchant of Venice,* V, 87).

Erī′nўes. See Eumenides.

E′ris, the goddess of Discord. See **Apple of Discord.**

E′rōs, in Latin Amor or Cupīdo, the god of love who bears sway over both gods and men. His arms consist of arrows (some tipped with gold to cause love, others with lead to repel love), which he carries in a golden quiver, and of torches which no one can touch with impunity. He is sometimes represented with wings, sometimes as holding or stringing his bow, and sometimes blind-folded. A statue of Eros by Praxiteles at Thespiae in Boeotia was specially famous.

The statue of Eros commemorates the seventh Earl of Shaftesbury, philanthropist and social worker, 1801–1855. The ' Shaftesbury

Memorial,' to give the statue its official title, was restored to its plinth in Piccadilly Circus on

Eros. (*From a gem*). *He is here represented as a winged boy stringing his bow.*

28 June, 1947, after nearly eight years' war-time exile.

Hermia swears

" by Cupid's strongest bow ;
By his best arrow with the
    golden head " ;

and Helena refers to the medieval notion of Cupid's blindness :

" Love looks not with the eyes,
    but with the mind ;
And therefore is wing'd Cupid
    painted blind."

The famous Latin version of the story of Eros and Psyche by Apuleius (interpolated into his *Golden Ass*) has been versified by Robert Bridges.

E′tĕoclēs. See **Antigone.**

Eu′clid, the celebrated mathematician of Alexandria who has given his name to the science of Geometry in every country in which his writings are studied.

' Todhunter's Euclid ' was an important mathematical text-book in our grandfathers' schooldays.

Eumāē′us, the faithful swineherd of Odysseus. Homer calls him " the prince of swineherds."

Eumĕ′nĭdēs, i.e. the kindly-disposed goddesses, the euphemistic name for the Erīnўes (or Furies, as the Romans called them), the Avenging Deities of Greek mythology. They are represented as winged goddesses of terrible appearance, with snakes twined in their hair. They carry torches and scourges. The crime which they especially punish is failure in duty to parents. Later writers give their names as Tīsi′phŏnē, Alēc′tō and Megae′ra.

It is worth noting here how the Greeks, in wholesome fear of their natural gods, tried to appease them by avoiding the use of their awful names and by giving them gentle ones—basically a form of *flattery*—often with directly opposite meaning to their harsher ones. Thus, the Erinyes become the Eumenides, the Pontus (at first called Axenos, i.e. the inhospitable sea, from the savage character of the peoples on its coasts and from its fogs and hidden rocks) becomes the Euxine, i.e. the sea hospitable to strangers. Similarly Nyx (the Roman *Nox*, Night) becomes Euphrŏnē, i.e. the kindly time. Perhaps with the same idea the Greeks called the left (or unlucky) side *aristeros*, i.e. " the better than the best." More modern (and we hope more enlightened) people have not hesitated to call the stormiest of the oceans the Pacific, or to re-christen the Cape of Storms the Cape of Good Hope.

Eurī′pĭdēs, the youngest of the three great Attic tragic poets, was born at Salamis, 480 B.C., on the very day that the Greeks defeated the Persians there. He is said to have written his tragedies on the island, within sight of the sea. He was twice married and both marriages were unfortunate—hence, possibly, his alleged hatred of women of which he was twitted by the comic poets. Eighteen of his ninety plays survive. Several of Euripides' plays in English rhyming verse by Prof. Gilbert Murray have been broadcast as well as acted on the stage.

See Browning's *Balaustion's Adventure* for translation of the *Alcestis*, combined with acute running commentary.

See **Alcestis**.

Euro'pa, daughter of the Phoenician King Age'nor. Zeus fell in love with her and in the form of a bull came to the spot where she and her maidens were sporting on the sea-shore. She ventured to mount his back; whereupon Zeus rushed into the sea and carried her in safety to Crete. She was the mother of Minos and Rhadama'nthus.

Europa.

Eury'ălus. See **Nisus**.

Euryclē'a, the fond old nurse of Odysseus who recognised the hero, on his return home after his twenty years' absence, by a scar from a wound he had received from a boar's tusk.

Eurў'dĭcē. See **Orpheus**.

Eury'sthēus. See **Heracles**.

Eute'rpē, the Muse of lyric poetry. See **Muses**.

Fā'bius. Quintus Fabius Maximus, offensively nicknamed ' Cunctator ' (i.e. ' Dilly-Dally '), was the dictator who saved Rome in the Second Punic War. His policy was to avoid pitched battles, indeed all direct contact with the enemy. Though his policy was not appreciated in Rome, he succeeded by his tactics in wearing down the strength of the Carthaginians. Hence ' Fabian tactics '=a cautious policy of delay.

The Fabian Society, founded in 1884, was named after Quintus Fabius. Its founders wished to avoid violent methods of propaganda in favour of Socialism, and to disseminate their views by means of lectures and tracts.

Fall of Man. Our first parents were originally without sin. The first act committed by man in violation of the laws prescribed for him by the Almighty constituted the Fall. Man fell at the moment when he first resolved to have experience of evil as well as of good. This experiment was suggested by the Tempter and consisted in making Adam and Eve believe that they would elevate themselves vastly, both intellectually and morally, by disobedience to God's commands. " Ye shall be as God knowing good and evil," the serpent told Eve (*Gen.* 3⁵, R.V.).

Babylonian cylinder-seal : Tree of Knowledge (?).

Literally, of course, there is no " tree of knowledge of good and evil," much less any " apple " which has been substituted for the "fruit" mentioned in the Bible story.
See **Fruit, Forbidden.**

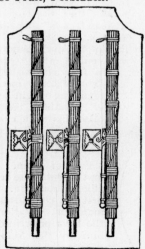

Fasces. (*From the original in the Capitol at Rome*). *They were bundles of birch or elm, with an axe in the middle, carried by lictors before the superior magistrates at Rome.*

Fa′scēs, rods of birch or elm bound together by a red thong in the form of a bundle, and containing an axe in the middle, the head of which projected from them. These rods were carried by lictors before the superior magistrates at Rome as symbols of their power.

Fates, the three sister-goddesses whom the Greeks called *Moirae* and the Romans *Parcae.* They determined the destiny of man, according to the counsel of the gods. Clōthō was the spinning fate, Lă′chĕsis wound the thread of man's fate and decided when enough thread had been spun ; and A′trŏpos, the eldest of the three sisters, inexorably cut the thread with her ' abhorred shears ' when man's life had reached its destined end. Thus the fate assigned to every being by eternal laws takes its course and Zeus, as well as the other gods and men, must submit. Not even the gods could alter the decrees of the Fates.

Milton makes Atropos one of the Furies and Pyramus, in *A Midsummer Night's Dream*, identifies (or more probably confounds !) the Fates with the Furies :
" Approach, ye Furies fell !
  O fates, come, come,
  Cut thread and thrum."

Fau′nus, grandson of Saturnus, an old Italian nature-god, the deity of the rural community. Hence his guardianship of country life and pursuits and of herds. At one time, he seems to have been identified with the Greek Pan, complete with goat's horns and cloven heel. The true Italian representation of this god was probably as a man of middle age, bearded, wearing a goat-skin over the shoulders and bearing a staff or club in one hand and a horn in the other. Afterwards the idea of several Fauns represented as Satyrs was borrowed from Greek mythology.

At the beginning of *Lycidas* Milton portrays his life and that of

A Faun. From an ancient gem. Represents the more familiar type due to the Greek influence which identified Faunus with Pan.

his friend Edward King at Cambridge in the true pastoral manner :
" Meanwhile the rural ditties
    (i.e. their youthful poems)
    were not mute ;
Tempered to the oaten flute
Rough Satyrs danced and Fauns
    with cloven heel
From the glad sound would
    not be absent long ;
And old Damœtas loved to
    hear our song."
By ' Satyrs ' and ' Fauns ' Milton probably intended undergraduate friends, and Damœtas may refer to a college tutor in the poet's Cambridge days.

Fig, Fig-tree. The fig-tree is very common in Palestine—a " land of wheat and barley and vines and fig-trees and pomegranates, a land of oil olive and honey " (*Deut.* 8⁸). Mount Olivet was famous for its

fig-trees in ancient times and they are still found there. Naturally, therefore, both *fig* and *fig-tree* occur many times in the Bible, and especially in the O.T., with both literal and emblematic meanings. " To sit under one's own vine and one's own fig-tree " became a proverb among the Jews for peace and prosperity (e.g. in 1 *Kings* 4²⁵). Figs were caked together to preserve them. Cakes of figs are given to the captured Egyptian as a restorative (1 *Sam.* 30¹²), and figs are laid on Hezekiah's boil and he recovers (2 *Kings* 20⁷). In the N.T. the barren fig-tree (*Mark* 11¹²⁻¹⁴) is used emblematically of the Jewish nation which was corrupt and therefore could not bring forth good fruit : it was merely "leaves without figs."

Flō′ra, the Roman goddess of flowers and spring.

Flora and fauna are the collective plants and animals of a particular region or epoch.

Fortū′na, the goddess of man's destiny, worshipped both in Greece and in Italy. She was represented with different attributes, especially holding a rudder (a goddess guiding the affairs of the world), a cornucopia (a goddess giving wealth and prosperity), or a wheel (a goddess representing the varying unsteadiness of fortune : cf. ' the giddy wheel of fortune '=inconstancy.)

" The wheel is come full circle," says Edmund towards the close of *King Lear.* In lighter vein Feste jestingly comments at the end of *Twelfth Night :* " thus the whirligig of time brings in his revenges." In *Henry V* Pistol with his usual alliterative rant has :
" giddy Fortune's furious fickle
    wheel,
    That goddess blind,

That stands upon the rolling
restless stone."
' Wheel ' and ' whirligig '(=spin-
ning-top) metaphorically symbolise
the vicissitudes of fortune.

Fortunate Isles, or the Islands of
the Blessed, to which the Greeks
regarded favoured heroes as passing
without dying, were supposed to
lie somewhere in the Atlantic Ocean
beyond the Pillars of Heracles.
The ancients may have had vague
knowledge of the existence of the
Canary Islands : anyhow, an island
is clearly spoken of as the abode
of the Blessed.

Tennyson represents Ulysses as a
vigorous man despite all his mis-
fortunes, sailing out to explore the
western ocean :
" My purpose holds
To sail beyond the sunset, and
the paths
Of all the western stars, until
I die.
It may be that the gulfs will
wash us down :
It may be we shall touch the
Happy Isles,
And see the great Achilles,
whom we knew."
(*Ulysses*, 59–64).

Forty. The Jews seemed to have
used *forty* (as the Latins used six
hundred) as a round number not
necessarily the product of ten and
four. Thus, in O.T. the flood was
forty days upon the earth, the
Israelites wandered forty years in
the wilderness before reaching the
Promised Land, Elijah was fed
forty days by the ravens ; and in
N.T. Christ fasted forty days and
forty nights before His Temptation
by the devil, after the Resurrection
He appeared to His apostles " by
the space of forty days."

In Shakespeare (and in other
Elizabethans) forty is similarly
used to mean ' a large number ' :

thus, Coriolanus affirms " On fair
ground I could beat forty of them" ;
and Hamlet avows :
" I loved Ophelia : forty thousand brothers
Could not . . . make up my
sum."

Forum. In the centre of ancient
Rome was the market-place or
' forum ', which in time became
the hub of the city's life. Here
bankers and money-lenders transacted their affairs, and here, too,
were the courts of law where
justice was dispensed. Cf. *forensic*,
applied e.g. to medicine, eloquence.

Furies. See **Eumenides.**

Fruit, Forbidden. " Of the tree
of the knowledge of good and evil,
thou shalt not eat " was God's
command in the Garden of Eden
to man in his state of original
innocence.
" Forbidden fruit " is a thing desired because not allowed (C.O.D.).
See **Fall of Man.**

Gae'a or **Gē,** goddess of the Earth
and mother of the Titans.

Galatē'a, a sea-nymph who loved
the Sicilian shepherd Ācis and was
herself loved by the Cyclops Polyphē'mus. The latter in mad
jealousy killed the shepherd by
rolling a heavy boulder down on
his head. Galatea could not be
consoled : she transformed him
into the Sicilian river that bears
his name.
See **Pygmalion.**
W. S. Gilbert wrote " an original
mythological comedy in three
acts, called *Pygmalion and Galatea.*

Galilee, the N. province of W.
Palestine, divided into Upper Gali-
lee and (to its S.) Lower Galilee.
In the N.T. Galilee is named in

35 chapters in the Gospels and Acts, the reference always being to Lower Galilee, including Nazareth (*Matt.* 2^{22}), Capernaum (*Luke* 4^{31}) and Cana (*John* 2^{11}). The province was in the tetrarchy of Herod Antipas (*Luke* 3^1). The dialect of Galilee differed from that of Jerusalem. St. Peter was sitting " without in the court " of the house of Caiaphas the high priest, when his Galilean accent betrayed him to two maids and a man— who had challenged him (*Matt.* 26$^{69-74}$, *Mark* 14^{70}, *Luke* 22^{59}).

The porch or chapel at the West entrance to some churches (e.g. the famous Galilee Chapel of Durham Cathedral) is called a ' Galilee,' possibly to imply that the porch or chapel is of less religious significance than the church itself, just as Galilee was less important than Judaea.

Ga′llio, elder brother of the philosopher Seneca and pro-consul of the Roman province of Achaia, with his headquarters at Corinth. The Jews rose against Paul's teaching at Corinth and wished to bring him before Gallio ; but as their accusations concerned their own laws only Gallio refused to listen to them. They then beat Sosthenes, an official in charge of the synagogue, " and Gallio cared for none of these things." (*Acts* 18$^{12-17}$). This does not imply indifference on the part of Gallio : it rather suggests a friendly Roman attitude towards the spread of Christianity.

Ga′nymēdē(s) was the most beautiful of all mortals. Homer says he was carried off by the gods to be the cupbearer of Zeus. Later writers state that Zeus himself, in the form of an eagle or by means of his eagle, carried him off

from Mount Ida to replace Hebe as his cupbearer.

Ganymedes, carried off from Mount Ida by the eagle of Zeus.

In *As You Like It* Rosalind took the name of Ganymede, ' Jove's own page ', when she assumed male attire.

See **Hebe.**

Gē′nius, a tutelary god who, according to both Greek and Roman beliefs, came into being with a person at his birth and was something of a guardian spirit throughout his life, sometimes with favourable fortune, sometimes with the reverse, dying with him or leaving him at his death. Man had his good genius and his evil genius (like Faust's Good Angel and Bad Angel) and these two were in constant opposition in their efforts to shape his destiny. Similarly divine protectors were imagined as watching over and influencing each place, as well as each person.

Antony calls Brutus " Caesar's angel," i.e. as inseparable from him as his guardian angel or genius

(Aldis Wright, who quotes " one of these men is Genius to the other " from a *Comedy of Errors*). Cf. Milton's " the unseen genius of the wood" (*Il Penseroso* 154), and Gray's

" Two angel forms were seen to glide,
The Genii of the stream."

Gē′rўŏn, a mythological monster with three heads (or with three bodies united together), was King in the island of Gades in Spain. He had a wonderful herd of cattle of which no one dared rob him

Heracles and Geryones. Geryones was the three-bodied monster king in Spain killed by Heracles.

because it was guarded day and night by Orthrus, a dog with two heads. As his tenth labour Heracles was ordered to fetch these oxen. He broke the dog's backbone with his club, killed the herdsman with his fist and finally had to wrestle with six-armed Geryon before carrying the oxen off.

Gethsemane, a place mentioned by name in *Matt.* 26³⁶ and *Mark* 14³² only. The word means ' oil-press '. It was apparently on the Mount of Olives which our Lord was wont to visit (*Luke* 22³⁹), and was a garden beyond the brook Kidron, not far from Bethany.

Here was the scene of Christ's Agony and Betrayal by Judas (*Mark* 14³²⁻⁵⁰).

Giants, The, beings of a monstrous size, with fearful countenances and legs ending in serpents. Armed with huge rocks and trunks of trees they made an attack upon heaven. The gods were told that they could not conquer the giants without the assistance of a mortal, so they summoned Heracles to their aid. The giants were then

Athena and Giant. Athena grasps Enceladus by the hair and her serpent has coiled round him.

killed one after another by the gods and Heracles and some of them were buried under volcanic islands. It is probable that the story of their contest with the gods took its origin from volcanic convulsions.

Glass. Of glass-work, only the scantiest notices are to be found in O.T., though Babylonians, Phoenicians and Egyptians were well acquainted with the art. The Israelites, too, must have known of it, though they evidently did not understand its manufacture until late in their history. Writing of the "tinkling ornaments" and other "bravery" used by women in their pride, Isaiah (3^{23}) refers to "the glasses", i.e. hand-mirrors ; but these were of polished metal. Doubtless it was this Mediterranean polished-metal mirror, which does not reflect all the light and in which therefore things seen in it are dimmer than natural, that St. Paul refers to in his magnificent chapter descriptive of the true idea of Christian love ($1\ Cor.^{13}$), concluding : "For now we see through a glass, darkly."

Golden Age, The.
See **Saturn**.

Golden Calf. Aaron, in the absence of Moses, made a molten calf of the gold earrings of the people to represent the God(s) who brought Israel out of Egypt. To punish the people for their loss of faith Moses burnt the calf and grinding the ashes to powder scattered them over the water.

See *Exodus* 32.

"The Golden Calf" symbolically represents wealth as an object of worship.

Golgotha, an Aramaic word meaning 'skull' (*Matt.* 27^{33} ; *Mark* 15^{22}), i.e. the skull-shaped hill outside the walls of Jerusalem, the site of the Crucifixion. The Latin translation of the Hebrew Golgotha is 'Calvaria' (*calvus* = bald. Doctors call the skull-cap or vault of the cranium the 'calvarium'). Prof. Weekley quotes from Wycliffe's translation of the Bible : "A place that is cleped Golgotha, that is, the place of Calvarie."

Goliath, the Philistine giant of Gath who "morning and evening for forty days" defied the armies of Israel. The youthful shepherd-boy David "took his staff in his hand and chose him five smooth stones out of the brook, and put them in his shepherd's bag which he had, even in a scrip ; and his sling was in his hand." Thus armed, David slew the Philistine ($1\ Sam.$ 17).

Good Samaritan. At the beginning of the Christian era the Samaritans lived in Central Palestine. They were intensely disliked by the Jews. "The Jews have no dealings with the Samaritans," said the woman of Samaria when asked by Jesus for a drink from the well (*John* 4^9). In answer to the lawyer's question "And who is my neighbour ? " Christ replied with the parable of the Good Samaritan (*Luke* 10^{30-7}).

A "good Samaritan", in general terms, is a kindly person who befriends a needy stranger.

Go'rdius, ancient King of Phrygia and father of Midas, was originally a peasant. When disturbances broke out in Phrygia, an oracle declared that a waggon would bring the inhabitants a king who should restore peace. Meanwhile Gordius, with his wife and son, appeared in his waggon and was acknowledged as king. Gordius at once dedicated his waggon to Zeus. The pole was fastened to the yoke by a knot of bark ; and an oracle declared that whosoever should untie the knot should reign over Asia. Alexander cut the knot with his sword and applied the oracle to himself. According to Aristobulas, Alexander's general, Alexander did not cheat by cutting the knot. What he did was to pull out the pin attaching the yoke to the pole. He could then slide the yoke bodily out of the knot, which was thus exposed to view and its secret revealed. It contained not two but many rope-ends.

The Archbishop of Canterbury, praising the political ability of the youthful King Henry V, says :
" Turn him to any cause of policy,
The Gordian knot of it he will unloose,
Familiar as his garter."

Hence, a ' Gordian knot ' is any problem difficult to solve.

Gorgons, three monstrous sisters with wings, brazen claws and enormous teeth, their heads covered with hissing serpents instead of hair. Medusa alone of the three was mortal. Anyone who looked at her head was changed into stone.

The Gorgon Medusa. (*Florentine gem*). *In archaic art the head was hideous and monstrous ; later the type became that of a beautiful face.*

Perseus cut off her head which was afterwards placed in the shield of Athene :
" that snaky-headed Gorgon shield
That wise Minerva wore, un-conquered virgin,
Wherewith she freezed her foes to congealed stone."
(*Comus,* 447).

A ' gorgon ' is a terrible sight, as in Macduff's words :

" Approach the chamber, and destroy your sight
With a new Gorgon,"
i.e. the murdered Duncan.
Tennyson has the verb ' to gorgonise ' :
" Gorgonised me from head to foot
With a stony British stare."
(*Maud* I, xiii, 21, 22).
See **Perseus.**

Gospel. This Anglo-Saxon word has the same meaning as the Greek *evangel,* i.e. good news. Hence *gospellers, evangelists,* used by various Protestant sects, the former = the followers of John Wycliffe and the latter = those (in particular) of Wesley.

The first three Gospels confine themselves almost exclusively to the events in our Lord's life which took place in Galilee until His last journey to Jerusalem. The fourth Gospel treats with precision of the occasions on which He visited Jerusalem.

Because they give a common outline or synopsis of our Lord's work the first three Gospels are usually called the *Synoptic* Gospels. St. John was more interested in the philosophy underlying Christ's teaching than in the incidents of His life.

Goths, a powerful German people who dwelt originally on the Baltic coast at the mouth of the Vistula but afterwards migrated south. In the third century they separated into two great divisions, the Ostro-goths (or E. Goths) and the Visi-goths (or W. Goths). The latter division under Alaric invaded Italy, and took and plundered Rome (A.D. 410). Later they settled in S.W. Gaul from which they invaded Spain. Here they established a kingdom which lasted more than two centuries and which was finally overthrown by the Arabs. The Ostrogoths, meanwhile, extended their dominions almost up to the gates of Constantinople. They plundered the Balkans, including Athens. Under Theodoric the Great they obtained possession of the whole of Italy where an Ostrogothic dynasty reigned until it was destroyed by Justinian, A.D. 553.

In general, a ' Goth ' is a rude, uncivilized person, a barbarian, a savage spoiler. Cf. Vandal, Hun. In Literature, Architecture and Art ' Gothic ' always implies barbarism. **' Gothic ' or (black-letter) type is opposed to roman or (Italian). All Caxton's books are printed in this type. Morris revived its use in some of his Kelmscott Press Books.**

Grai'ae, i.e. ' the old women ' who had but one eye and one tooth between them. In his story of Perseus Kingsley describes them as if they were ice-bergs : ' The surge [of the Northern waters] frosted the hair of the three Grey Sisters, and the bones in the ice-cliff above their heads.'' They were sisters of the Gorgons whom they protected.

Greek Kalends. The first day of each month in the Roman Calendar was called ' Kalendae ' (the Kalends). But the Greeks had no Kalends, so ' on/at the Greek Kalends ' in a merely humorous way expresses ' never.'

Greeks. Various names given to the Greeks are a frequent cause of confusion. They themselves called their country *He'llas* and its inhabitants *He'llēnes.* Neither of these names is found in Latin. Hellas was in most ancient times a small district in Thessaly. The inhabitants of this district, the Hellenes, gradually spread over the surrounding country and the name was at last adopted by all Hellenic countries. The Romans called the land of the Hellenes *Graecia* (whence our Greece) and its people the *Graeci.* Then they were called *Achaii* or *Achīvi* (in English form *Achaeans*), with *Achaea* the name of the country, from Achaeus, grandson of Hellen, whose descendants they were regarded as being. A common name in Homer for Greeks is *Argeioi* (in Latin *Argivi,* anglicized as *Argives*) because Argos was in Homeric times the most important part of the Peloponnesus. From Dă'năus, mythical King of Argos, the Greeks were often called *Danaoi* (in English form, *Danaans*). Virgil also calls the Greeks *Pelasgi,* though the Pelasgians are usually regarded as the inhabitants of the peninsula before the arrival of the Achaeans.

Gryps, or griffin, a fabulous animal which according to Greek belief lived in Scythia and guarded the gold of the north. The story probably came from the fact that the Ural Mountains abound in gold.

Gytheum, a seaport of Laconia, near the mouth of the river Eurotas, said to have been built by Heracles and Apollo. It is the port of Sparta, some twenty-five miles inland.

Hā'dēs, the god of the Nether World, brother of Zeus and Poseidon, the ' infernal Zeus '. Only twice did he leave his realm—when he went to Sicily and carried off Perse'phonē, daughter of Dēmē'ter, to be his wife, and when he went to Olympus to be cured of the wound dealt by Heracles. He was called Pluto when he came to be regarded as the god of the wealth and fruits of the earth.

The Kingdom of Hades, i.e. the underworld, was a dark sunless abode, the approach to which was

Hermes presenting a Soul to Hades and Persephone. *An important function of Hermes was to conduct the shades of the dead from the upper to the lower world. Cf. cut under Charon.*

cut off by the underground Styx, Cocȳ'tus and A'chĕrōn. Here the ghosts of the dead flittered about, twittering like bats. Tartarus, divided from the rest of Hades by the blazing Phlĕ'gĕthōn, was reserved for the punishment of the most guilty of men. In the asphodel meadows were those who deserved neither great bliss nor punishment. The places of reward were elsewhere in Elȳ'sium.

Ha'drian, Roman Emperor, A.D. 117–138. Before his death Trajan (both he and Hadrian were of Spanish descent), under whom Hadrian had fought against the Dacians and the Parthians, appointed him as his successor. He spent the greater part of his reign in travelling through the various provinces of the empire in order that he might see for himself what remedies were necessary to counter mismanagement. In Britain he caused a wall to be built from the Solway to the mouth of the Tyne,

the Roman Wall or Hadrian's Wall, (or, as locally known, the Picts' Wall), terminating at the modern shipbuilding town of Wallsend at its E. end.

Hălĭcarna'ssus, a city of Asia Minor, opposite the island of Cos. It was the birthplace of the historians Hĕrŏ'dŏtus and Dionȳ'sius. It was celebrated for the Mausoleum which was built as a tomb for Mausō'lus and which was adorned with the works of the most eminent sculptors of the age. Fragments of these sculptures are now in the British Museum. This tomb was one of the Seven Wonders of the World.

Hămădrȳ'ădes. See **Nymphs.**

Haman, the favourite minister of Ahasuerus (Xerxes), King of Persia. He was hanged on a gallows fifty cubits high which, as a courtier opportunely suggested, stood ready for the purpose. Haman had prepared it for the execution of his enemy Mordecai.

" *Thy* portion, jailbird ! " exclaimed Cromwell of Roger Wildrake in Scott's *Woodstock*, " the gallows—thou shalt hang as high as Haman if thou betray counsel ! "

Hands, to wash one's. Pilate " took water and washed his hands before the multitude, saying, I am innocent of the blood of this righteous man " (*Matt.* 27[24]), i.e. he declined responsibility for the condemnation of Jesus. The title of Jesus, ' the Messiah (=anointed), King of the Jews ', as fulfilling the O.T. prophecies of a deliverer of Israel, was a religious one and not in any sense political, so the Procurator of Judæa, a Roman official, was not interested in it.

In general, to " wash one's hands " of a person or issue is to withdraw and decline to accept responsibility for him or it. This is the sense in which Richard uses the expression (*Richard II*, iv, 1, 239) :
" . . . some of you with Pilate
    wash your hands,
Showing an outward pity ; yet
    you Pilates
Have here deliver'd me to my
    sour cross,
And water cannot wash away
    your sin."

Harmŏ′nĭa, daughter of Ares and Aphrodī′tē and wife of Cadmus. All the gods of Olympus were present at her marriage. Cadmus gave his bride the necklace which he had received from Hēphae′stus and which proved fatal to all who possessed it. Cadmus and Harmonia were finally changed by the gods into serpents. These " two bright and aged snakes "
" Bask in the glens or on the
    warm sea-shore,
In breathless quiet, after all
    their ills ;

Nor do they see their country,
    nor the place
Where the Spinx lived among
    the frowning hills,
Nor the unhappy palace of
    their race,
Nor Thebes."
    M. Arnold :
      Cadmus and Harmonia.
See **Cadmus.**

Harpies, i.e. the ' robbers ' or ' snatchers ', are represented as monstrous birds with the hands of maidens, long claws and faces pale with hunger. In Homer they are personified storm-winds.

A Harpy (British Museum. From a tomb at Xanthus), represented in the act of carrying off a maiden.

" Suddenly from the hills with
    awful swoop
And loudly flapping wings the
    Harpies pounce
And rend our food ; all round
    with dirty taint
They dabble mid dread screams
    and loathsome smells."
    (Virgil, *Aen.* iii, 225–8,
      tr. by Richards).

Shakespeare must have remembered the Virgilian story of the Harpies swooping on the Trojans and carrying off their food. In *The Tempest* (iii, 3), stage directions read : " Enter Ariel, like a harpy ; claps his wings upon the table ; and, with a quaint device, the banquet vanishes."

Hē′bē, goddess of youth, daughter of Zeus and Hera. She was the attendant of the gods in Olympus whose cups she filled with nectar. One story relates that she lost her place as cup-bearer to the gods because she had once stumbled and fallen while carrying out her duties. She was replaced by Ganymēdē(s) whose beauty had captivated the gods and who was carried up to Olympus by the sacred eagle of Zeus.

Milton refers to
  " wreathed smiles
Such as hang on Hebe's cheek "
  (*L'Allegro* 28, 9).
Referring to the Lady's brothers, Comus asks
  " Were they of manly prime, or
    youthful bloom ? "
to which the Lady replies :
  " As smooth as Hebe's their
    unrazored lips."
  (*Comus* 289, 90).

Hebrew Poetry. We are so accustomed to metre and rhythm and rhyme in our own poetry that we find the form of Hebrew poetry in the translation difficult to appreciate. There are two main characteristics to be remembered. Imagery is a vital factor—simile, metaphor, personification. Figures of speech abound that would seem ludicrous to us if the Bible had not made them familiar. Personification was a favourite figure, and simile, because the simile also explained and interpreted. The heavens as a curtain, the deep as a garment, hoar-frost like ashes—these are the similes that are the foundation of Hebrew poetry. The hills skipping like rams, the clouds dropping fatness, the floods clapping their hands, a land flowing with milk and honey—these are the figures that represent its colour and vividness. But the characteristic corresponding with our rhyme was repetition, of word, phrase, or thought. There are examples everywhere : the reiterated questions in the passage from the epic of Job ; the account of Sisera's death ; the actual refrain " O that men would praise the Lord " in Psalm cvii ; the climax of appeal in David's elegy ; the signs of old age in the poem from the book of Ecclesiastes. But actual repetition is only a part of a much wider and more characteristic element—parallelism of thought and phrase. It is, in reality, a kind of thought-alliteration. The expression of one poetic idea seems to find an echo and re-echo in another. One note of music lingers in the next :
" He paweth in the valley and rejoiceth in his strength ;
He goeth on to meet the armed men.
He mocketh at fear and is not affrighted ;
Neither turneth he back from the sword.
He swalloweth the ground with fierceness and rage ;
Neither believeth he that it is the sound of the trumpet."
This " parallelism " was a characteristic of all Hebrew poetry. It is the commonest element in the Psalms : it occurs in the songs of War and Nature as well as in the poems of wisdom and philosophy. " Like the swing of a pendulum to and fro," says Professor Moulton, " like the tramp of an army marching in step, the versification of the Bible moves with a rhythm of

parallel lines.'' That is not the least of the secrets of the Bible's songs. See Peake: One volume *Commentary on the Bible*, p. 23, for a clear account of Hebrew parallelism, with examples.

He′cătē, a mysterious goddess identified with Selē′nē in heaven, Ar′temis on earth and Perse′phonē in the lower world. Hence she is represented with three heads. It is possible that her triple form was derived from the three phases of the new, the full and the waning moon ; but the triple form may be derived from her statue being placed at the fork of roads, looking each way. She was the patron-goddess of night and darkness, of ghosts and nightly apparitions, and of magic and sorcery.

Hecate. *As a moon-goddess she is represented with torches ; as portress of Hades with keys. Her triple form may be derived from the three phases of the new, full and waning moon.*

Most Elizabethan dramatists use classical proper names in various forms to suit their rhyme and metre. So, except in one doubtful passage, Shakespeare always scans 'Hecat'. Milton in *Comus* follows his example, as does Byron in *Childe Harold*. Keats, too, in his sonnet on the sea, has :
" till the spell
Of Hecate leaves them their old shadowy sound.''

He′ctor, the chief hero of the Trojans in their war with the Greeks, the eldest son of Priam and Hecuba, husband of Andro′-machē and father of Astÿ′ănax. He fought with the bravest of the Greeks and at length slew Patro′clus, the friend of Achilles. The death of his friend roused Achilles to the fight. The other Trojans fled before him into the city. Hector alone remained without the walls, though his parents implored him to return ; but when he saw Achilles, his heart failed him and he took to flight. Thrice he raced round the city pursued by the swift-footed Achilles, and then fell pierced by Achilles' spear. Achilles tied Hector's body to his chariot and thus dragged him into the camp of the Greeks ; but later traditions relate that he first dragged the body thrice round the walls of Troy. At the command of Zeus, Achilles surrendered the body to the prayers of Priam who buried it at Troy with great pomp.

The common noun ' hector ' = a bully, and the verb ' to hector ' = to bully, to swagger, are derived from Hector, the bullying braggart of popular drama.

Hĕ′cŭba, wife of Priam and mother of numerous children including Hector, Paris and Cassandra. On the capture of Troy she fell to the lot of Odysseus and was carried away as a slave to the Thracian Chersonesus, where her daughter Poly′xĕnă was sacrificed

on the demand of the shade of
Achilles who had loved her. Further
sorrow awaited Hecuba. Her
youngest son Polydŏ′rus, a mere
boy, had been murdered by Poly-
mēstor, the Thracian King, and
his body was brought to her. She
appealed in vain to Agamemnon
for vengeance and then put out the
eyes of Polymestor and slew his
sons. Later she was transformed
into a dog and leaped into the sea.

Hamlet contrasts his own in-
activity, his failure to carry out
the Ghost's instructions, with the
Player's emotion over the woes of
Priam's Queen. And yet, he says,
" What's Hecuba to him, or he
    to Hecuba,
    That he should weep for her ? "
He himself, on the other hand,
confesses himself a ' John-a-
dreams ', incapable of translating
his motive into action.

            (*Hamlet* II).

Helen, according to the best-
known legend the daughter of Zeus
and Lēda and half-sister of Castor
and Pollux, a woman of surpassing
beauty. She was the wife of
Měnělāus, King of Sparta. She
was carried off by Paris, son of
Priam, and this was the cause of
the Trojan war. On the capture of
Troy she became reconciled with
Menelaus and returned with him
to Sparta.

Marlowe twice refers to Helen's
beauty :
" Helen, whose beauty sum-
     moned Greece to arms,
And drew a thousand ships
     to Tenedos."
     (*Tamburlaine II*, ii, 4, 87) ;
" Was this the face that launch'd
     a thousand ships,
And burnt the topless towers
     of Ilium ? "
     (*Doctor Faustus*, v, 1, 107).
With these quotations from Mar-

Helios. (*From the metope at Ilium*). *Represents the four horses and chariot
with which Helios traverses the heavens.*

lowe cf. what Troilus says of Cressida :

> " She is a pearl
> Whose price hath launcht above
>   a thousand ships
> And turn'd crown'd kings to
>   merchants."
> (*Troilus and Cressida*, 2, 2, 81).

Hĕ'lĕnus, a son of Priam and Hecuba, gifted with prophetic powers. After the fall of Troy he fell to the share of Pyrrhus to whom he foretold the sufferings which awaited the Greeks who returned home by sea. He prevailed on Pyrrhus, Achilles' son, to return by land and, as a reward for thus saving his life, he was allowed to marry Andro'machē, widow of his brother Hector.

Hĕ'lĭcōn, range of mountains in Boeotia, sacred to Apollo and the Muses. Here sprang the celebrated fountains of the Muses, Agan'ippē and Hippocrē'nē.

Hē'lĭos, the god of the sun. See Hyperion.

He'llēn, son of Deucalion and Pyrrha. He is the mythical ancestor of all the Hellēnes, whose abode was the country which they called Hellas and which the Romans called Graecia, whence we have derived the name of Greece.

He'llespont, the long narrow strait connecting the Propontis (the Sea of Marmora) with the Ægean. It is fifty miles long and its width varies from one to six miles. The narrowest part is between Sestus and Abȳ'dos, where Xerxes made his bridge of boats and where legend says Leander swam across to visit Hero.

The name of the Hellespont, i.e. the Sea of Helle, was derived from the story of Helle's being drowned in it. Helle and her brother Phrixus were rescued by their mother Ne'phelē from the wrath of Ino. They were riding through the air to Colchis on the Ram with the golden fleece when Helle fell off and was drowned in the waters to which she gave her name.

Hĕ'lots, originally inhabitants of Hĕlos, a town of Laconia, who were enslaved by the Spartans and were employed by them as drudges. Any dangerous Helots were liable to liquidation by the Krupteia or Secret Police. Cf. the Biblical story of the wily Gibeonites who were punished by being made " hewers of wood and drawers of water."

Hēphae'stus, called Vulcānus by the Romans, the god of fire, son of Zeus and Hera. He was so much disliked by his mother that she threw him down from Olympus. After nine years he returned. On one occasion he took Hera's part in a domestic scene against Zeus who in anger seized his son by the

Hephaestus. (From an altar in the Vatican). He carries a blacksmith's instrument and wears a workman's outer garment which leaves the right arm and shoulder free.

leg and hurled him down from heaven. His lameness, accounted for in mythology by one of these two falls, was a source of " Homeric laughter " to the gods. He was the blacksmith of the gods, an artist who, with his workshop and anvil in Olympus, built all their palaces. He made the armour of Achilles and the fatal necklace of Harmonia.

Milton calls Hephaestus ' Mulciber ', i.e. the ' softener ' (of metals) and makes him the builder of Pandemonium :

" in Ausonian land
Men call him Mulciber ; and
   how he fell
From Heaven they fabled,
   thrown by angry Jove
Sheer o'er the crystal battle-
   ments . . ."

              (*P.L.*I, 739).

Hē′ra, called Juno by the Romans, sister and wife of Zeus. Though treated with the same reverence as her husband, she is far inferior to him in power : she is not the ruler of gods and men, but simply the wife of the supreme god. She is of a jealous and quarrelsome disposition and hence arise frequent disputes between her and Zeus. Owing to the judgement of Paris she was hostile to the Trojans and sided with the Greeks in the Trojan war. She persecuted all the children of Zeus and mortal mothers and so appears as the enemy of Diōnysus, Heracles and others. Hera was represented as a majestic woman, carrying a sceptre in her hand. Sometimes her sacred bird, the peacock, is painted by her side. She is said to have transplanted the hundred eyes of Argus ' the all-seeing ' to the peacock's tail.

Hē′raclēs, in Latin writers Hercules, the greatest of the deified heroes, was the son of Zeus and Alcmēnē. Following her policy of persecuting children of Zeus and mortal mothers, Hera sent two serpents to destroy the child in his cradle, but the infant hero strangled them. When he was eighteen years old, two tall beautiful women, Virtue and Pleasure, appeared to him and offered him respectively the choice between a life of toil leading to glory and one of ease and enjoyment. He chose the former. Soon after his marriage with Megara, daughter of the Theban King Crĕōn, he was driven mad by Hera, and in his madness killed his own children and those of his half-brother Īphicles. In consequence he was ordered by the oracle at Delphi to serve Eurystheus, King of Argos, for twelve years, after which he was promised immortality. During these years Heracles executed his twelve labours at the King's command. These were :

Heracles and Hydra. (*From a marble at Naples*). *This nine-headed monster dwelt in a swamp near Argos.*

(i) *Fight with the Nemean lion.* Heracles strangled it and later wore its skin. [See **Nemea**].
(ii) *Fight against the Lernean hydra.* [See **Hydra**].
(iii) *Capture of the Arcadian stag.*

Heracles pursued this swift animal with golden antlers and brazen

Heracles and Arcadian Stag. (*From a group at Naples*). *The animal had golden antlers and brazen feet. It had been dedicated to Artemis.*

feet for a year, captured it and carried it away on his shoulders.

(iv) *Destruction of the Erymanthian boar.* When Heracles appeared with the huge beast, alive, on his

Heracles and Boar, with Eurystheus. (*From a marble at Naples*). *When Heracles appeared carrying the huge beast on his shoulders Eurystheus in panic took refuge in a tub.*

shoulders, Eurystheus in panic took refuge in a tub.

(v) *Cleansing of the stables of Augeas.* [See **Augean Stables**].

(vi) *Destruction of the Stymphalian birds.* Athene helped Heracles in this task by providing him with a brazen rattle by the noise of which he startled the carnivorous birds, killed some of them and drove others away.

(vii) *Capture of the Cretan bull.* The bull had been driven mad by Poseidon and had caused great havoc in Crete. Heracles brought it home on his shoulders ; but he then set it free again and it roamed through Greece. [See **Theseus**].

(viii) *Capture of the mares of the Thracian Diŏmēdes.* They were fed on human flesh. Heracles killed Diomedes whose body he threw to the mares which became tame after eating the flesh of their master.

(ix) *Seizure of the girdle of the Queen of the Amazons.* Hippo′lÿtē, Queen of the Amazons, possessed a girdle which she had received from Ares. Admete, Eurystheus' daughter, wished to obtain it and Heracles was sent to fetch it. When he reached the country of the Amazons Hippolyte promised him the girdle ; but Hera again intervened and incited the Amazons against him. In battle he killed Hippolyte and took the girdle.

(x) *Capture of the oxen of Gērÿōnes.* [See **Geryon**].

(xi) *Fetching the golden apples of the Hesperides.* [See **Apple** (ii)].

(xii) *Fetching Cerberus from the lower world.* This was the most difficult of the twelve labours of Heracles. He descended into Hades, accompanied by Hermes and Athene, and obtained permission from Pluto to carry Cerberus to the upper world provided he could accomplish it without force of arms. Heraclès succeeded in seizing the monster and carrying it to the upper world ; and after he had shown it to Eurystheus he carried it back again to the lower world.

Heracles and Cerberus. *The dog that guarded the entrance of Hades is here pictured as having three heads and the tail of a serpent.*

After he had performed the twelve labours, Heracles was released from the servitude of Eurystheus and returned to Thebes. Later, in a fit of madness, he killed his friend Īphitus, and in atonement he served **Omphalē** for three years. Then he married Dēĭănī′ra who was the unwilling cause of her husband's death. She presented to him the poisoned robe which the centaur Nessus had given her, and when the garment became warm on his person the poison entered his limbs and caused him most excruciating agony. Heracles erected a funeral pile for himself and ordered it to be set on fire. A cloud came down from heaven and carried him to Olympus where he was honoured with immortality, and married Hera's daughter Hebe.

Figuratively, a ' Heracles ' is a strong man (cf. Samson, the Hebrew personification of strength). An abnormally large baby is facetiously called a ' pocket Hercules '.

Hercula′nĕum, an ancient city in Campania, between Naples and Pompeii. In A.D. 63 a great part of it was destroyed by an earthquake, and in 79 it was overwhelmed with two other popular resorts, Pompēii and Stăbĭae, by the great eruption of Mt. Vesuvius. It was buried under showers of ashes and streams of lava from 70 to 100 feet under the present surface of the ground. The ancient city was accidentally discovered by the sinking of a well in 1720. Excavations have been carried on since : besides the remains of ancient buildings, many works of art and several MSS., written on rolls of papyrus, have been discovered.

He′rmēs, called Mercŭrĭus by the Romans. At the entrance to the cave in which he was born he found a tortoise. He took its shell, drew strings across it and thus invented the lyre. (The Latin *testūdo* = tortoise, often means lute or lyre). He was the herald of the gods (and therefore the god of ready speech) and was specially employed by them as messenger when readiness of speech was necessary. An important duty of Hermes was to conduct the shades of the dead into the lower world. His excellencies were combined with cunning, both in word and actions, and even fraud, perjury and the inclination to steal. Naturally enough, therefore, he was the god of thieves. A Pompeian wall-painting shows Hermes the messenger starting off with a bag of money in his hand. His principal attributes in art are :

(i) a pĕtăsus or winged cap, signifying the traveller ;

(ii) the staff, a gift from Apollo, which he bore as a herald ;

(iii) the sandals, golden and provided with wings, which carried him across land and sea with the rapidity of wind.

Our phrase " hermetically sealed " only accidentally refers to Hermes ; for the Egyptian god Thoth, the inventor of magic and god of alchemy, was known also under the name of Hermes Trismegistos (i.e. the thrice-greatest).

Hē′rō, see **Lēander.**

Herod. (i) the Great, King of the Jews, an Idumaean. He was a shrewd but merciless man. When he died in 4 B.C. his son

(ii) Herod Antipas obtained the tetrarchy of Galilee and Peraea (*Acts* 13¹). In A.D. 38, through the intrigues of Herod Agrippa, who was high in the favour of the Roman emperor, Antipas was deprived of his dominions and banished.

(iii) Herod Agrippa I was made King of the whole of Palestine by the Emperor Claudius as a reward for helping him to gain possession of the empire. He beheaded James, the brother of John, and " proceeded to seize Peter also " (*Acts* 12¹···). He was "eaten of worms" at Caesarea (*Acts* 12²³).

(iv) Herod Agrippa II, at the time of his father's death, was seventeen years old. He and his sister heard Paul's defence at Caesarea (*Acts* 25¹³, 26). He sided with the Romans in the Jewish war, and after the capture of Jerusalem in A.D. 70 he went with Berenice, his sister, to Rome where he died in A.D. 100.

Herod is the stock braggart and bully of the old religious or miracle plays. Hamlet (iii, 2) refers to him. " It offends me," he tells the players in the Castle Hall of Elsinore, " to hear a robustious periwig-pated fellow tear a passion to tatters . . . it out-herods Herod ", i.e. it is worse than the ranting speech and

action of the Herod of the miracle plays. Cf. the similar expression " to out-Hector."

Hērŏ′dŏtus (480–425 B.C.), the " Father of History." He travelled extensively to collect materials for his work, sifted them for accuracy as far as he could and arranged them in a delightful form. He divided his work into nine books, each of which he named after one of the Muses.

Hēsĭ′ŏnē, daughter of Lāo′medon, King of Troy, was chained by her father to a rock to be devoured by a sea-monster, that he might thus appease the anger of Apollo and Neptune. Heracles promised to save her if Laomedon would give him the six horses he had received from Zeus as a compensation for Ganymedes. Heracles killed the monster, but Laomedon refused to keep his promise. Thereupon Heracles took Troy, killed Laomedon and gave Hesione to his friend Telamon. She became the mother of Teucer.

Hespĕ′rĭdes, the nymphs who guarded the golden apples, with the assistance of the dragon Lādōn. It was one of the labours of Heracles to obtain possession of these apples.

See **Apple** (ii).

He′stĭa, called Vesta by the Romans, the goddess of the fire burning on the hearth. As the hearth was looked upon as the centre of domestic life, so Hestia was the giver of all domestic happiness. As such she was believed to dwell in the inner part of every house. The hearth itself was the sacred asylum where supplicants implored the protection of the inhabitants of the house.

Hewers of wood and drawers of

water, i.e. servile workers who perform the most menial of tasks. The Gibeonites lived in the central hilly part of Palestine. As Joshua was advancing successfully into the country the Gibeonites succeeded by a trick in making terms with him. They ' did work wilily ' and pretended to be ambassadors from a very far country. To bolster up their pretence they wore old clouted shoes and old garments and the bread they brought with them was dry and mouldy. They sought to make a league with Joshua " because of the name of the Lord thy God." Joshua was thus beguiled into making a league with them and when he discovered the trick he would not go back on his word ; but he reduced them to a state of semi-slavery and made them " hewers of wood and drawers of water for the congregation and for the altar of the Lord." (*Jos.* 9³⁻²¹).

High Places (frequently mentioned in O.T. and always a puzzle to students). It was a wide-spread custom to worship on sacred mountains or elevated spots and the character of the ' high place ' would depend on the deity worshipped. The towns of Palestine were often built on hill-slopes and the ' high place ' above the town was the place for worship and social intercourse (see 1 *Sam.* 9¹¹⁻¹⁴). Till the erection of the Temple the worship of Jehovah on the ' high-places ' was not improper (1 *Kings* 3²). The Israelites found on every side high places at which the Canaanites worshipped the local deities or *baalim.* As this worship was associated chiefly with agricultural life, it insidiously gained influence over the Israelites even when they persuaded themselves they were doing honour to their own God. Thus Israelite and

Canaanite had a common place of worship. Similarly to-day in Palestine and Syria there are ' high places ', often bearing the name of some saint buried in the place and supposed to have the power of conferring special benefits. Muslims and Christians alike make visits to these places and pay vows at them. Hezekiah in his reform is said to have removed the ' high places ' (2 *Kings* 18⁴) ; but they reappear under his successors. Josiah's reformation was more thorough and there is no mention of ' high places ' under the kings who followed him.

Hi′ppocrē′nē (i.e. the ' Horse-Fountain '), the fountain raised in Mt. Helicon by a stroke from the hoof of Pegasus.

In the *Ode to a Nightingale* Keats talks as though the fountain ran wine :
" O for a beaker full of the warm South,
Full of the true, the blushful Hippocrene."

Hippŏ′lўtē, queen of the Amazons and sister of Antī′ŏpē. One legend has it that Hercules was sent to obtain the girdle which her father Ares had given her and that he killed her in a battle that ensued. Another legend says that she marched with an army of Amazons against Attica to take vengeance on Theseus for having carried off her sister.

In *A Midsummer Night's Dream* Hippolyta is betrothed to Theseus, Duke of Athens, who tells her
" Hippolyta, I woo'd thee with my sword,
And won thy love, doing thee injuries ;
But I will wed thee in another key,
With pomp, with triumph, and with revelling."

Titania accuses Oberon of being in love with Hippolyta,

" the bouncing Amazon,
Your buskin'd mistress and your warrior love."

Hippŏ'lўtus, a son of Theseus and Hippolyte. Theseus afterwards married Phaedra who fell in love with Hippolytus and hanged herself in despair, leaving a letter in which she blamed her stepson. Theseus thereupon cursed his son and begged Poseidon to destroy him. As Hippolytus was driving in his chariot along the sea-coast, Poseidon sent a bull from the water. The horses were frightened, upset the chariot and dragged Hippolytus along the ground till he was dead.

Hippŏ'tădēs, son of Hippotes, i.e. Aeŏlus, the King of the Winds which he kept shut up in a mountain.

" They (the felon winds) knew not of his story ;
And sage Hippotades their answer brings."
(*Lycidas*, 95, 6).

Holland House Vase.
See **Portland Vase, The.**

Hŏ'mer, the great epic poet of Greece whose poems formed the basis of Greek literature. Every Greek of liberal education had learnt the epics by heart at school. Homer's date and birthplace are equally matters of dispute. His date is variously given between 1050 and 850 B.C. As to his birthplace

" Seven wealthy towns contend for Homer dead,
Thro' which the living Homer begg'd his bread."
Tradition relates that he was the son of Maeon :

" Old Maeonides the blind
Said it three thousand years ago." (J. S. Flecker).

Equally, tradition relates that he was blind and poor in his old age. For his epics see **Odyssey** and **Iliad**. Some scholars have contended that these two long poems are not the work of one man, but small, separate epic songs, celebrating single exploits of the heroes, which were chanted and recited by minstrels at banquets and great religious festivals, but not committed to writing until some compiler(s) undertook this task centuries later. Modern scholarship is more inclined to regard the epics as the work of a single poet. Samuel Butler even suggested that a woman was the authoress of the *Odyssey !*

Homeric laughter, like that indulged in by the gods in Olympus as they watched lame Hēphae'stus limping about the godly palace. So, too, an *Homeric struggle* is one such as Homer's heroes might have taken part in.

Homer sometimes nods, i.e. even the greatest poet has occasional lapses. Horace admits that this is so, but asserts that he is annoyed whenever it happens. Pope, too, defends Homer when he writes in his *Essay on Criticism :*

" Those oft are stratagems which errors seem,
Nor is it Homer nods, but we that dream."

Horace, the Roman lyric poet. Some of his poems attracted the notice of Virgil who introduced him to Maecenas. This patron of literature became his intimate friend and gave him a Sabine farm from which the poet derived infinite pleasure and which was the source of some of his happiest poems. For exquisite finish and mastery of metre the " Odes " (on which Horace based his claim to be remembered) are unsurpassed.

Horace was a wise and sincere man, tolerant of a great deal he knew to be amiss in Roman society, and a witty commentator on the public and private life of his day. He teaches a lofty morality, he preaches moderation and contentment, endurance and integrity. His moral teaching is well summed up in his own words, thus translated by Lonsdale and Lee : " You would not rightly call ' blest ' the man who has great possessions ; more rightly does he assume the title of ' blest ' who has learned how to use wisely the gifts of Heaven, and to endure stern penury, and who fears disgrace worse than death."

Some fifteen of these odes have been translated by C. S. Calverley, a scholar and poet of the Victorian age. More recently translations by Sir Edward Marsh and Lord Dunsany have been published and broadcast.

Horā'tii and Curiā'tii.

Three brothers of the ancient patrician family at Rome (the Horā'tia gens) fought, according to legend, with the Curiatii, three brothers from Alba, to determine whether Rome or Alba was to be supreme. The battle was long undecided. Two of the Horatii fell ; but the three Curiatii, though alive, were severely wounded. Seeing this, the surviving Horatius who was still unhurt pretended to flee, and vanquished his opponents by encountering them severally. He returned in triumph, bearing his threefold spoils. As he approached the Capēne Gate leading to the Appian Way his sister Horatia met him and recognised on his shoulders the mantle of one of the Curiatii, her betrothed lover. Her grief drew on her the wrath of Horatius who stabbed her, exclaiming " So perish every Roman woman who

bewails a foe ! " For this murder he was sentenced to be scourged and hanged on the accursed tree. He appealed to his peers, the burghers, who prescribed a nominal punishment. With veiled head, led by his father, Horatius passed under a yoke or gibbet—*tigillum sororium* or sister's gibbet.

Horse, the Wooden. The Greeks had pretended to abandon the siege of Troy and had withdrawn their fleet behind the island of Tenedos. On the beach they left a large wooden horse filled with armed warriors, pretending that it was an offering to Athene for a safe return home. When night came Sīnon, a cunning Greek who had allowed himself to be captured by the Trojans, persuaded Priam to have the horse brought inside, though Lāo'cŏon, the priest of Neptune, urged him not to do so : " Trojans, trust not the horse. Whate'er it means, I fear even gifts from Greeks." But a breach was made in the wall and the horse was dragged inside amid great rejoicing. Then Sinon opened the door in the side of the Horse and released the warriors :

" The city sunk in sleep and
    wine
They enter, kill the sentries
    and admit
Through open gates the
    accomplice host of Greeks."

Hour, the Eleventh, i.e. the last moment, just in time to avoid losing some benefit. " Hopes of an eleventh hour settlement " of an industrial strike is a common newspaper report of our day.

See the Parable of the Labourers in the Vineyard (*Matt.* 20$^{1-16}$). Those who had worked but one hour received the same reward as those who had ' borne the burden and heat of the day.'

House divided against itself, A.
Jesus had healed a man blind and
dumb and the Pharisees, who
could not deny the miracle, explained it away by saying : " This
man doth not cast out devils but
by Beelzebub, the prince of the
devils." The reply of Jesus was :
" Every kingdom divided against
itself is brought to desolation ;
and every city or house divided
against itself shall not stand ", i.e.
the accusation of the Pharisees was
patently absurd, because evil is
not likely to destroy evil.

(*Matt.* 12²²⁻⁸).

Houses, Eastern. Eastern houses
were built of stone in hill districts
and of sun-dried bricks in the
plains. The roofs were formed of

*Hebrew houses were usually one-
storeyed and the roof is either flat or
(when of stone) has a central dome.*

brushwood laid on rude rafters,
and were easily removed (*Mark* 2⁴ ;
Luke 5¹⁹). The house was usually
one-storeyed and often there was
an outer staircase leading to the
roof. The flat-roofs were surrounded by a battlement. The
windows were small and high up,
often closed by a wooden lattice.
Frequently there were no outside
windows, all light and air being
obtained from an inner courtyard.
Greek and Roman houses often
followed the same plan. The
" guest-chamber " (*Luke* 22¹¹) was
sometimes an " upper chamber "
(*Acts* 1¹³, 9³⁷) and even a third
storey is mentioned (*Acts* 20⁹).
The roof was used as a sleeping-
place in summer, for taking the
air and for private communication
(1 *Sam.* 9²⁵,²⁶ ; 2 *Sam.* 11², *Acts*
10⁹).

Huns. See **Attila.**

Hy̆ăcin'thus, a youth of extra-
ordinary beauty, beloved by Apollo
and Zephyrus. As he was once
playing at quoits with Apollo,
Zephyrus in a fit of jealousy turned
the quoit so that it struck the boy
and killed him. From his blood
sprang the flower, the hyacinth,
on the petals of which appeared
the exclamation of woe, AI, AI
(i.e. Alas ! Alas !) or the letter Υ,
the initial of the Greek form of
the youth's name. The myth
seems to refer to the effect of the hot
summer sun in withering the spring
flowers, the quoit being the sun's
disk.

Milton in *Lycidas* makes poetic
use of the myth : " that sanguine
flower inscrib'd with woe," referring
to the hyacinth. Similarly, in
Keats' *Endymion :*

" They might watch the quoit-
    pitchers, intent
On either side ; pitying the
    sad death

Of Hyacinthus, when the
cruel breath
Of Zephyr slew him.''

Hȳ′dra, a legendary monster
(evidently some kind of water-
snake. Greek ' hudōr ' means
water) which lived in a swamp and
ravaged the country of Lernae
near Argos. It had nine heads of
which the middle one was immortal.
Heracles struck off its heads with
his club ; but in the place of the
head he cut off, two new ones grew
each time. With the assistance of
his faithful servant Ĭŏlā′us he
burned away the heads of the hydra
and buried the immortal one under
a huge rock. Having thus conquered the monster he poisoned his
arrows with its bile so that the
wounds inflicted by them became
incurable.

Shakespeare refers to this monster several times, e.g. " Another
King ! " cries Douglas in 1 *Henry
IV,* " they grow like Hydra's
heads." In *Henry V* we have
Canterbury's compound ' hydra-
headed ' = constantly recurring.

Hȳpe′riŏn, in Greek accented
Hyperíon, but from Elizabethan
times onward in English poetry,
noticeably in Shakespeare, accented
Hypérion.

He was a Titan, the son of
Urănus (Heaven) and Gē (Earth),
the father of Helios (the Sun),
Selēnē (the Moon) and Eōs (Dawn).
He has been identified by poets
from the time of Homer with
Hēlĭos, the sun-god.

Hamlet expresses the contrast
between his dead father and his
uncle as " Hyperion to a satyr ",
i.e. as a curly-headed sun-god to
a half-human, half-goat sylvan god.

I′cărus. See **Daedalus.**

Ichabod, the son of Phineas and

grandson of Eli, so named by his
dying mother because the news of
the capture of the Ark by the
Philistines arrived as she gave him
birth (1 *Sam.* 4[19-22]). The word
means " no glory."

I′da (*a*) the " many-fountain'd "
range of mountains bordering the
S. of the plain of Troy. Mt. Gar-
garos was one of its peaks. It is
the source of the Sĭmŏĭs and
Scamander. Homer says the gods
watched the battles in the plain of
Troy from the summit of Mt. Ida.
See Tennyson's *Oenōnē.*
(*b*) a mountain in the centre of
Crete. It was connected with the
worship of Zeus who was said to
have been brought up in a cave
in this mountain.

Ĭdes. There is an Etruscan or
old Roman dialectical verb *iduo*
= to divide : hence, literally, the
Ides is the day of the divided or half
month—the 15th day of March,
May, July and October, the 13th of
the other eight months.

Ĭdes of March, i.e. March 15th.

Julius Caesar was assassinated
on the Ides of March, 44 B.C.
In the street before the Capitol,
Shakespeare represents Artemidorus
and the Soothsayer warning Caesar
of his danger on this morning.
Caesar merrily " chips " the Soothsayer who softly and gravely
insists on his warning :
Caesar : The Ides of March are
come.
Soothsayer : Ay, Caesar ; but
not gone.

Ĭdŏ′mĕnēus, King of Crete. Once
in a storm he vowed to sacrifice
to Poseidon whatever he should
first meet on his landing, if the
god would grant him a safe return.

This was his own son, whom he sacrificed. As Crete was in consequence visited by a plague, the Cretans expelled Idomeneus for his inhuman conduct.

Cf. the Jewish story of **Jephthah.**

I'liad. The Iliad is an epic in 24 books, telling some of the incidents in the last two months or so of the 10-year-long Trojan war. The opening line of the poem gives its scope :

" Sing, goddess, the wrath of
Achilles, Peleus' son."

The Iliad is not, then, the story of Troy and its siege, but that of the wrath of Achilles and what came of it. Achilles and Agamemnon quarrelled about a captive, Chryseis, who had been allotted to Agamemnon. Her father, a priest of Apollo, came to the Greek camp to secure his daughter's release; but Agamemnon received him in anger and hence Apollo sent a plague on the camp which lasted nine days. Achilles urged that Agamemnon should follow the advice of Calchas, the seer, and should give Chryseis up in order that the plague might cease. This he was compelled to do, but he took another captive, Briseis, from Achilles who thereupon retired to his tent and sulked.

Like its companion, *The Odyssey*, the epic has many episodes : e.g. the story of Diomēʹdēs and his great deeds, the duel between Hector and Ajax, the death of Hector. One entire book is devoted to a description of the shield of Achilles. These episodes are closely interwoven with the action of the epic as a whole—a fact which supports modern scholarship in its belief that the poem is the work of one poet.

W. H. D. Rouse's " Achilles and the Great Quarrel at Troy " (Murray) is a simple retelling of the *Iliad*.

Iʹō, daughter of the first King of Argos. Zeus loved her, but on account of Hera's jealousy he changed her into a white heifer. Hera, who was aware of the change, obtained the heifer from Zeus and placed her under the care of Argus Panoʹptēs. Zeus sent Hermes to slay Argus and deliver Io. Hera then tormented Io with a gad-fly and drove her in a state of frenzy from land to land. At length she swam the Bosporus (= the ford of the ox) and reached the banks of the Nile where she recovered her original form.

Ĭŏlāʹus, faithful friend and charioteer of Heracles whom he helped to slay the Lernean Hydra. After Heracles' death, he helped his children to kill Eurystheus.

Iphĭgĕnīʹa, daughter of Agamemnon and Clytaemnestra. Agamemnon had once killed a stag in the grove of Artemis. So the goddess sent a calm which detained the Greek fleet at Aulis, and the seer Calchas declared that the sacrifice of Iphigenia was the only means of propitiating her. At the last moment the goddess carried her in a cloud to Tauris where she became the priestess of Artemis. Here it was her duty to sacrifice all strangers who came to the country. Her brother, Orestes and his friend Pȳʹladēs came to carry off the image of the goddess, and Iphigenia recognised Orestes just as she was about to sacrifice him. She and they fled, carrying the image with them.

See Tennyson's " A Dream of Fair Women," in particular the lines suggesting Iphigenia's feelings before her ordeal :

" The high masts flicker'd as
they lay afloat ;
The crowds, the temples,
waver'd, and the shore ;

The bright death quiver'd at
   the victim's throat ;
Touch'd ; and I knew no
   more."

I'ris. In the *Iliad* Iris is the
messenger of the gods, especially
of Zeus and Hera ; in the *Odyssey*
Hermes is the messenger and Iris
is not mentioned. The rainbow is
the road on which Iris travels,
and it therefore appears whenever
the goddess wants it and vanishes
when it is no longer needed.

*Iris, the goddess of the rainbow, and
in the later poets wife of Zephyrus.
(From an ancient vase). She was
regarded as the swift messenger of the
gods, and so has wings on her
shoulders and the herald's staff in her
left hand.*

Iris is a character in the
masque Shakespeare intro-
duces in *The Tempest*, Act 4.
Here is Ceres' description of
her :
   " Hail, many colour'd mess-
      enger, that ne'er
   Dost disobey the wife of
      Jupiter ;
   Who with thy saffron
      wings upon my
      flowers
   Diffusest honey-drops,
      refreshing showers ;

And with each end of thy blue
   bow dost crown
My bosky acres and my un-
   shrubb'd down,
Rich scarf to my proud earth."

Ishmael, son of Abraham and
Sarah's bondmaid Hagar. He
became the cause of bad feeling
between Sarah and Hagar and
procured his mother's expulsion
from the house. With her fifteen-
year-old son she wandered in the
wilderness of Beersheba and would
have died from thirst had it not
been for a miraculous interposition.
   An 'Ishmaelite' is an outcast
from the society of man, one
" whose hand is against every
man and every man's hand against
him " (*Gen.* 16¹²).

Ismē'nē, daughter of Oedipus
and Jocasta, and sister of Antigone.

I'thăca, a small island in the
Ionian Sea, the traditional birthplace and home of Odysseus.

I'tys. See **Pandion.**

Ixī'ŏn, a King of Thessaly who
treacherously murdered his father-
in-law, a crime for which he could
receive no rites of purification on
earth. Zeus took pity on him,
purified him, carried him to heaven

Sisyphus, Ixion, and Tantalus.

and caused him to sit down at his table. But Ixion repaid Zeus by foul ingratitude and was fearfully punished. His hands and feet were chained by Hermes to a wheel which is said to have rolled perpetually in the air.

In *The Glove*, Browning remarks :
   " Joys prove cloudlets :
   Men are the merest Ixions "
i.e. men are subject to the whims of fortune.

In her *Song of the Cold* Edith Sitwell has
   " I, an old man,
   Bent like Ixion on my broken
      wheel the world,
   Stare at the dust."

Jā′nus, an old Latin deity, represented with two heads, facing opposite ways. He was the god of all ' openings ' or ' beginnings ' both in public and in private life. His own month, January, was the first month of the year in the later Calendar. He was the god of the doorway (*janua*) who watched over all that went out and came in ; who kept off evil influence (as in the superstitions of many nations) from crossing the threshold. He was the god of the city gates as of the house door and of the havens

Head of Janus. (*From a coin* (ās) *of the 4th century B.C.). As the god of the doorway, watching all who went out and came in, Janus is represented with two heads, so that he looks both ways.*

or wharfs of the Tiber, for which reason a ship appears on the Janus coins. He was most of all celebrated for his guardianship of the state in time of war. The ' temple ' of the national Janus was in the Forum. Its doors were opened in time of war, for it was regarded as a bad omen to close what represented the gates of the state against the citizens who had gone out to war. They were closed in time of peace.

Our word *janitor* (a pure Latin word, by the way) = doorkeeper, is derived ultimately from Jānus through *iānua*, a door.

In *The Merchant of Venice* Salarino swears 'by two-headed Janus', the point being that he is speaking of both solemn people who will " not show their teeth by way of a smile " and frivolous people " who laugh like parrots at a bagpiper."

Jā′son, son of Aeson, King of Iˊolchus. His father was deprived of his kingdom by his half-brother Pĕˊlĭas who tried to kill the infant Jason. The boy was saved and entrusted to the care of the centaur Chiˊrōn. When he reached man's estate he returned to Iolchus to demand his kingdom. Pelias consented to surrender it if Jason would command an expedition to fetch the Golden Fleece from Colchis and so soothe the spirit of Phrixus. [See **Argonauts.**] With the aid of the magician Mēdēa Jason was successful. He married her and they returned to Iolchus. Later they went to Corinth where Jason deserted Medea and married Glaucē, Creōn's daughter. In revenge Medea sent Glauce a poisoned robe which burnt her to death when she put it on. Medea also killed her own two children and then fled to Athens in a chariot drawn by winged dragons.

In his *Life and Death of Jason*
William Morris follows the story
that Jason was killed by the fall
of the Argo's sternpost which
crushed him to death.

Jehu, a colloquialism for 'driver';
in particular, a furious driver.
"The driving is like the driving of
Jehu the son of Nimshi; for he
driveth furiously" (2 *Kings* 9²⁰).

Jephthah's daughter. Jephthah,
Judge of Israel, had been outlawed
but was received back by the
people as their chief when the
Ammonites were threatening. Before the battle in which he defeated
Ammon, he *devoted* (i.e. promised
to sacrifice) whoever first came
out of his home to meet him when
he returned in peace (Jephthah's
rash vow). His daughter came
out with timbrels and dances and
"she was his only child." He
allowed her two months to live
upon the mountains and lament
her fate, and then "did with her
according to his vow."

See Tennyson's "A Dream of
Fair Women" (177-244) for this
story of

"The daughter of the warrior
  Gileadite,
A maiden pure; as when
  she went along
From Mizpeh's tower'd gate
  with welcome light,
With timbrel and with song."

Cf. the Classical stories of Idomeneus and his son, and of Agamemnon and his daughter Iphigenia.

Jeremiad, a tale of woe, a lamentation, like those of the prophet
Jeremiah of whom it has been said
that he had "no friends but God
and death."

Jericho, a royal Canaanite city
with walls. Probably it was a

trading centre having an inn. Such
inns were kept by women, but were
not regarded as respectable places.

Joshua sent two men to spy
secretly upon the defences of
the city. They lodged with a
woman named Rahab who hid
them under flax laid out to dry
on the roof of the house. In return
for thus saving their lives she
asked that she and her family
might be spared when Jericho was
taken. The spies agreed provided
that she would indicate the house
by binding a line of scarlet thread
in the window by which she had
lowered them over the city wall.
After a miraculous crossing of the
Jordan in flood Joshua was given
instructions by a divine being for
the capture of the city. The
Israelite army was to march round
the walls, preceded by the priests
blowing trumpets, for six days.
On the seventh day the walls were
to be compassed seven times.
Then all the people were to shout
with a great shout and the walls
would fall down. The city was
razed to the ground and all the
inhabitants, except Rahab and
her family, were slain, and, says
the chronicler, "she dwelleth in
Israel even unto this day."

Gordon Daviot has made a
successful one-act play out of the
story of Rahab and the spies—
"Rahab" in *Leith Sands*.

Jesse, father of David. The
"son of Jesse" was a contemptuous
term for David in his lifetime (see,
e.g. 1 *Sam.* 20²⁷, 2 *Sam.* 20¹;
1 *Kings* 12¹⁶); but the phrase
"root of Jesse" is a Messianic
title (*Is.* 11¹⁻¹⁰), full of dignity.

(*a*) Jesse Tree. In the ecclesias-
tical art of the Middle Ages, a vine
tracing the genealogy of Christ
from the "root of Jesse."

(*b*) Jesse Window, one adorned
with the Jesse Tree.

Palestine in the time of Christ

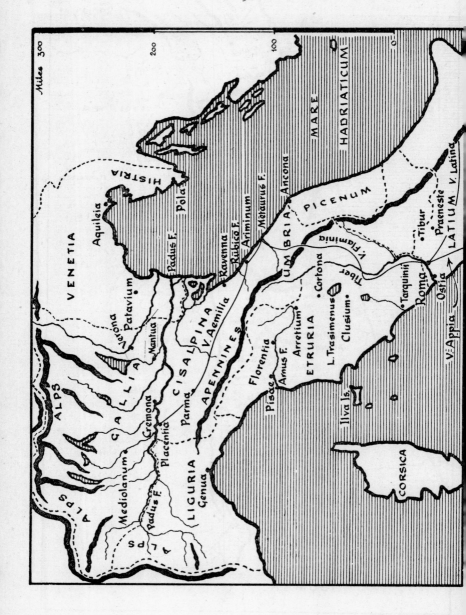

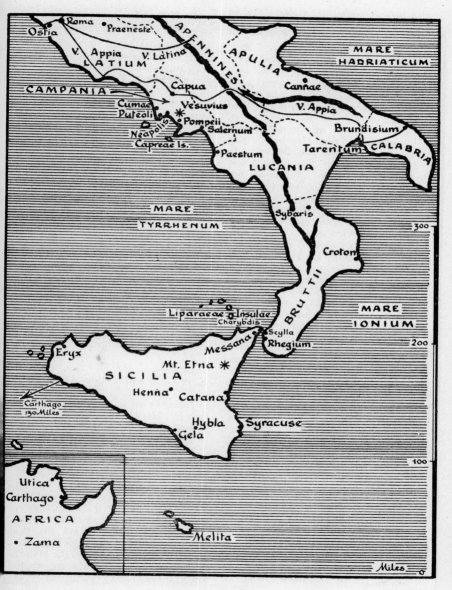

South Italy

Jezebel, wife of Ahab King of Israel. She was a Phoenician, a daughter of a King of Tyre, in whose hands Ahab became a mere puppet. From Phoenicia she introduced into Israel the worship of Baal and Astarte. At length, at the instigation of Elijah, the people rose against her prophets and slaughtered them at the foot of Carmel. Ahab was tempted into submission ; but Jezebel's only answer was one of defiance to Elijah : " So let the gods do to me, and more also, if I make not thy life as one of them by to-morrow at this time " (1 *Kings* 19¹,²). The next instance of her power and unscrupulousness is found in the story of **Naboth.** After Ahab's death she became the special mark for the vengeance of Jehu. As he neared Jezebel she painted her face and tired her head and stood at the window over the city gate, looking down on him. He ordered her to be hurled from the window and she fell in front of the usurper's chariot. Later in the day Jehu ordered the body to be buried, but only " the skull and the feet and the palms of her hands remained " (2 *Kings* 9³⁰⁻³⁷). Her name became a term of reproach for any who indulged in idolatrous practices. To-day a " Jezebel " is a harridan, especially one who paints her face.

In Scott's *Woodstock* Cromwell calls Woodstock " Jezebel's Palace " because of the traditional stories (including that of her murder by Queen Eleanor) connecting the Fair Rosamond, Henry II's mistress, with the palace.

Job. (*a*) as a type of patience. Satan obtained leave of God to tempt this great O.T. hero, the prosperous and wealthy Job ; but Job remained steadfast. " In all this Job sinned not nor charged God foolishly."

(*b*) as a type of poverty. " The Lord giveth and the Lord taketh away," he said when Satan had deprived him of all his possessions —his oxen, his asses, his sheep and his camels—all that meant wealth to an oriental.

(*c*) Job's three friends tried to comfort him, maintaining that he must have been guilty of some terrible sin to merit such misfortunes ; but he rejected their efforts : " I have heard many such things : miserable comforters are ye all."

A ' Job's comforter ' is one who, while apparently trying to sympathize with a man's misfortunes, only aggravates them by hinting that he has brought them on himself.

At the beginning of 2 *Henry IV*, Falstaff, accused of misleading the youthful prince, admits to the Lord Justice : " I am as poor as Job, my lord, but not so patient."

" Was Job the instructor of the ant ? " asks Mr. de la Mare. Patience is the characteristic of the ant, as well as of Job.

Joca'stē, wife of the Theban King Lāïus and mother of Oe'dïpus.

John evidently came of a wealthy family. His father must have been a well-to-do fisherman on the Sea of Galilee. John was known to the high-priest (*John* 18¹⁵). His mother, Salome, asked that her sons James and John might sit on either hand of Jesus in His Kingdom, and stood by the Cross. John was one of the three chief Apostles who, only, were allowed to witness the raising of Jairus's daughter (Mark 5³⁷), the Transfiguration (9²), (this time with Andrew) the prophecy on the Mount of Olives (13³) ; and the Agony in the Garden (14³³). John was " the disciple whom Jesus loved " (John 13²³). After the Ascension, Peter and John were persecuted by the Sadducees when the lame man had been healed (*Acts* 3¹–4²²). Long afterwards, James (our Lord's brother), Peter and John were the three pillars at the time of the Apostolic Conference, and this is the last direct mention of John in N.T. We know he was exiled to Patmos where he saw the Revelation. He was not the mild character he is often considered to be, but eminently stern and impetuous. Not for nothing did our Lord call the sons of Zebedee ' sons of thunder ', e.g. James and John wished to call down fire on the Samaritans (*Luke* 9⁵⁴). Nothing (doubtful tradition apart) is known of his death.

Jonah was bidden by God to go to Nineveh and " cry against it," i.e. warn its inhabitants of the wrath of God if they did not repent. Instead of doing so he took ship for Tarshish. And the Lord sent a mighty tempest " so that the ship was like to be broken." In their fear the sailors cast lots to discover " for whose cause this evil is upon us." The lot fell on Jonah who thereupon told the men to cast him into the sea " so that the sea be calm unto you." Jonah was swallowed by a great fish and " he was in the belly of the fish three days and three nights," after which he was miraculously cast ashore by the monster. Many modern scholars prefer to regard the Book of Jonah as allegorical.

By a ' Jonah ' we mean a bringer of ill-luck. Meredith uses " to Jonah " = to throw overboard : " Rather he is the Jonah whose jettisoning would do more than anything else to save the ship "— (quoted by Weekley).

Jonah's gourd. Though opinions differ, the probability is that the gourd which afforded shade to the prophet Jonah before Nineveh is the ' castor-oil plant '. Its leaves are large and palm-shaped, and would afford an excellent shelter.

See *Jonah* 4⁶ : " The Lord God prepared a gourd and made it to come up over Jonah, that it might be a shadow over his head, to deliver him from his grief."

Jordan, wash in. Read the story of Naaman, the Syrian leper (2 *Kings*, 5). Naaman learnt that leprosy, a living death, could be cured by the God of Israel who was thereby proved to be much more powerful than his own native gods. The cure was not brought about by a grand display of ritual, but by the simplicity of washing seven times in Jordan. The insignificant Jordan was the vehicle for cleansing used by the prophet, and not the grander Abana and Pharpar of Syria. " There is no god in all the earth but in Israel," Naaman confessed, cured indeed of his leprosy, but not completely freed from the heathen ideas of his country.

Jot and Tittle. " Till heaven and earth pass away, one jot or one tittle shall in no wise pass away from the law, till all things be accomplished " (*Matt.* 5¹⁸). *Jot* = iota, the smallest letter of the Greek alphabet. The corresponding Hebrew letter was called " yōdh." Cf. our " not a *jot* ", " to *jot* down." " Tittle " is a mistranslation of the Greek keration = little horn or hook, i.e. ' waw ', the sixth letter of the Hebrew alphabet. In spelling certain Hebrew words it is permissible to omit both ' yodh ' and ' waw ' without altering the pronunciation. Hence they both represent trivialities whose absence makes no difference.

Jubilee. The Jewish Year of Jubilee, the year of restoration and emancipation, was held every fifty years. During that year, all land that had passed out of the hands of the original owners was restored to them, and all Hebrew slaves were liberated. During Jubilee Year the land was to lie fallow, the owner was not permitted to gather the produce of his field or vineyard into his storehouse, as all such produce became common property for the use of all men and beasts.

The word ' Jubilee ' comes from a Hebrew word meaning ' ram ' and hence 'ram's horn', which was blown on the day when the jubilee was proclaimed.

Nowadays, the word means a fiftieth anniversary (but cf. *Silver, Diamond* jubilee, celebrations of the 25th and 60th anniversaries respectively) and then any time of general rejoicing, as in Wordsworth's *Ode :*

" I see
The heavens laugh with you in
  your jubilee."

Judas (Iscariot, i.e. man of Kerioth in Judaea), the only non-Galilean Apostle, an able but avaricious and dishonest double-dealer " who also betrayed Him " (*Matt.* 10⁴). He is always mentioned last in the lists of the Apostles. After the crisis in the Upper Room, Judas " went out," not merely from the upper room but from Christ's discipleship, and hanged himself.

We call a foul traitor a ' Judas '; an act of treachery done under the guise of friendship a ' Judas kiss ' (*Matt.* 26⁴⁸,⁹) ; a small grating in the door of a prison-cell through which prisoners within may be privily watched a ' Judas hole ' or ' Judas slit '.

Jews' ear, fungus, is a mistaken rendering of *auricula Judae*, Judas' ear, so called because commonly found on the elder (Judas tree), the tree on which Judas traditionally hanged himself (Weekley).

There was a medieval legend that once a year on Christmas Eve, the soul of Judas was permitted to leave hell for a night and a day. Matthew Arnold (followed by Kipling) improved the legend by causing Judas to cool himself by floating on an iceberg. See his *Saint Brandan* and the poem *Judas Iscariot's Paradise* by Sebastian Evans, the artist and poet ; and Kipling's " The Last Chantey " :

" Then said the soul of Judas
    that betrayéd Him :
  ' Lord, hast thou forgotten
    Thy covenant with me ?
  How once a year I go
  To cool me on the floe ? ' "

Julian Calendar. In 46 B.C. Julius Caesar was responsible for a most important measure—the reformation of the Roman **Calendar.** The Roman year was now three months in advance of the real time, so Caesar added 90 days to this year which he thus made one of 445 days. He guarded against a repetition of similar errors for the future by adapting the year to the sun's course, adding 10 days to the original 355 days of the year and an extra day (which we call ' leap-day ') every fourth year.

But it was found that the Julian Year is more than 11 minutes too long, so in 1582 Pope Gregory the Great ordered that 10 days should be omitted that year. Moreover, he arranged that the last year of centuries should not be leap years except when the first two figures in the date are divisible by 4. (Thus 1900 was not a leap year, but 2000 will be). This Gregorian reformation was termed ' New Style.' It was adopted in England in 1752 by which time a further extra day had crept into the calendar. When the correction was made there was an outcry by the ignorant of " give us back our 11 days." The New Style is now in almost universal use. Russia and Turkey adopted it as late as 1917 when the error had grown to 12 days.

Jū′no, an old Italian deity afterwards identified with the Greek Hera. She was a moon goddess. As Jupiter is the King of heaven, so Juno is the queen. She was regarded as the guardian spirit of women from birth to death. She was the model of dignified womanhood and, as the ' giver of good counsel ', she was called *Juno Monêta.* A temple under this title was dedicated to her on the Capitol. To this temple the mint was attached, so that from her title comes our word *money.*

In *The Tempest,* Juno as the patroness of marriage, sings :
" Honour, riches, marriage-
blessing,
Long continuance and
increasing,
Hourly joys be still upon you !
Juno sings her blessings on
you."

Ju′p(p)iter, called Zeus by the Greeks, was peculiarly the Great deity of the Latin nation. His name signifies ' the bright heaven '. He was worshipped as the god of rain, storms, thunder and lightning. His chief temple at Rome was that of Jupiter Capitolinus, in which Juno and Minerva had shrines ; but in the temple he reigned as Jupiter Optimus Maximus (Jupiter, best and greatest), the head of the State and the giver of its power and wealth.

Lacedae′mon. See **Spartans.**

G

Lă′chĕsis, the Fate who assigns the good and ill in man's fate and decides when enough thread has been spun.

See **Fates.**

Lā′dŏn, the dragon guarding the apples of the Hesperides, slain by Heracles.

Lāe′rtēs, King of Ithaca and father of Odysseus. He was still alive when his son returned to Ithaca after the fall of Troy. The description in the last book of *The Odyssey* of the meeting between the aged Laertes, " wearing a filthy, patched and disreputable tunic " and digging on the vineyard terrace, and Odysseus, triumphant over the suitors, is most touching.

Lāŏ′cŏon, priest of Apollo in Troy. He tried to dissuade his countrymen from drawing into the city the wooden horse which

Laocoon. (*From the group found at Rome in 1506 and now in the Vatican*).

the Greeks had left behind them. But as he was preparing to sacrifice a bull to Poseidon, suddenly two serpents were seen swimming towards the Trojan coast from Tenedos. They made for Laocoon, and killed him and his two sons.

Lăŏdămi′a, wife of Prōtesilā′us, a Thessalian king who went with the rest of the Greeks to fight against Troy. The oracle at Delphi had doomed to death the Greek who first set foot on the Trojan shore. Protesilaus, though he knew of this doom, was the first to land and was killed by Hector. Laodamia begged the gods that she might talk with her dead husband, and they allowed him to revisit the upper world for three hours. When he died a second time, Laodamia died with him.

Wordsworth had been re-reading the classics, Virgil in particular, with his son who was preparing for the university. His *Laodamia* resulted from this reading.

" Such grace hath crown'd
     thy prayer,
Laodamia, that at Jove's
     command
Thy husband walks the path
     of upper air :
He comes to tarry with thee
     three hours' space ;
Accept the gift, behold him face
     to face."

Lăŏdĭcē′a. Laodicea was a town of some consequence in the Roman province of Asia, situated in the valley of the Maeander. It was a place of great wealth (*Rev.* 3^17). Christianity was introduced into Laodicea which in subsequent times became the See of a bishop. But the Christians were lukewarm and St. John was commanded to write to them and say : " I know thy works, that thou art neither cold nor hot. I would thou wert cold

or hot. So then, because thou art lukewarm . . . I will spue thee out of my mouth." (*Rev.* 3^15,16).

We speak, e.g. of *Laodicean zeal,* i.e. half-hearted fervour.

Lăŏ′mĕdon. See Hesione.

Lă′pĭthae, a mythical race dwelling in Thessaly. At the marriage-feast of their ruler Peiri′thŏus and Hippodamī′a, a furious battle was fought in which the Lapithae defeated the Centaurs. The latter had in their drunkenness tried to carry off the bride and the other women.

The battle was a favourite subject for sculptors and other artists. It was represented on friezes of the Parthenon as well as in the Elgin Marbles (now in British Museum) and on countless vases.

Lār or **Lars,** an Etruscan title, signifying lord, king or hero.

Lars Porsena, in Macaulay's *Horatius,* was King of Clusium, the most powerful of the Etruscan cities. There were twelve cities in Etruria, each headed by a priest-prince with the title ' Lucumo '.

Latī′nus, King of Latium and mythical founder of the Latins. When Aeneas and he were allied he gave him in marriage his daughter Lavi′nia, who had been betrothed to Turnus.

Lātō′na, see **Lēto.**

Lavi′nia, see **Turnus.**

Lazarus, the brother of Martha and Mary of Bethany, the family which " Jesus loved." When our Lord received the sisters' message that Lazarus was sick, He waited two whole days and then announced plainly that Lazarus was now dead. By the time of Christ's arrival,

Lazarus had been in the grave four days. First Martha and then Mary slipped away to converse with Christ while He was still outside the village. The Jews followed, weeping. At sight of so much sorrow, " Jesus wept." Nevertheless, He bade them take Him to the grave itself. When they arrived there, in spite of Martha's scruples, the stone that closed the entrance was removed. Then Jesus with a loud voice commanded Lazarus to come forth, and the dead obeyed His voice, bound though he was hand and foot with grave-clothes.

The full story is given in *John* 11$^{1-46}$.

Lēa′nder, a youth of Abydos who was in love with Hērō, the priestess of Aphrodite in Sestos. Every night he swam across the Hellespont to visit her, and returned before daybreak. One stormy night he was drowned and next morning his body was washed ashore at Sestos. Hero in grief threw herself into the sea.

" The winds are high on Helle's wave,
As on that night of stormy water,
When Love, who sent, forgot to save,
The young, the beautiful, the brave,
The lonely hope of Sestos' daughter."

Byron's *The Bride of Abydos.*

Leaven is fermented dough, for which yeast is now found to be a more convenient substitute. When it is mixed with fresh flour and water, and baked, ordinary *leavened* bread results. The use of leaven was forbidden for bread baked for use in religious rites. Both the Passover cakes and the shewbread were *unleavened*. In the figurative sense, the underlying thought is

' permeating '. The word is thus used in a good sense when leaven is likened to the Kingdom of Heaven (*Matt.* 13^{33}), and in a bad sense of the hypocrisy of the Pharisees (*Matt.* 16^6).

Lē′da, daughter of Thestius and wife of Tyndărĕus, King of Sparta. Zeus took the form of a swan when he visited her. She brought forth two eggs, from the one of which issued Helen and from the other the Dioscuri, Castor and Pollux.

Lent, the period of the Christian fast from Ash-Wednesday to Easter, commemorating our Lord's " forty days and forty nights " fast in the Wilderness before He was " tempted of the devil " (*Matt.* 4^{1,2}).

The adjective *lenten* (= frugal, meagre as food during a fast) is used by Rosencrantz in *Hamlet* ii, 2, 332 (' lenten entertainment ') and by Maria to the Clown in *Twelfth Night* i, 5, 9 (' a good lenten answer '). Tennyson has :

" but none can say
That Lenten fare makes Lenten thought."

(*Tiresias,* 30, 1).

Leō′nidas, King of Sparta, famous for his defence of Thermŏ′pўlae, the pass between Thessaly and S. Greece. He had only 300 men while the army of Xerxes was enormous ; but the Spartan defence was successful until a traitor allowed the Persians to attack from the rear. Leonides and all his men were annihilated.

C. M. Yonge tells the story of " The Pass of Thermopylae " in her *Book of Golden Deeds.*

Lē′thē (i.e. oblivion), a river of the nether world. The souls of the departed drank of this river and thereby forgot all they had said or done in the upper world.

> " What ! rate, rebuke, and
>   roughly send to prison
> The immediate heir of Eng-
>   land ! Was this easy ?
> May this be washed in Lethe,
>   and forgotten ? "

This is the question King Henry IV asks the Lord Chief Justice who had imprisoned the King in his days of wild youth for striking him " in his very seat of judgement."

Milton has this description of the river :

> " A slow and silent stream,
> Lethe, the river of oblivion, rolls
> Her watery labyrinth, whereof
>   who drinks
> Forthwith his former state and
>   being forgets,
> Forgets both joy and grief,
>   pleasure and pain."

(*P.L.* ii, 582–6).

Lē'to, called **Lātōna** by the Romans, the mother of Apollo and Artemis. Hera was her enemy and

Leto (Latona). (From a painted vase). The serpent Pytho was sent by Hera to follow her on her wanderings. She has her two children, Apollo and Artemis, in her arms.

sent the serpent Pytho to follow her. Leto finally came to Delos, which was then a floating island ; but Zeus fastened it by adamantine

chains to the bottom of the sea that it might be a secure resting-place for his beloved Leto.

Leviathan. The word occurs in four passages of the A.V., viz. *Job* 41^1, *Ps.* 74^{18}, 104^{26}, *Is.* 27^1. In the first two of these passages the Egyptian crocodile is probably the monster referred to ; in the third some species of the whale family, and in the passage in Isaiah, some type of rock-snake or python. The beast called ' Behemoth ' in *Job* 40^{15-24} without doubt is the hippopotamus. Since ' leviathan ' usually denotes the crocodile, ' behemoth ' seems to point to its associate in the Nile, the hippopotamus. The description of behemoth lying under " the shady trees", among the reeds and willows, is perfectly applicable to the hippopotamus. In former days, hippopotamuses were found in Lower Egypt, although they have now receded far up the Nile.

Milton's ' leviathan ' is the whale :

> " there Leviathan,
> Hugest of living creatures, on the
>   deep
> Stretched like a promontory
>   sleeps or swims
> And seems a moving land, and
>   at his gills
> Draws in, and at his trunk spouts
>   out a sea."

(*P.L.* vii, 412–6).

His ' behemoth ' is undoubtedly the elephant :

> " Scarce from his mould
> Behemoth biggest born of earth
>   upheav'd
> His vastness."

(*P.L.* vii, 470–2).

Keats (*Endymion*, iii, 134-5), probably remembering these Miltonic passages, lists behemoth, leviathan and elephant together.

Li'chas, an attendant of Heracles who brought his master the poisoned garment which destroyed him. In his anguish Heracles threw Lichas into the sea.

Livy, the Roman historian whose literary talents secured the patronage and friendship of Augustus. His great work is a History of Rome in 142 books. Only 35 of these are extant, but we have epitomes of all the other books except two.

Loaves and Fishes, i.e. the material advantages to be had out of something ; an eye to the main chance for one's own benefit.

Jesus said to the people who had crossed the Sea of Galilee and come to Capernaum in search of Him : " Ye seek me, not because ye saw the miracles, but because ye did eat of the loaves and were filled " (*John* 6²⁶). Jesus was referring to His feeding of the 5,000, besides women and children, with 5 loaves and 2 fishes.

Loins, gird up the. The expression is frequent throughout the Bible ; e.g. " Elijah girded up his loins " (1 *Kings* 18⁴⁶) ; " Let your loins be girded " (*Luke* 12³⁵) ; and, metaphorically, " Gird up the loins of your mind " (1 *Peter* 1¹³). The expression means : " Gather up your loose Jewish outer garments and fasten them by means of a girdle so that you may not be impeded in your movements ", i.e. prepare for vigorous effort.

Lots. ' Lot ' originally means the object (counter, die, straw, etc.) used in drawing (casting) lots. Cf. ' to cast in one's lot with ' (*Prov.* 1¹⁴); "thou hast neither part nor lot in this matter" (Peter of Simon Magus, *Acts* 8²¹). Hence the word is applied to a tract of land originally assigned by lot ; cf. *allotment* (Weekley).

The custom of deciding doubtful questions by the casting of lots is one of great antiquity. It was deemed an appeal to the Almighty and prevailed extensively among the Jews ; but after the election of Matthias, the method was not used by Christians in N.T. times. Instances of its use are for the

(i) choice of men for an invading force (*Judges* 20⁹) ;
(ii) partition of land or other spoils (*Numb.* 26⁵⁵ ; *Matt.* 27³⁵) ;
(iii) settlement of doubtful questions, such as
　(*a*) detection of criminals (*Jos.* 7¹⁴⁻¹⁸) ;
　(*b*) appointment to duties : Saul (1 *Sam.* 10²⁰, *Matthias* (*Acts* 1²⁴) ;
　(*c*) selection of scapegoat on the Day of Atonement (*Lev.* 16⁸⁻¹⁰).

The Scriptures themselves were used to obtain guidance by opening a Bible at random and drawing inference from the first passage read in it. Cf. the method of divination practised among the Italian nations, the *Sortes Vergilianae*, in which a copy of Vergil's poems, opened at random, was used in a similar way.

Lōtus, a plant which grew (and probably still grows) on the N. coast of Africa. Its honeyed fruit caused the eater of it to lose all wish to return to his native country. " All they now wished for was to stay where they were with the Lotus-eaters, to browse on the lotus and to forget that they had a home to return to " (from the story told by Odysseus in Homer. E. V. Rieu's translation).

See Tennyson's poem *The Lotos-Eaters*, which he based on this account given in Homer. Mr. Weekley, in the preface to his *Etymological Dictionary*, humorously remarks : " These distinguished scholars . . . would probably regard an eight-hour day as approximating to the existence of the Lotus-eaters."

Love your enemies. " Unto him that smiteth thee on the one cheek offer also the other " (*Luke* 6²⁹).

In these words Christ replaces the Mosaic Law of retaliation : " an eye for an eye and a tooth for a tooth."

Lū′cǐfer, the morning star which the Greeks called ' Phosphorus '. Both words mean ' light-bringer '.

Lūcu′llus, Roman general and statesman. As a general, he carried on the war with Mithridates for eight years (74–67 B.C.) with great success, but as he could not finish it satisfactorily he was superseded, ultimately, by his old rival Pompey. During these eight years, having amassed great wealth in Asia, Lucullus ceased to take further part in public affairs and began to gratify his taste for luxury and magnificence. He was the first to introduce cherries into Italy, bringing them from Cěrăsus in Pontus. He is said to have spent £2000 on a single dinner. It was more to his credit that he was a patron of literature and collected a valuable library which was open to the use of the literary public.

To gain some idea of what is implied by a " Lucullan banquet," see Landor's Imaginary Conversation between Lucullus and Caesar.

Luke was probably the son of a Roman father and a Greek mother. He was not a Jew. That the writer of the third Gospel and the Acts was a physician is highly probable. Both books abound in medical terms and in descriptions of cures accurate according to the standard

of his time. Luke met Paul at Troas during Paul's second journey (the ' we ' of *Acts* 16¹⁰ shows that Luke had now joined the party) and went with him to Philippi, where he remained after Paul had left. Six years later they met again at Philippi and went together to Jerusalem. Luke accompanied Paul to Rome and was with him there until his death. " Only Luke is with me " (2 *Tim.* 4¹¹) wrote the great apostle as he waited for death.

Lū′na, goddess of the moon. See **Selēnē.**

Lūpercal, probably the most ancient of Roman festivals, held every year on Feb. 15. Connected with the festival were two guilds of priests (Julius Caesar instituted a third, the head of which was Mark Antony) who ran " the course " round the city walls, bearing strips of skin cut from the hides of sacrificial goats. With these they struck the bystanders, women especially, in token of purification. The Latin name for these strips of skin was *februa,* which gave its name to the month February, i.e. the month of purification (Latin *februāre*=to purify).

The first ten lines or so of *Julius Caesar,* I, 2, give some details of the *Lupercā′lia,* the games of which (i, 2, 178) Caesar would watch on his way to the Forum.

Lūtē′tia, modern Paris.

Lўcē′um, the name of the gymnasium or school, sacred to Apollo Lycēus, in a grove on the banks of the river Īli′ssus, where Aristotle taught.

Ly′ncēus, the keen-sighted Argonaut.

Maean'der, a river in Asia Minor, proverbial for its wanderings. Hence our verb ' to meander ', to wander aimlessly about.

See Gray's *The Progress of Poesy :*

" . . . where Maeander's amber waves

In lingering lab'rinths creep " ;

and Milton's *Comus :*

" By slow Maeander's margent green " ;

and Coleridge's *Kubla Khan :*

" Five miles meandering with a mazy motion

. . . the sacred river ran."

Cf. Robert Montgomery's sentence so castigated by Macaulay : " streams meander level with their fount."

Maecē'nas, Roman Knight coming of a wealthy and powerful family, friend of the Emperor Augustus. In the latter years of his life he lost the favour of the Emperor and retired entirely from public life. His name lives as that of a patron of literature. Virgil owed much to him, and it was at his request that the poet undertook the *Georgics,* the most finished of all his poems. Maecenas died in 8 B.C.

In general a ' Maecenas ' is a generous patron of literature or of art.

Magi. The Magi, or wise men of the East, of *Matt.* 2 were probably astrologers who may have come to Jerusalem from the Yemen in S. Arabia. The inhabitants of that region were brought much into contact with the Jews by trade, and it may well be that they had heard of the expectation among the Jews of the coming of the Messiah about this time. Anyhow, there was a widespread feeling outside Judaea that the time was ripe for the coming of a Deliverer who should rule the world in peace.

The Yemen was rich in gold, frankincense (an aromatic gum) and myrrh (a gum-resin used in incense). The Queen of Saba had brought Solomon gifts of gold and spices (1 *Kings* 10). The people of the Yemen worshipped the sun and the moon and to these deities tributes in gold and incense were paid. The Magi, accordingly, made costly offerings symbolic of Kingship to the young Christ of Bethlehem.

Mā'lĕa, a cape on the S.E. of Laconia, the passage round which was dreaded by sailors.

Mammon, riches personified and regarded as the devil of covetousness. " Ye cannot serve God and Mammon " (*Matt.* 6^{24}). The " mammon of unrighteousness " (*Luke* 16^{9}), the " unrighteous mammon " (*Luke* 16^{11}) is ill-gotten wealth.

Mā'nēs (i.e. the good beings), the name given by the Romans to the souls of their dead, which they revered and propitiated. There are many religions in which men worship their ancestors in one way or another.

Manlius (i) Marcus. He took refuge in the Capitol when Rome was taken by the Gauls in 390 B.C. One night, when the Gauls endeavoured to ascend the Capitol, Manlius was roused from his sleep by the cackling of the geese in the temple of Juno. Collecting hastily a body of men, he succeeded in driving back the enemy who had just reached the summit of the hill. From this act he is said to have received the surname of **Capitōli'nus.**

(ii) Titus. In 361 B.C. he earned immortal glory by slaying a gigantic Gaul. From the dead body of the barbarian he took the chain (*torques*) which had adorned him, and placed it round his own neck. From this circumstance he obtained the surname of **Torquātus**. When consul in 340 he ordered his own son to be put to death for slaying his adversary singlehanded in defiance of a proclamation that no Roman should engage in single combat with a Latin on pain of death.

Manna : the mysterious food on which the Israelites were fed for forty years in the desert. The word is said to be a corrupt form of the enquiry " What is it ? " which the Hebrews made when they first saw it on the ground. From various passages in the O.T. we learn that it came every morning except the Sabbath, in the form of a small round thing resembling hoar-frost ; that it had to be gathered each day early, before the sun could melt it ; that on the attempt to lay aside for a succeeding day, except on the day before the Sabbath, the substance became wormy and offensive ; that it was white and its taste like fresh oil ; that the whole nation ate it forty years ; that the supply suddenly ceased when the Hebrews first got the new corn of Canaan ; and that it was always regarded as a miraculous gift from God. See *Ex.* 16¹⁴⁻³⁵.

There is a sugary whitish substance, still called ' manna ', which falls from the tamarisk tree and is eaten as a relish by the Arabs.

Metaphorically, ' manna ' is anything that refreshes, e.g. food or drink or good news. Thus, at the very end of *The Merchant of Venice*, Lorenzo replies to Nerissa who has just announced Shylock's " special deed of gift " to him and Jessica :

" Fair ladies, you drop manna
    in the way
Of starved people,"
    (i.e. good news).

Mantle of Elijah, The. Elijah the Tishbite was the Hebrew prophet during the reign of Ahab, King of Israel. He was a man of great physical strength, capable of long fasts (1 *Kings* 19⁸), of living on the most scanty food (1 *Kings* 17⁶,¹⁶), and he could run a distance of 16 miles in front of the royal chariot (1 *Kings* 18⁴²⁻⁶). He wore the ordinary articles of dress, viz. girded under-robe and the ' mantle ' (2 *Kings* 2¹⁴) which has given us one of our most familiar Biblical expressions. The events connected with his life are to be found chronicled in 1 *Kings* 17—2 *Kings* 2. When Elijah " went up by a whirlwind into heaven " Elisha took up " the mantle of Elijah that fell from him " (2 *Kings* 2), the mantle clearly being the symbol of authority to which Elisha succeeded.

Mă'răthon, a village 26 miles or so from Athens, famous for the battle in which the Athenians under Miltiades defeated the Persian army in 490 B.C. ; and for the exploit of Pheidippides (q.v.) in running thence to Athens to announce the victory.

Mark was the son of a Mary who was an influential member of the church at Jerusalem, the church meeting at her house. Paul and Barnabas took him with them on Paul's First missionary journey ; but he would go no further with them than Perga. He returned to his mother's house in Jerusalem, and Paul refused to take him on his Second journey. We next hear of John Mark with Paul at Rome. The two are completely reconciled. The last notice in N.T. of Mark shows that he and Peter had become more in harmony with Paul. At the last Mark found it possible to be equally loyal to Peter and to Paul. Mark was probably Peter's interpreter because he knew Greek better than the humbly-born prince of the Apostles did. The second Gospel was universally believed in the ancient Church to have been written by Mark under Peter's influence.

Market-place. 'A'gora,' the Greek word for market-place, signified any open space, originally used for the purpose of assembly. Hence it suggests meetings in any open or public place, in contrast with what goes on in privacy. It is found in the N.T. in connection with business dealings (*Matt.* 20³), with children's games (*Matt.* 11¹⁶), with the greetings of passers-by (*Matt.* 23⁷), with trials (*Acts* 16¹⁹) and (in Athens) with public discussions (*Acts* 17¹⁷).

A person who has a morbid dread of being alone in a large open space suffers from ' agoraphōbia ' (the opposite of claustrophōbia).

Mars was an ancient Italian deity, later identified with the Greek **Ares** merely because both had come to be regarded as peculiarly gods of war. Primarily, Mars was the god of the vigorous growth of the year in spring : hence he was worshipped especially in his own month, March. Among herdsmen he was worshipped as a god who averted evil from herds. But to the later Romans he was **Mars Grādīvus,** i.e. Mars who ' strides forward ' to the fight. To him the fierce, predatory wolf was sacred. The great open space in which the youths of Rome were trained in military exercises was called the Campus Martius, or Field of Mars. The god had his altar in the Campus and there was a temple of Mars on the Appian Way. He was the reputed father of Rŏ'mulus and Rē'mus who were reared by a she-wolf and later fed by a woodpecker—a bird sacred to Mars.

Mar'sўas, a Phrygian satyr or peasant who was rash enough to challenge Apollo to a musical contest, on condition that the victor should do what he pleased with the vanquished. The Muses were the umpires. Apollo played on the cithera or lute and Marsyas on the flute. Apollo was declared victor. The fable evidently refers to the struggle between the Dorian ' mode ' or scale played on lutes, and the more warlike Phrygian ' mode ' played on flutes. The reeds of which the flutes were made grew on the banks of the river Marsyas.

Martha, elder sister of Mary and Lazarus (*Luke* 10³⁸ⁱⁱⁱ; *John* 11¹ⁱⁱⁱ, 12²). These three were honoured in being specially loved by our Lord, and at their home in Bethany He spent much of the last few days of His life on earth. Martha is the busy, active house-keeper, anxious to entertain her guests almost with an excess of hospitality, rather than, like her sister, to profit by their society. This characteristic is especially marked when her guest was the Son of Man, and He gently rebukes her for this fault.

To call a lady a ' Martha ' is to imply that she is a slave to her household duties.

Massi'lia, modern Marseilles.

Matthew, a " publican ", i.e. a collector of customs, in the service of Herod Antipas at Capernaum on the sea of Galilee. He was probably the same person as the Levi whose call is described in *Luke* 5²⁷⁻³². At the call of Christ " he forsook all and rose up and followed Him." He then made a feast to which he invited many publicans and sinners (i.e. fellow customs-collectors and Gentiles)—thereby incurring criticism from some Scribes and Pharisees. The N.T. gives us no further information : he is reputed to have led a strictly ascetic life, to have visited Ethiopia and India and not to have suffered martyrdom.

Mausō′lus, King of Cārĭa in S.W. Asia Minor. To perpetuate his memory his wife (and sister) Artĕ-

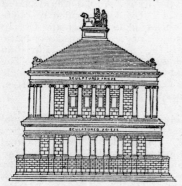

The Mausoleum of Artemisia as restored by Mr. Fergusson. The sculpture and architecture, 140 feet high, were in Parian marble of the finest quality.

mĭ′sĭa built at Halicarna′ssus the ' Mausoleum '—one of the Seven Wonders of the World.

Any costly monument or tomb may be called a ' mausoleum '.

Measures, Greek and Roman.
(*a*) *Choenix*, translated " measure " in *Rev.* 6⁶. The margin explains : " the word *choenix* signifies a measure containing one wine quart and the twelfth part of a quart." As a dry measure the choenix contained 1½–2 pints, which Thucydides says was a slave's daily allowance.

(*b*) *Bushel* or *modius*, the principal dry measure of Romans, = ⅓ amphora and so nearly 2 galls. English or ⅙ medimnus. The *medimnus* was the common Attic

corn-measure containing nearly 12 gallons.

(*c*) *Firkin* (*John* 2⁶) was the Greek metrētēs, the principal Greek liquid measure = ¾ medimnus, i.e. nearly 9 gallons. The Roman *amphora* held ⅔ of this.

Measures of Length, Roman.
(*a*) *Smaller Measures.*
   Uncia (i.e. twelfth part of a *pes* or foot) = inch.
   Pes, foot.
   Cubitus, ell or cubit.
   [These three Roman measures fall short of our *inch, foot* and *foot-and-a-half* only by less than ₁₀, ₁₀ and ₁₀ of an inch respectively.]
(*b*) *Larger Measures.*
   Gradus, a step or pace (slightly more than 2 ft. 5 in.).
   Passus, a double-step = 2 gradus.
   1000 double-steps = 4854 feet. Thus the Roman mile (i.e. 1000 passus) differs from the English only by less than ₁₀ (4854 as against 5280 ft.).

The most important Roman measure of surface was the *iugerum*. It measured 240 by 120 feet, i.e. 28,800 sq. feet, or about ⅝ of an English acre.

Mēdē′a, the celebrated magician of Colchis. She helped Jason to win the Golden Fleece, was deserted by him at Corinth, destroyed his new bride Glauce by a poisoned garment, killed her own two children and fled to Athens in a chariot drawn by winged dragons.

See **Absyrtus; Argonauts; Jason.**

Medes and Persians, Law of the. Something proverbially unalterable. " Now, O King, establish the decree, and sign the writing, that it be not changed, according to the law of the Medes and Persians, which altereth not." (*Daniel*, 6⁸).

The Medes were an Aryan tribe, closely connected with the Persians in language and descent. They are first spoken of as living in the province we now know so well as Azarbaijan.

Medū′sa, one of the three monstrous Gorgons. She alone of the three was mortal.
See **Gorgons ; Perseus.**

Megae′ra. See **Eumenides.**

Mĕlĕā′ger, a king of Calydon. When he was seven days old, Atropos declared that he would die as soon as the piece of wood which was burning on the hearth should be consumed. His mother Althaea extinguished the firebrand and concealed it in a chest. As a man Meleager took part in the Argonautic expedition, and slew the monstrous boar which ravaged the fields of Calydon. He gave its head to Atalanta, thereby enraging his uncles whom he slew. Althaea was now full of resentment against her son. In the words of Swinburne : " she waxed for wrath and sorrow like as one mad, and taking the brand whereby the measure of her son's life was meted to him, she cast it upon a fire ; and with the wasting thereof his life likewise wasted away . . ."
See Swinburne's " Atalanta in Calydon," one chorus from which is reprinted in The Oxford Book of English Verse (No. 808).

Mĕlĭta. The island of Malta on which Paul's ship was wrecked in A.D. 62. The traditional scene of the shipwreck is St. Paul's Bay on the N.E. of the island. Luke calls the natives of the island " barbarians ". All he means is they were non-Greeks : they were of Phoenician origin. (*Acts* 28[1-10]).

Mē′los, the most westerly of the Cyclades. Here the " Venus of Milo ", now in the Louvre, was found in 1820.

Melpo′menē, the Muse of Tragedy. See **Muses.**

Me′mnōn, an Aethiopian prince of marvellous beauty, son of Eōs. He came to the aid of his uncle Priam in armour made for him by Hephaestus, and slew Antĭ′lŏchus, the son of Nestor, but was himself slain by Achilles after a long and fierce combat.

Roman travellers attached the name of Memnon to two gigantic statues of the Egyptian King Amenōphis, one of which was said to emit a musical note when struck by the light of the rising sun. See Tennyson's *The Palace of Art*, 171 :
" . . . from her lips, as morn from Memnon, drew
    Rivers of melodies."

Menelā′us, son of Atreus and younger brother of Agamemnon. He was King of Lacedaemon and married to Helen. In the Trojan war he was under the special protection of Hera and Athene, and

Menelaus and Helen.

would have slain Paris but for the direct intervention of Aphrodite. After the fall of Troy he lived in peace and wealth with Helen at Sparta.

Me'ntor. When Odysseus left his home in Ithaca he entrusted its care and that of his son Tēle'machus to his friend and fellow-Ithacan Mentor. The youthful son of Odysseus was often in need of wise advice, for he lacked his father's energy and power of making decision. The bright-eyed goddess Athene in the *Odyssey* assumed the name and form of Mentor when she flashed down from the heights of Olympus " to instil a little more spirit into Odysseus' son."

Hence, a ' mentor ' is a faithful and older counsellor of a young man, a tutor.

Mercury, the Roman god of traders and thieves, of commerce and traffic generally. He was identified with the Greek Hermes.

See **Hermes.**

The Clown (in *Twelfth Night*), hinting that what Olivia has just said in praise of fools has been at the expense of truth, says to her : " Now Mercury endue thee with leasing (i.e. falsehood), for thou speakest well of fools." Obviously, in the clown's opinion, Malvolio is a fool. In 1 *Henry IV*, 4, 1, 106 we have ' feathered Mercury ' and in *King John* 4, 2, 174 ' Be Mercury, set feathers to thy heels '—allusions to Mercury's winged sandals.

Mess of Pottage. Jacob was the younger son of Isaac and Rebekah and (younger) twin-brother of Esau. One day, returning from hunting, faint and hungry, Esau asked his brother to feed him with the red pottage he was preparing. Taking advantage of Esau's distress, Jacob demanded his brother's birthright

(i.e. his rights as the elder son) as the price, and later he completed the usurpation by obtaining his father's blessing by a subterfuge suggested by his mother. Thus Esau " sold his birthright for a mess of pottage " (*Gen.* 25$^{29-34}$). ' Jacob ' means ' supplanter.'

' Pottage ' is a dish of boiled vegetables ; ' mess ' a plate of food.

Methuselah, the longest-lived antediluvian, Noah's grandfather. *Gen.* 5^{27} says he lived 969 years.

John Donne (1572–1631), preaching about God's Day (i.e. Eternity) said : " Methuselem, with all his hundreds of years, was but a mushroom of a night's growth to this Day."

Me'tope. (3 syllables). In Greek temples such as the Parthenon and the so-called Theseum there is a stone beam resting on columns. Above this beam is the frieze (a decorated band of sculpture) of three-grooved tablets called trigraphs and between these tablets is a flat space called a *metope*. The metopes are ornamented, and the subjects of ornamentation are usually various contests in battle such as those of the Gods and the Giants, or the Lapithae and Centaurs, or the Labours of Heracles or of Theseus.

Mi'das, the fabulously wealthy son of Gordius, King of Phrygia. Sīlē'nus, companion of Diony'sus, on one occasion was hospitably received by Midas. In recompense the god allowed Midas to choose any favour he wished, and in his folly he asked for the power to turn into gold everything he touched. But even the food he tried to eat now became gold and Midas besought Dionysus to take his favour back. He was ordered to bathe in the Pactōlus. He was saved and from that time the river had an abundance of gold in its sand. On another occasion Midas showed his folly by deciding in favour of Pan in a musical contest between him and Apollo ; whereupon Apollo changed his ears to those of an ass. Midas contrived to conceal this humiliating fact under his Phrygian cap, but the servant who used to cut his hair discovered it. As he was not allowed to mention the disgraceful fact to anyone, the servant dug a hole in the earth and whispered into it " King Midas has ass's ears." Reeds sprang up on the same spot and, as they were agitated by the wind, in their whispers they betrayed the secret.

For the wealth of Midas cf. the story of Croesus.

See Keats's Sonnet " On the Sonnet " :

" Misers of sound and syllable,
    no less
Than Midas of his coinage, let
    us be
Jealous of dead leaves in the
    bay wreath crown."

Keats was endeavouring to find a better sonnet stanza than already existed so, just as Midas was greedy to increase his immense wealth, poets should not cease to experiment with new metrical forms.

Milk and Honey, A Land of. In the song which God gave Moses before he went up to Mount Nebo to view the promised land, this land is described as one " that floweth with milk and honey," i.e. it is a land wonderfully fertile (*Deut.* 31²⁰).

Figuratively, the blessings of Heaven comprise milk and honey, as in J. M. Neale's version of the 12th century poem :

" Jerusalem the golden
    With milk and honey blest."

Mī′lo, a celebrated athlete of prodigious strength. He is said to have carried a four-year old heifer on his shoulders through the stadium at Olympia. He met his death in a strange way. He was passing through a forest when he saw the trunk of a tree partially split open by woodcutters. He tried to rend it further, but the wood closed on his hands and held him fast. In this state he was attacked and devoured by wolves.

Miltī′ădēs, an Athenian statesman and general. When Attica was threatened with invasion by the Persians, he was chosen one of the ten Generals to meet it. The ten were equally divided as to whether they should risk a battle, and Miltiades persuaded Callĭm′ăchus, the military Commander-in-Chief, to give his casting vote in favour of fighting. The result was the victory of **Marathon.** Shortly afterwards Miltiades attacked the island of Paros to gratify a private enmity. He was unsuccessful, was impeached at Athens and condemned ; but owing to the great services he had rendered to the state the penalty was commuted to a fine sufficient to cover the expenses of the expedition. Being unable to pay this, he was thrown into prison where he died of a wound he had received at Paros. The fine was subsequently paid by Cīmon, Miltiades' son.

Mine′rva, one of the three great Roman divinities, only Jupiter and Juno being considered greater than she. Worshipped as the goddess of wisdom, she was the patroness of all the arts and trades and was invoked by all who desired to distinguish themselves in any art or craft such as painting, poetry, medicine and the like. This character of the goddess may be perceived by the proverb ' *sus Minervam* (docet) ' (a pig shows Minerva how), i.e. the foolish instruct the wise. Like Athena, Minerva came to be regarded as a goddess of war. She was believed to be the inventor of musical instruments, especially the wind instruments used in war.

Mī′nos (i) a legendary King of Crete and brother of Rhadama′nthus. After his death he became supreme judge of the shades in Hades.

(ii) His grandson, also King of Crete, kept the Minotaur in the labyrinth constructed by Daedalus. When Daedalus escaped from the labyrinth by flying, Minos pursued him to Sicily where he was slain by Cōcălus, the king of the land.

Mī′nŏtaur, the half-man, half-bull monster, son of Pāsĭphăë (the wife of Minos), was kept in the labyrinth at Cnōsus in Crete. Aided by Pasiphae's daughter Aria′dnē, who gave him the "clue" of

Theseus and Minotaur. (From a painted vase).

thread by means of which he was able to retrace his steps from the centre of the labyrinth and so to leave it, Theseus slew the Minotaur and sailed off home, taking Ariadne with him.

Mite, a tiny copper coin, the least valuable of any that existed in Palestine. Two of them were equal to a farthing. In our money the ' mite ' was worth about $\frac{1}{20}$ of a denarius, i.e. of $9\frac{3}{4}$d.

Cf. the Elizabethan *doit* which was originally a Dutch coin of infinitely small value. Shylock would " take no doit of usance for his moneys "; Trinculo in *The Tempest* says when people " will not give a doit to relieve a lame beggar, they will lay out ten to see a dead Indian."

Mnēmŏ′sўnē, mother of the " Sisters of the Sacred Well," the nine Muses.

Moabite Stone, a monument of black basalt found in South Palestine in 1868 by a missionary. It was badly damaged, but was pieced together again and is now in the Louvre. It chronicles, in Hebrew-Phoenician characters, the victory of Mesha, rebellious Moabite king, over Israel, the story of which is to be found in 2 *Kings* 3. This is one of the oldest (9th century B.C.) records of a Semitic alphabet in existence.

Moi′rae. See **Fates.**

Molech or **Moloch,** the sun-god of the people of Ammon whose worship was accompanied by human sacrifices, especially of children (see 2 *Kings* 23[10]).

Milton makes Moloch one of the fallen angels :

" Moloch, horrid king, besmeared with blood
   Of human sacrifice, and parents' tears,

Though, for the noise of drums
and timbrels loud,
Their children's cries unheard,
that passed through fire
To his grim idol."
(*P.L.* i, 392–6).

See also the " sullen Moloch "
stanza (xxiii) in the *Nativity Ode*.
A modern poet, Ralph Hodgson,
has a " Hymn to Moloch "—to be
found in the Zoo section of the
Week End Book.

Mōly, the name of the magic
herb " with a black root and a
milk-white flower," given by
Hermes to Odysseus to protect
him from Circe's spells.

See Milton's *Comus* 636, 7 :
" more med'cinal is it than
that Moly
That Hermes once to wise
Ulysses gave " ;
and Tennyson's *Lotos-Eaters* (Choric
Song 88) :
" Propt on beds of amaranth and
moly."

Mo'psus, a celebrated seer, a son
of Apollo. He contended in prophecy with Calchas at Cŏlŏphōn
in Asia Minor and showed himself
superior in prophetic power. Thereupon Calchas died of grief.

Mo'rpheūs, the son of Sleep and
the god of dreams. He was generally
represented with a bunch of poppies
in his hand. Hence our ' morphia ',
for opium is the narcotic juice of
poppies.

In *Il Penseroso* Milton refers to
" the fickle pensioners of Morpheus' train," i.e. dreams which
are the bodyguard of Morpheus.
(Queen Elizabeth's personal bodyguard had the official title " Pensioners.").

Mote and Beam. The illustrations
used by our Lord in his teaching
" Judge not that ye be not judged "

are to be taken literally. A *mote*
is a chip of wood, a particle of dust,
and a *beam* is a rafter supporting
the roof of a house. Metaphorically,
the mote and the beam are an
insignificant fault and a considerable one. " Why beholdest thou
the mote that is in thy brother's
eye, but considerest not the beam
that is in thine own eye ? " (*Matt.*
7³) is Christ's condemnation of the
Pharisees' hypocritical character.

Weekley quōtes the Prologue of
the *Reeves Tale* where Chaucer has :
" He kan wel in myn eyë seen a
stalke,
But in his owene he kan not
seen a balke."
Stalke is the mote, and *balke* the
beam.

Mourning. A marked feature of
Oriental mourning is what may be
called its studied publicity and the
careful observance of the prescribed ceremonies. Among the
particular forms observed were :

(*a*) Rending of the clothes ; e.g.
Reuben " rent his clothes " when
he found that Joseph was not in
the pit (*Gen.* 37²⁹).

(*b*) Dressing in sackcloth. This
was a coarse-textured material
made of goats' hair, not unlike the
sacking we got to know during the
war under its glorified name ' Hes-
sian '. It was used for the rough
garments of mourners, worn sometimes next the skin (e.g. in 1 *Kings*
21²⁷ we read that Ahab " put sackcloth upon his flesh.")

(*c*) Ashes, dust or earth sprinkled
on the person ; e.g. Hushai came
to meet David " with his coat rent
and earth upon his head " (II *Sam.*
15³²).

Cf. what Homer has to say about
Achilles mourning the death of
Patroclus. " A black cloud of
sorrow fell upon Achilles. With
both hands he caught up handfuls
of ashes and sprinkled them over

his head, until his face was covered and his clothes were full. Then he lay all along in the ashes and tore his hair. And there was weeping and lamentation of all the household " (Dr. Rouse, *Achilles*).

(*d*) Employment of professional mourners ; e.g. in the ruler's house Jesus saw " the flute-players and the crowd making a tumult " (*Matt.* 9²³). To " wear sackcloth and ashes " metaphorically expresses repentance, regret for a course of action.

Mu'lciber, the ' softener ' (of metals), i.e. ' smelter ', the Romans' euphemistic name for Hēphae'stus or Vulcan.
See **Hephaestus**.

Muses. Among the lesser divinities of Olympus were the Muses, daughters of Zeus and Mnem'osynē. They were born in Pĭĕrĭa at the foot of Mount Olympus. They presided over the different kinds of poetry and over the arts and the sciences. Apollo was their leader. They had a temple on Mount Helicon in Boeotia, in which mountain their sacred springs, Hippocrēnē and Aganippe, had their source. *Muse* is often used, under

Melpomene, the Muse of Tragedy. (*From a statue in the Vatican*). *She is wearing the cothurnus, her head is surrounded with vine leaves, she is holding a tragic mask.*

the collective name or under individual names, as a synonym for poetic inspiration. Poets, too, use *muse* = one inspired by the Muses, a poet, as in *Lycidas* :
" So may some gentle Muse
  With lucky words favour my
      destined urn."
             (i.e. my grave).

Their names were :

Name of Muse	Muse of	Her attributes
1. Clī'o . .	History . .	Open roll of paper, or chest of books.
2. Eute'rpē .	Lyric poetry . .	Flute
3. Thal'īa .	Comedy ; merry and idyllic poetry	Comic mask ; shepherd's staff ; wreath of ivy
4. Melpo'menē	Tragedy . .	Tragic mask ; club of Heracles ; cothurnus
5. Terpsi'chorē	Choral dance and song	Lyre and plectrum
6. E'ratō .	Love songs . .	Lyre
7. Polyhy'mnia	Sublime hymn .	Pensive and meditating attitude
8. Ūră'nĭa .	Astronomy . .	A staff pointing to a globe
9. Calli'opē .	Epic poetry . .	Tablet and stylus.

Thalia, the Muse of Comedy. (*From a statue in the Vatican*). *She appears with a comic mask and a tambourine.*

Music, Hebrew. The Hebrews were obviously enthusiastic musicians. Music was associated with every phase of their life, private and public. The parting guest was sped " with songs, with tabret (i.e. tabouret, a little tabor or tambourine) and with harp " (*Gen.* 31²⁷). The householder enjoyed in his leisure the sound of the timbrel (or tabret), the harp and the organ (*Job* 21¹²). At the wine-press or in the vineyard work was lightened by songs. Prominent mention is made of music in connexion with national victories (*Judges* 5² ; 1 *Sam.* 18⁶). Music was cultivated by the early prophets to promote an access of inspiration, or to calm the mind and prepare it to receive the divine message (2 *Kings* 3¹⁵). Naturally it was employed at royal coronations (1 *Kings* 1³⁹˙˙), and at state and private banquets (*Amos* 6⁵). Very striking is its application to mental disorder in the case of Saul, who obtained relief from David's playing on the kinnor (harp). The presence of musicians

was general at funerals (2 *Chron.* 35²⁵ ; *Matt.* 9²³), and the memory of the dead was often celebrated in the wailing song, of which David's lament over Saul and Jonathan (2 *Sam.* 1¹⁷) and over Abner (3³³) are conspicuous examples. Music thus entered into the Hebrews' whole life.

Among the musical instruments mentioned in the Bible are :

(i) the *harp*, the Hebrew *kinnor*, the national instrument of the Hebrews. Its invention is ascribed to Jubal, " the father of all such as handle the harp and organ " (*Gen.* 4²¹).

(ii) the *shawm*, a reed-instrument, akin to the clarionet.

(iii) the *dulcimer*, possibly a sort of bagpipes still used by peasants in E. Europe.

(iv) *psaltery*, a stringed instrument to accompany the voice, a sort of guitar or lute. David's psalteries were made of fir wood (2 *Sam.* 6⁵), those of Solomon of almug (1 *Kings* 10¹²).

(v) The " instruments of music " (1 *Sam.* 18⁶) are probably, as R.V. margin has it, triangles, or three-stringed instruments.

(vi) *sackbut*, a wind instrument, probably a bass trumpet, with a slide, somewhat like the modern trombone (*Dan.* 3).

It is only reasonable to add that most of these Biblical instruments have been equated at one time or another with almost every other type.

Mȳcē′nae, an ancient fortress-town in Argolis, nine miles inland from Tī′ryns. Its massive walls were regarded as the work of the Cyclopes. The princes of Tiryns most probably built Mycenae to give them an outlet to the Corinthian gulf. Hence it outstripped Tiryns and in the Homeric story is regarded as Agamemnon's capital

H

and the first city of all Greece. The chief known remains of the ancient city were the ' Lion Gate ' and some ' beehive tombs ', the

Lion Gate of Mycenae. This was the chief entrance to the city through the Cyclopean walls that guarded it.

largest 50 feet high. The latter consisted of a long passage leading to a vaulted chamber and are traditionally said to be the graves of Agamemnon and his companions. The excavation of the royal palace, with its gates and walls, its courts and its apartments for men and women, shows how interesting and valuable it is regarding life in the palace of an Achaean prince in Homeric times.

My′rmïdons, a Thessalian tribe of warriors led against Troy by Achilles. According to legend Thessaly, under King Ae′ăcus, had suffered severely from plague which had killed off most of the males. Aeacus prayed Zeus to re-people his country and Zeus did so by changing the hordes of ants (Greek myrmēkes = ants) into men whom Aeacus in consequence called ' Myrmidons.'

' Myrmidons ' colloquially means a band of ruffians under a daring leader. Policemen, who do their

work without fear or favour, are sometimes called ' myrmidons of the law ' (of course without any implication of their being either ants or ruffians !) In *Twelfth Night* the clown, seeking to impress the foolish Sir Andrew by means of long words and abstruse references, tells him " my lady has a white hand, and the Myrmidons are no bottle-ale houses ", meaning— nothing sensible.

My′ron, one of the greatest of Greek sculptors, an older contemporary of Pheidias. His greatest

Copy of the Discobolus of Myron. The player in the game, standing on a slight elevation, raised the discus to the level of his right shoulder and then threw it with all his force.

works were nearly all in bronze. His most famous statue is the Discobolus (the discus- or quoit-thrower).

Naboth's Vineyard. Naboth was a victim of Ahab and Jezebel. He was the owner of a vineyard which adjoined the royal precincts and which thus became an object of desire to the king. Naboth refused to sell it or to exchange it for a better. Ahab was cowed by the refusal, but the proud spirit of Jezebel was roused. She took the matter into her own hand. She caused two suborned witnesses to accuse Naboth of having " cursed God and King " at a solemn fast and he and his children were stoned to death—the usual punishment for blasphemy. See 1 *Kings* 21 ; for Ahab's punishment 1 *Kings* 22$^{34-8}$; for that of Jezebel 2 *Kings* 9$^{30-7}$.

A " Naboth's vineyard " is a possession coveted by a stronger man than its owner, who will secure it by fair means or foul.

Nāïădes. See **Nymphs.**

Narci'ssus, a beautiful youth, untouched by love. Echo, who was in love with him, died of grief [See **Echo**]. As a punishment Nemesis caused him to fall in love with his own image reflected in a

Narcissus. (From a Pompeian painting. His death is signified by Eros with inverted torch.

fountain, but as he could not approach it, he gradually pined away and was changed into the flower which bears his name.

In *The Sensitive Plant* Shelley has :

" . . . narcissi, the finest among
  them all,
Who gaze on their eyes in the
  stream's recess,
Till they die of their own dear
  loveliness,"

and in *Adonais :*

" To Phoebus was not Hyacinth so
  dear
Nor *to himself* Narcissus."
See **Echo.**

Nau'plia, the port of Argos, situated on the Saronic Gulf. It was in modern times a flourishing seaport up to the days of the Axis occupation of Greece.

Nausi'căa, daughter (' tall and beautiful as a goddess ') of Alcĭ'nŏus King of the Phaeā'cians. Phaeacia is likely to be the modern Corcyra, an island in the Ionian Sea. When Odysseus was shipwrecked on the island Nausicaa, prompted by Athene, set food and drink before the stranger, and clothed him and brought him to the palace of Alcinous.

Na'xos, the largest island in the Cyclades group. It was famous for its wine and so appears in the legends about Dionysus. Here the god is said to have found Ărĭa'dnē after she had been deserted by Theseus.

Nazarene, a native of Nazareth in Galilee. Christians were called ' Nazarenes ', a term of contempt used by the Jews for the followers of Jesus of Nazareth (*Acts* 24^5). This remains the usual term for Christians in Asia to the present day.

Nazirite (or **Nazarite**), one who is "separated" for a religious reason from the rest of the people. The Nazirite was to abstain from wine; no razor was to come on his head, and he was not to defile himself by contact with a dead body, even that of his nearest relative. For "the law of the Nazirites in their separation" see *Numb.* 6$^{1-21}$. The name is applied to Samson who is commanded by the angel to be "a Nazirite of God from the womb"; to Samuel who was devoted to God's service by his mother; and to John the Baptist. There were "Nazirites of days" and "Nazirites for life." Cf. the modern "Rechabites" = total abstainers, for whose name and tenets see *Jeremiah* 35.

Milton (*Samson Agonistes* 318) correctly calls Samson "this heroic Nazarite"; but when Shylock (*Merchant of Venice* i, 3, 32) sardonically says to Bassanio (who had invited him to dinner): "Yes, to eat of the habitation which your prophet the Nazarite conjured the devil into," he must have known that Jesus was a Nazarene. Scott in *Anne of Geierstein* strangely enough makes the same mistake. He calls Samson "the mighty Nazarene."

Nehemiah was a Jew who had risen to the position of cupbearer to the Persian King Artaxerxes. His grief on hearing of the ruinous state of Jerusalem was noted by the king who granted his prayer to be allowed to go to Jerusalem to rebuild its walls. When he began the work the Samaritans, between whom and the Jews there was bitter enmity, threatened an armed attack on the workers. But Nehemiah arranged that half his servants should work on the rebuilding while the other half "held both the spears, the shields and the bows" ready to repel the attackers. In 52 days the walls were rebuilt and then Sanballat, Tobiah and Geshem, the leaders of the Samaritan conspiracy, tried to assassinate Nehemiah, or at least force him to leave Jerusalem. They failed, and Nehemiah, assisted by the influential priest Ezra, went on to reorganize the political and religious life of the city. Several years later Nehemiah again returned to Jerusalem to find that many of the former abuses had recurred. He saw "some treading wine presses on the Sabbath and bringing in sheaves and lading asses. Men of Tyre brought fish and sold on the Sabbath. Jews had married wives of Ashdod, of Ammon and of Moab." All these abuses and many others Nehemiah reformed with vigour.

Nehemiah presents to us the picture of a shrewd, devout, upright statesman. He sacrificed his own interests and ran endless risks for the welfare of his people. He was a man of action, prompt and vigorous. His book concludes with his prayer: Remember me, O my God, for good.

Nĕ'mĕa, a valley in Argolis where Heracles slew the Nemean lion. In this valley there was a splendid temple of Nemean Zeus, surrounded by a sacred grove in which the Nemean Games were celebrated every other year.

Nĕ'mĕsis, a Greek personification of reverence for law. She measures out happiness and unhappiness to mortals; and he who has too many gifts of fortune is visited by her with losses and sufferings in order that the arrogant may become humble. Hence she came to be regarded as an avenging or punishing fate, i.e. retribution.

But Whittier is nearer to the original view :

" The Fates are just ; they give us but our own ;
Nemesis ripens what our hands have sown."

(*To a Southern Statesman*).

Neoptŏ'lĕmus, also called Pyrrhus from his fair hair, one of the Greek heroes concealed in the wooden horse. At the capture of Troy he killed Priam, whose daughter, Pŏly'xĕna, he sacrificed on her father's tomb. When the Trojan captives were distributed, Hector's widow Andro'machē was given to him. Later, he married Hermi'onē, daughter of Menelā'us, who had been promised to Orestes. In revenge Orestes slew him and married Hermione.

Neptune, the chief sea-god of the Romans, identified with the Greek Poseidon. As the early Romans were not a maritime people they had few myths about the sea. Neptune's temple stood in the Campus Martius. At his festival (July 23) the people formed tents (*umbrae*) of the branches of trees, in which they enjoyed themselves in feasting and drinking ; cf. the practice of using tents for entertaining friends at English cricket festivals.
See **Poseidon.**

Nē'rēĭds, the fifty daughters of Nēreūs, the unerring old man of the sea. They are described as dwelling with their father at the bottom of the sea and were believed to be propitious to all sailors. Thetis, the mother of Achilles, was one of the most celebrated of them.

Nē'reūs, the father of the fifty sea-nymphs of the Mediterranean, called the Nērēĭds. He is described as the wise, unerring old man of the sea. He was believed to have,

like other deities of the sea, the power of prophesying and of appearing to mortals in different shapes. Heracles obtained his counsel as to what route would bring him to the Hespe'rides ; but he had first to subdue him by wrestling. A similar account is given of Prōteūs in the story of Odysseus, and of Glaucus in that of the Argonauts.

Ne'ssus, a centaur who carried Dē'ianī'ra across the river Ēvēnus, but who, in attempting to run away with her, was shot by Heracles with a poisoned arrow.
See **Heracles, De'ianīr'a, Centaurs.**

Ne'stor, King of Pylos in the Peloponnesus. He is mentioned among the Calydonian hunters and the Argonauts. Although far advanced in age, he sailed with the other Greek heroes against Troy. Having ruled over three generations of men he was deemed the equal of the immortal gods in authority. In the *Iliad* silver-tongued Nestor, whose voice ran from his lips sweeter than honey, is praised for his eloquence and wisdom, his justice and his knowledge of wars.

Any wise old counsellor may be called a ' Nestor '. Salarino, in *The Merchant of Venice*, introduces him as a type of gravity, and Biron in *Love's Labour's Lost* mentions, among the scenes of foolery he has seen, ' Nestor playing at push-pin with the boys.'

Nī'kē, called Victoria by the Romans, the goddess of Victory. She is shown as a winged figure and often carries a palm or a wreath. A favourite attitude in the Roman period showed Nike holding a shield on which she is inscribing a record of victory. Her temple on the Acropolis, the temple of ' Wingless Victory', small but of great beauty, was built, probably in the time of Pericles, in honour of Athena-Nike, who was called 'Wingless' in distinction to the goddess Nike.

Nimrod, grandson of Ham. He is described as "a mighty one in the earth" and "a mighty hunter before the Lord" (*Gen.* 10⁸,⁹).

A 'Nimrod' of to-day is a big-game hunter, or a great sportsman.

Nineveh and **Tyre,** wealthy cities destroyed because of the wickedness of their inhabitants.

See *Jonah* c. 4, and more especially *Ezekiel* cc. 25, 26.

Kipling in *The Recessional* links these two cities as examples of faded greatness :

" Lo, all our pomp of yesterday
   Is one with Nineveh and
     Tyre."

The ruins of Nineveh are in Iraq, on the upper Tigris, opposite the modern city Mosul. Tyre, under King Hiram, was allied to Solomon, and supplied him with material for the Temple. In later years it was captured by Alexander after a memorable siege. The site of Tyre, the ancient capital of Phoenicia, is now occupied by a small fishing village in South Syria.

Nĭ′ŏbē, daughter of Tantalus and wife of Amphī′on, King of Thebes. Proud of her twelve children, she deemed herself superior to Lētō, the mother of two children only, Apollo and Artemis who slew all Niobe's children with their arrows. Niobe herself was changed by Zeus, the father of Apollo and Artemis, into stone on Mt. Sipylus in Lydia, which periodically during the summer wept for her children in streams trickling down the rock. The story of Niobe and her children was frequently taken as a subject by ancient artists. Our illustration shows the group, consisting of Niobe holding her youngest daughter on her knees and 13 statues of her sons and daughters (only the central figures are here given).

Niobe is therefore the type of a mother inconsolable by reason of the loss of her children ; an emblem of grief. Hamlet refers to his mother following his

The Group of Niobe. *Only the central figures of the larger group are here given. Niobe is holding her youngest daughter on her knee.*

" poor father's body,
Like Niobe, all tears."
Cf. the Jewish story of **Rachel.**

Nĭ'sus and **Eury'ălus.** Trojan
friends who accompanied Aeneas to
Italy and perished in a night attack
against the Rutulian camp. Their
friendship is proverbial, like that
of Damon and Phintias.

Nōnes. Latin nōnus = ninth.
The Nones are the ninth day
(inclusive reckoning) before the
Ides. Therefore the Nones = the
5th of eight months ; in March,
May, July and October the 7th.

Nŭ'ma Pompi'lius, the second
King of Rome, belongs to legend
and not to history. He was renowned for his wisdom and his
piety. His reign was long and
peaceful : the temple of Janus,
which he founded, remained shut
throughout his reign. He devoted
his chief care to the establishment
of religion among his rude subjects.
He courted Ēge'ria, a nymph of
Arīcia in Italy, who became his
adviser and (according to Ovid)
his wife. That he might more
successfully introduce his laws and
new forms of worship into the state,
he solemnly declared before the
Roman people that they were previously sanctified and approved by
the nymph. In consequence her
name is used to denote a female
source of inspiration.

Numbers. Round numbers are
widely used in the Bible when
there is no intention of exact
determination. Certain numbers
were used to express abstractions
such as completeness, abundance,
perfection (or their opposites). The
context would determine what
these ideas were. Thus " five "
would be associated with the fingers
of the hand ; " seven " would
derive prominence from the days
of the week—itself a natural division of time, the fourth part of the
lunar month ; " twelve " would be
a prominent number owing to the
twelve tribes or the twelve months.
" Forty " is especially used in
connexion with periods of time as
a result of its association with the
wanderings in the wilderness. Often
little more is intended than the
idea of plurality. Thus " two "
(' behold, I am gathering two
sticks,' I *Kings* 17^{12}), or more
frequently " three " (Laban ' set
three days' journey betwixt himself and Jacob,' *Gen.* 30^{36}). Large
numbers are expressed roundly, as
100 (' Obadiah took an hundred
prophets ', I *Kings* 18^4) or 1000
(Samson ' slew a thousand men '
with the jawbone of an ass, *Judges*
15^{15}). " Thousand " with its multi-
ples is frequently used in hyperbole
(Daniel in his vision saw that
' thousand thousands ministered
unto God, and ten thousand times
ten thousand stood before Him ',
Dan. 7^{10}).
See **Seven.**

Nymphs. The early Greeks and
Romans saw in all the phenomena
of nature some divine agent.
Springs, rivers, grottoes, trees and
mountains all seemed to them
fraught with life. Over these
powers of nature watched so many
deities—nymphs as they were
called. They may be classed
according to the different parts of
nature of which they are the
representatives :
1. *Ŏc'ĕanĭdes :* daughters of
Oceanus, the nymphs of the outer
Ocean.
2. *Nēre'ĭdes :* the fifty daughters
of Nereus, the sea-nymphs of the
Mediterranean.
3. *Naï'ădĕs :* the nymphs of
fresh water.
(Greek *naō* = I flow).

4. *Orĕădes :* the nymphs of mountains and grottoes. (Greek *oros* = mountain).

5. *Drў'ădes* and *Hămădrў'ădes :* the nymphs of trees and groves. The life of these nymphs depended on that of the trees to which they were attached. (Greek *drūs* = oak-tree).

Ŏcĕă'nĭdes. See **Nymphs.**

Ŏcĕ'ănus, god of the water which was believed to surround the whole earth, the father of all the river-gods and water-nymphs. The early Greeks regarded the earth as a flat circle which was encompassed by a river perpetually flowing round it, and this river was Oceanus. As geographical knowledge advanced, the name was applied to the great *outer* waters of the earth, and especially to the Atlantic (i.e. the sea west of the Pillars of Heracles as distinguished from the Mediterranean). Thus the Atlantic is often simply called Oceanus.

Ody'sseus or **Uly'ssēs,** one of the principal Greek heroes in the Trojan war. He was son of Lāertēs, King of Ithaca, husband of Pēnĕ'lŏpē and father of Tēlĕ'măchus. As a young man, he was wounded by a boar in the knee, by the scar of which he was afterwards recognised by Euryclei'a. During the siege of Troy he distinguished himself as a warrior and a negotiator. He contended with Ajax for the armour of Achilles and gained the prize. But the most celebrated part of his story consists of his adventures after the destruction of Troy. He visited the land of the Lotus-eaters, escaped from the clutches of the Cyclops Polyphē'mus, was enabled to resist the magic of Ci'rcē by means of the moly given to him by Hermes. After a visit to Hades to consult Tire'sias, he reached Calypso's island where he stayed eight years. He was hospitably entertained by King Alci'nŏus and his daughter Nausi'căa. Finally, after twenty years' absence he reached his native Ithaca where his old dog Argus alone recognised him. Supported by Athene and Telemachus he destroyed all Penelope's suitors by means of his famous bow. Sixteen years later he was unwittingly slain by his son Tēlĕ'gŏnus whom his mother Circe had sent in search of his father.

Stephen Phillips' play *Ulysses* will be found interesting.

Frederic Prokosch describes him in a poem called " Sunburned Ulysses " :

" Black-eyed Ulysses, being an
    astute and eagle-hearted man,
A heavily loined, lumbering man
    with a bird's eye and a bird's
    unrest . . ."

Tennyson's *Ulysses* is the noblest of all his classical poems.

Odyssey. *The Odyssey*, an epic of 24 books, tells the story of the return of Ody'sseus (in Latin Uly'ssēs) to his home in Ithaca from the Trojan war, of his ten years' wanderings and his final overthrow of Penelope's suitors. As in *The Iliad* there are many episodes, such as the story of Nausĭcăa ; that of Odysseus and Calypso, the nymph of Ŏgy'gia; that of the Cyclops of Sicily, and of Circē, the sorceress of Aeāē'a ; followed by that of the landing of Odysseus in Ithaca, his meeting his son Telemachus, his recognition by his old nurse Euryclei'a, and his final battle with the suitors in his hall. It may well be that the poet of *The Odyssey* is not the poet of *The Iliad*, though scholars are certain that the whole of *The Odyssey* is the work of one poet.

An eminently suitable version

for non-Greek readers is the modern one in prose made by E. V. Rieu (Penguin Classics).

See Andrew Lang's sonnet " The Odyssey " (841 in *The Oxford Book of English Verse*), concluding :
" They hear like Ocean on a western beach
     The surge and thunder of the Odyssey."

Oe'dĭpus, son of Lā'ĭus and Jŏcast'a of Thebes. Laius had been informed by an oracle that he would perish by the hands of his own son, so, when the boy was born, his parents pierced his feet, bound them together and exposed him on Mt. Cĭthae'rōn. He was found by a shepherd of the King of Corinth, who called him Oedipus, i.e. ' Swollen-Feet '. As a man he was informed by the oracle at Delphi that he was destined to slay his father and to marry his mother. He thought he would avoid this destiny by not returning to Corinth. On the road, however, he met Laius (whom, of course, he did not know) and in a dispute about right of way he slew Laius. Meanwhile, Oedipus solved the riddle of the **Sphinx** and as a reward the Thebans gave him the Kingdom to rule and Jocasta as his wife. In consequence of this marriage Thebes was visited by a plague and the oracle ordered that the murderer of Laius should be expelled. Oedipus pronounced a solemn curse on the unknown murderer, but was told by the seer Tīrĕs'ĭas that he himself was the parricide and the husband of his own mother. In horror Oepidus put out his eyes and Jocasta hanged herself. Some years later popular feeling rose against him and he was expelled from Thebes. His sons did not interfere to save him, but his daughters voluntarily went into exile with him. Anti'gonē led him to Colō'nus near Athens where

he mysteriously died in the sacred grove of the Eumenides.

Oenō'nē, daughter of a river-god. She lived in the Troad where she was beloved of Paris before he forsook her for Helen of Troy.

See Tennyson's *Oenone* and Laurence Binyon's tragedy in one act, *Paris and Oenone.*

Ōgў'gĭa, the mythical island of Calypso on which Odysseus was shipwrecked.

Oil. In the Bible the olive-berry is the most frequently mentioned source of oil. The olives themselves were eaten : in addition the chief uses of the oil were :

(i) *Edible.* Dried wheat, boiled with butter or oil, is a common dish for all classes in Syria.

(ii) *Cosmetic.* As is usual in hot climates, oil was used by the Jews for anointing the body, e.g. after the bath. " Wash thyself therefore, and anoint thee . . . but make not thyself known unto the man [Boaz] until he shall have done eating and drinking " (*Ruth* 3³).

(iii) *Funereal.* The bodies of the dead were anointed with oil, probably as a partial antiseptic.

(iv) *Medicinal.* In fevers, oil was applied externally with friction. The good Samaritan poured " oil and wine " into the victim's wounds (*Luke* 10³⁴). The Twelve " anointed with oil many that were sick, and healed them " (*Mark* 6¹³).

(v) *Light.* Olive-oil was used for the great lamps at the Feast of Tabernacles and for domestic lamps. See the Parable of the Ten Virgins (*Matt.* 25¹⁻¹³).

(vi) *Ritual.* Kings, priests and prophets were anointed with oil ; but Scripture mentions the anointing as actually taking place only with Saul, David, Solomon, Jehu and Joash.

Olive Branch, (a) the emblem of peace. Representatives of a defeated nation when suing for peace carried olive branches in their hands. An olive leaf provided the dove's message of hope when the waters of the Flood began to retire.

(b) = child. "Thy children [shall be] like olive plants round about thy table" (Ps. 128³) is explained by the fact that suckers spring up round the bole of any old olive tree.

Oly'mpia, a plain on the West coast of the Peloponnesus in which was the sacred grove of Olympian Zeus, known as the *Altis*. With its temples and statues and the public buildings in the immediate neighbourhood the Altis formed what was called Olympia ; but there was no town of this name. Here, once in every four years, the Olympic Games, the greatest of the Greek national festivals, were held. The contests included foot-racing, wrestling, boxing, horse-and-chariot racing. Persons from all parts of the Greek world assembled at these games. "Booths were erected for their accommodation. Beggars, hucksters, mountebanks and fortune-tellers all flocked in as at Epsom on Derby Day" (C. E. Robinson : *Everyday Life in Greece*). The only prize given to the victor was a garland of wild olive, cut from a sacred olive-tree which grew in the grove ; but the victor's fame throughout Greece was universal and he received not only substantial money prizes but special privileges for himself and his family from his own state on which his victory was held to confer honour.

The four-year interval between one celebration of the festival and the next was called an *Olympiad*. In recent years there has been a revival of the Olympic Games, first in 1896 in Athens, later in

Paris, the U.S.A., London, Stockholm, Antwerp, Amsterdam, and Berlin (1936). The games were revived in London in 1948.

Oly'mpias, wife of Philip II of Macedon, and mother of Alexander the Great.

Oly'mpus, a mountain, 10,000 feet high, in the north of Greece. Its summit is covered with perpetual snow. In Greek mythology Olympus was the abode of the gods of whom Zeus was the head. Homer describes the gods as having their palaces on Olympus. On the summit is the council-chamber where they meet in solemn conclave. The Muses entertain them with the lyre and song. They are shut in from the view of men upon the earth by a wall of clouds, the gates of which are kept by the Hours.

O'mphălē, wife of Tmōlus, King of Lydia. After his death she under-

Omphale and Heracles. (*Farnese Group, now at Naples*).

took the government herself. Heracles spent three years in bondage with Omphale as atonement for a murder. During these years he is said to have lived an effeminate life, wearing women's garments and spinning wool, while Omphale wore his lion's skin.

Saint-Saëns' symphonic poem, " Le Rouet d'Omphale " " Omphale's Spinning Wheel," is well-known.

Ops, a Roman goddess of plenty and fertility. She was regarded as the wife of Saturnus and the protectress of everything connected with agriculture. Her temple was on the Capitol.

Oracle : (i) the means whereby divine purpose was revealed to man, (ii) the place where such revelation was to be expected, (iii) the deity making such revelation. In O.T. we read, for example, of the arrangements made for " the oracle " in Solomon's Temple (1 *Kings* 6¹⁶). For the means by which the divine utterance was sought see **Urim and Thummim.** In N.T. ' oracles ' means ' divine utterances ', with special reference to the law of Moses, e.g. St. Stephen speaks of Moses " receiving living oracles " (*Acts* 7³⁸), as distinct from those given by false gods such as those of Delphi and Dodona.

The most famous oracles in Greece were those dedicated to Zeus at Dodona in Epirus and at Olympia, and those of Apollo at Delphi—' the Pythian's mystic cave ', as Byron calls it—and at Delos.

See **Delphi** and **Dodona.**

In general, an ' oracle ' is a person claiming profound wisdom.

" I am Sir Oracle,
And when I ope my lips, let no dog bark "

was Gratiano's claim in *The Mer-*chant of Venice. Further, we speak of ' working the oracle ', i.e. helping our own interests surreptitiously.

Orbĭ'lĭus, the ' flogging ' schoolmaster who taught the poet Horace.

Orcădes, the Orkney and Shetland Islands.

Orĕădes. See **Nymphs.**

Ore'stes, son of Agame'mnon and Clytemne'stra. As an infant he was saved by his sister Ele'ctra from being murdered by his mother and was taken to Phōcis in N. Greece where he was brought up with the King's son Pў'lădes. Their friendship became proverbial. Accompanied by Pylades Orestes went in secret to Argos where, helped by Electra, he avenged his father's murder by killing his mother and her friend Aegi'sthus. He was now seized with madness and fled from land to land, pursued by the Furies. He finally took refuge with Athene in Athens. He asked Apollo how he could be freed from his madness and was advised to fetch from Tauris (the Crimea) the image of Artemis, which was believed to have fallen there from heaven, and to take it to Athens. The two friends went to Tauris together and were on the point of being sacrificed to Artemis when Iphigeni'a, priestess of Artemis there, recognised her brother, and all three escaped to Greece with the statue. Orestes had now recovered his sanity and become King of Argos. He gave his sister Electra in marriage to his friend and he himself married Hermi'onē, daughter of Menelā'us and Helen, after slaying Neopto'lemus. He is said to have died of snake-bite and his body was buried in Sparta.

Ori′ōn, a handsome giant and hunter of Boeotia. After his death he was placed among the stars, where his constellation appears as a giant with a girdle of three stars, sword, a lion's skin and a club.

O′rpheūs, a mythical personage, called by Pindar ' the Father of Songs '. Legend represents him as a son of Calli′opē, living in Thrace at the time of the Argonauts. Presented with the lyre by Apollo and instructed by the Muses in its use, he enchanted with its music not only the wild beasts but the trees and rocks on Olympus so that they followed the sound of his golden harp. Cf. the song sung in *Henry VIII* to Queen Katharine :

" Orpheus with his lute made trees,
 And the mountain tops that freeze,
  Bow themselves when he did sing."

The Argonauts sought his aid and his harp helped them to avoid the Clashing Rocks and to lull to sleep the Colchian dragon guarding the Golden Fleece.   His wife

Orpheus. (*From a mosaic*). *With his music of the lyre—the gift of Apollo himself—he enchanted not only the wild beasts, but the trees and rocks on Olympus, so that they followed him.*

Eury′dicē died from a serpent bite. Orpheus followed her to Hades where the charms of his lyre won her back ; but his prayer was granted only upon condition that he should not look back upon her till they had arrived in the upper world.   At the very moment when they were about to pass the fatal bounds he looked round to see that Eurydice was following him ; and she was caught back into the infernal regions.   His grief for her loss led him to treat with contempt the Thracian women, who in revenge tore him to pieces.   The Muses collected the fragments of his body and buried them at the foot of Olympus ; but his head still muttering ' Eurydice ' was thrown into the Hebrus, down which it rolled to the sea.

See Milton's *L'Allegro* 145–150 ; *Lycidas* 58–63 ; and *Paradise Lost* vii, 32–39.

There are English translations of the fine poem on this theme by the Austrian poet Rainer Maria Rilke.

Ossa, a mountain in Thessaly. The giants piled it on the adjacent Mt. Pelion in their war against Olympus.
See **Pelion.**

Ostĭa, a town at the mouth of the Tiber, the harbour of Rome from which it was distant sixteen miles by land.   It is now a mere village, two or three miles from the coast.

Ovid (Publius Ōvĭdĭus Nāso), Roman poet, 43 B.C.—A.D. 17. Till his fiftieth year he lived in Rome, enjoying the friendship of distinguished men and the favour of Augustus himself ; but in A.D. 1 he was suddenly exiled to Tŏmi at the mouths of the Danube.   The reason for his exile is not precisely known ; but how bitterly the town-loving man of culture felt his banishment to the very extremity of the Roman world may be judged from his *Tristia*. He was a master of form and grace of diction : his verses reflect the grace and ease of the most polished society of the Augustan age. Ovid was a great teller of stories. His *Metamorphō'sēs* in fifteen books is a store-house of mythological legend. In 1565 a translation of this long work, in rhyming hexameters, was made by Arthur Golding, a Cambridge scholar, and this translation is of peculiar interest to us, for it was the main source of Shakespeare's knowledge of classical mythology.

Pălămē'des, a Greek chief who was the means of getting Odysseus to join in the fight against Troy. Odysseus did not want to go : he was quietly settled with his wife, child and aged father in Ithaca ; so he feigned madness. He yoked a horse and an ox and used them to plough the sands and to sow them with salt. But Palamedes proved Odysseus' sanity by placing young Tēle'machus in front of the plough and seeing Odysseus save the child by turning the plough aside. Odysseus revenged himself by forging a letter supposed to have been sent by Priam to Palamedes regarding the proposed surrender of the Greek army. Palamedes was accused of treachery, the forged letter was found in his tent, and he was stoned to death. Palamedes is described by Greek poets as famed for wisdom and ingenuity. He is said to have invented lighthouses, measures, scales, the discus and the dice, and to have added letters to the Greek alphabet.

Palinū'rus, pilot of the ship of Aeneas. He fell into the sea and was murdered on the coast by the natives.

Pallă'dĭum, an image of Pallas Athene which fell from heaven and was kept hidden in a temple at Troy and revered, for the safety of Troy was believed to depend on it. It was carried off by Odysseus and Diomē'dēs. Another story says that Aeneas brought a palladium from Troy to Italy. In general, a ' palladium ' is a national safeguard.

See Arnold's *Palladium :*
" Backward and forward roll'd the
        waves of fight
    Round Troy—but while this
        stood, Troy could not fall."

Pa'llas, a surname of the goddess Athene. It is an ancient word meaning ' maiden '.

Palm Sunday is the Sunday before Easter day, the day on which Christ made His triumphal entry into Jerusalem (*John* 12$^{12-19}$). The people " took branches of palm trees and went forth to meet Him "—hence ' Palm Sunday '. Weekley compares this with the French ' Pâques fleuries ', literally ' flowery Easter '.

Read Chesterton's marvellous poem " The Donkey " :
    " I also had my hour ;
One far fierce hour and sweet :
    There was a shout about my
        ears,
And palms before my feet."

Pān : god of flocks and shepherds among the Greeks. Arcadia was always the principal seat of his worship. During the heat of midday he was supposed to slumber and the peasants feared to disturb his rest. Like all gods who dwelt in forests Pan was dreaded by travellers, whom he startled with sudden awe or terrors. His

supposed dreadful shout was doubtless imagined from the unexplained
sounds heard in the depths of

Pan with syrinx. (*From a bas-
relief*). *The syrinx was the approp-
riate musical instrument of Grecian
shepherds who regarded it as the
invention of their tutelary god Pan.*

forests. Hence sudden fright without any visible cause was ascribed
to Pan and was called a Panic fear.
In works of art Pan is represented
as having horns and goats' feet and
sometimes as playing on the shepherds' pipe or syrinx which he was
believed to have invented.

See E. B. Browning's " A Won-
derful Instrument." It describes
how Pan fashioned the syrinx :
" What was he doing, the great
    god Pan,
  Down in the reeds by the river ? "
See **Syrinx.**

Pandī'ōn, King of Athens and
father of Procnē and Philomēla.
He gave Procne in marriage to the
Thracian King Tēreus : their son
was Ītys. In time Tereus tired of
Procne. He invited Philomela to
his court where he ill-treated her
and then cut out her tongue so
that she could not tell of her
sufferings. But she wove the story
into a tapestry which she gave
secretly to Procne. When Procne
learned how her sister had been

wronged she murdered Itys and
served him up as food to Tereus.
The sisters fled from the court
pursued by Tereus. Just as he
was on the point of slaying them,
they were all three transformed
into birds, Procne becoming a
swallow, Philomela a nightingale
and Tereus a hoopoe.

See Barnfield's poem to " The
Nightingale " in Palgrave's *Golden
Treasury.* In *Itylus* Swinburne
seems to confuse the stories of Itys
and of Itylus. Cf. also Arnold's
" Philomela."

Pandō'ra, the name of the first
woman on earth. When Promē'theūs
had stolen fire from heaven, Zeus in
revenge caused Hēphae'stus to
make a woman out of earth, who
by her charms should bring misery
upon the human race. Aphrodī'tē
adorned her with beauty ; Hermes
bestowed on her boldness and
cunning ; and the gods called her
Pandora, or *Allgifted.* Hermes
took her to Epimētheus, who made
her his wife, forgetting the advice
of his brother Prometheus that he
should not receive any gifts from
Zeus. In the house of Epimetheus
was a closed box which he had been
forbidden to open. But the curiosity
of a woman could not resist the
temptation to know its contents ;
and when she opened the lid all
the evils incident to man poured
out. She had only time to shut
down the lid and prevent the
escape of Hope.

Milton compares Eve in Adam's
bower to Pandora. She was, he says,
" More lovely than Pandora, whom
    the gods
  Endow'd with all their gifts."
Orpheus, according to William
Morris, sang to the Argonauts the
story of
    " the bitter life
  Pandora brought to luckless
    man,"

Panem et Circenses. The Circus Maximus between the Palatine and the Aventine Hills in Rome was an immense oval enclosure where the " ludi circenses " were held. The most characteristic of the ludi were the chariot races. These sporting exhibitions were extremely popular with idle Roman crowds who could not or would not work. In early times four races were run in a day : later the races frequently lasted the whole day. Intervals between sets of races were filled up by exhibitions of rope-dancing, tumbling and feats of horsemanship, very like those of a modern circus.

The satirical poet Juvenal tells us that as the Romans degenerated the only things they really cared for were ' bread and circuses '— as we might perhaps with equal cynicism say to-day ' food-subsidies and football.'

Panop'tēs, see **Argus.**

Panthē'on or **Pa'nthēon,** a circular temple built in honour of Mars and Venus by Agrippa in 27 B.C. Its great characteristic is the magnificent dome—a solid mass, $142\frac{1}{2}$ feet in diameter and in height, standing by its own coherence and not by the principle of the arch. It was consecrated as a Christian Church by Boniface IV in 608. The name is now applied to a memorial to national heroes, such as the Panthéon at Paris. This was originally a church, but was secularised during the Revolution and renamed Panthéon. These two buildings are used as burial-places for illustrious Italians and Frenchmen.

Parable. The Greek word means a " comparison ". A parable is distinguished from a fable by its truth to nature. The fables of the O.T. taught by Jotham (*Judges* 9[8...])

and Jehoash (2 *Kings* 14[9]) have no parallels in the teaching of any prophet : they teach the wisdom of this world only. A parable is, in the familiar words, an earthly story with a heavenly meaning. It is a homely and concrete story to illustrate some abstract idea, and it is not necessary to find an interpretation for each of the details. In the allegory every detail has its abstract counterpart, e.g. The Sower, The Man who planted a Vineyard. The parables of the N.T. combine exquisite grace and ease. Christ uses them for a double purpose—to present abstract ideas in a form more readily intelligible to the uneducated mind (a common oriental device that may be noted in *The Arabian Nights*) and as a test of character.

Bishop Westcott classifies Christ's parables by subjects :

(*a*) Parables drawn from the material world, e.g. The Sower, The Tares, The Mustard Seed, The Leaven ;

(*b*) Parables drawn from the relations of men

    (i) to the lower world, e.g. The Barren Fig-tree, Lost Sheep, Lost Coin,

    (ii) to their fellow men
      (*a*) in the family, e.g. Unmerciful Servant, Two Debtors,
      (*b*) in social life, e.g. Friend at midnight, Unjust Judge,

    (iii) to Providence, e.g. Hid Treasure, Rich Fool.

Pa'rcae, see **Fates.**

Păris, the second son of Priam and He'cuba. He spent his early life on Mt. Ida, tending his flocks. He deserted Oenō'nē, the nymph of Mt. Ida, and carried away Helen, the wife of Menelā'us, thus causing the Trojan war. He awarded the prize for beauty to Aphrodī'tē [see **Apple** (i)]—a decision which called forth in Hera and Athene fierce hatred against Troy. In the Trojan war he fought in single combat with Menelaus to decide the whole issue ; he was defeated

Paris. (*Aegina Marbles*). *Paris is represented as a beautiful youth, wearing a Phrygian cap.*

but was saved by Aphrodite. With Apollo's aid he is said to have killed Achilles. On the capture of Troy, he was wounded by Phīloctē'tes and then returned to his long-abandoned wife Oenone. She refused to heal the wound and Paris returned to Troy and died. Oenone quickly repented and hastened after him, but she came too late and in her grief hanged herself.

See Laurence Binyon's one-act tragedy, " Paris and Œnone."

Parna'ssus, the highest point in a mountain range in N. Greece, celebrated as one of the chief seats of Apollo and the Muses. Hard by was the far-famed Castalian spring the waters of which inspired those who drank of them with the gift of poetry.

Păros, one of the larger of the Cyclades group of islands in the Aegean, famous for its marble.

The Parthenon : *slightly damaged by mortar-fire during the Axis occupation of Athens, April 1941 to October 1944.*

Pa´rthĕnōn, the temple of Athena Parthenos (i.e. Athena the maiden goddess), the chief glory of the Acropolis, built entirely of marble. It contained the statue of Athena by Pheidias and was adorned within and without with sculptures, the masterpieces of Greek art, executed in part by Pheidias himself. The whole building was surrounded by a number of pillars. Many of the sculptures were brought to England early in the nineteenth century by Lord Elgin. They were bought by the British Government and are now in the British Museum. They are known as the " Elgin Marbles." The temple remained nearly intact until 1687 when it was half destroyed by an explosion during the war between the Turks and the Venetians. During the Axis occupation the east end of the temple was slightly damaged by mortar-fire.

Par´thians, an Iranian tribe which revolted under Ar´săcĕs somewhere about 250 B.C. and became an independent monarchy. They were a warlike people, especially celebrated as mounted archers. Their mailclad horsemen spread like a cloud round the hostile army, and poured in a shower of darts. Then they evaded any closer conflict by a rapid flight, during which they continued to shoot their arrows over their shoulders upon the enemy.

' A Parthian shot (shaft, glance) ' is a last shot, fired at the moment of departure (C.O.D.).

" Arm me, audacity, from head
    to foot !
Or, like the Parthian, I shall
    flying fight."
    (Iachimo in *Cymbeline*.)

Pāsĭ´phaē. See **Minotaur.**

Passover. One of the ten plagues

inflicted on the Egyptians to secure the exodus of the Israelites was the slaying of their firstborn, " from the firstborn of Pharaoh that sat on his throne unto the firstborn of the captive that was in the dungeon." The Israelites were commanded to strike sacrificial blood on the two side posts and on the upper door post of their houses so that the Angel of Death might " pass over " them. Their freedom from the plague was marked by the festival of the Passover held on the evening of the 14th day of the Hebrew month Abib or Nisan, and the following seven days.

Pa´tmos, one of the Sporades group of islands in the Aegean. On it is the celebrated monastery which bears the name of " John the Divine." Halfway up the hill on which the monastery stands is the cave or grotto where tradition says that St. John received the Revelation.

Patro´clus, the kinsman and friend of Achilles whom he followed to Troy. When the Greeks were hard pressed he begged Achilles to allow him to put on his armour and with his men to hasten to their assistance. Achilles agreed and Patroclus drove the Trojans back and extinguished the fire which was raging among the ships. But he was slain by Hector with Apollo's help. Achilles now left his tent, in which he had been sulking, to avenge his friend's death.

See **Achilles.**

Paul, a native of Tarsus, a Pharisee and a son of Pharisees. He was educated in Jerusalem under Gamaliel. It seems certain that he never met Jesus Christ and must have been absent from

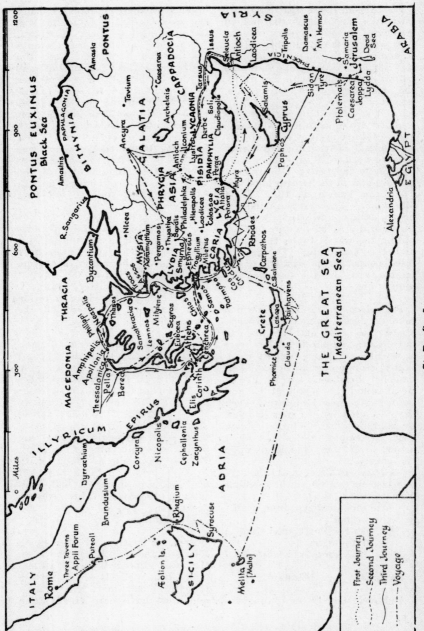

St. Paul's Journeys

First Journey ....
Second Journey — — —
Third Journey ————
Voyage —·—·—·—

Jerusalem at the time of the Crucifixion. The story of his conversion in A.D. 31 is given three times : (i) in the historian's account (*Acts* 9) ; (ii) by Paul in Hebrew to the crowds in Jerusalem (*Acts* 22) ; (iii) by Paul in Greek before the authorities at Caesarea (*Acts* 24). The apostle's three great missionary journeys are detailed in the *Acts* : (i) 13⁴—14²⁸ ; (ii) 15⁴⁰—18²² ; (iii) 18²³—21¹⁵. Two years' imprisonment at Caesarea were followed by the journey to Rome, in the course of which he was shipwrecked on the island of Malta. In Rome he suffered a further two years under military confinement, though preaching unhindered " in his own hired dwelling." Such in briefest outline is St. Paul's story as given in the *Acts*. Tradition says that after his release he journeyed possibly as far as Spain. He was, however, again arrested and sent to Rome where he was beheaded under the tyranny of Nero.

Pax, called Irē'nē by the Greeks, the goddess of Peace. She is represented on coins as a young woman, holding in her left arm a cornucopia and in her right an olive branch or the staff of Mercury. The olive branch is thus used as a symbol of peace or reconciliation.

Pē'gasus, the winged horse which sprang from the blood of Medusa

Coin of Corinth, of 4th cent. B.C Obv., Pegasus, under which Koppa, the initial of the city's name in early times, and retained on its coinage ; rev., head of Pallas.

when her head was struck off by Perseus. When the Muses engaged in a contest with the Pīĕ'rĭdes, all nature stood still to listen to the Muses' song and Mt. Helicon rose heavenward with delight. But Pegasus, by command of Poseidon, stopped its ascent by kicking it with his hoof. From this kick there arose Hippocrēnē, the inspiring well of the Muses, on Mt. Helicon. See **Bellerophon**.

Peirē'nē, a fountain in the citadel of Corinth. Here with a bridle studded with gems and adorned with a golden bit, the gift of Athena, Bellerophon caught Pegasus while he was drinking at the fountain.

Pē'leūs, a King of Thessaly who married the Nereid Thetis. Eris (Strife) was the only goddess not invited to the wedding, and she revenged herself by throwing the ' apple of discord ' among the guests [see **Apple** (i)]. Achilles was their son.

Pe'lias, twin brother of Nēleus. The brothers seized Iolchos, to the exclusion of Jason's father Aeson. When Jason came to claim the kingdom as his right, Pelias sought to get rid of him by sending him to Colchis to fetch the Golden Fleece. [See **Argonauts**]. After the return of Jason, Pelias was cut in pieces and boiled by his own daughters who had been told by Medea that in this way they would restore their father to vigour and youth.

Pē'lion, a lofty range of mountains in Thessaly. Its sides were covered with pine-woods, timber from which was felled and shaped for the building of *Argo*. Achilles' spear was fashioned from a tree that grew on its slopes. Near its summit was the cave of the Centaur, Chīron. In their war with the gods the giants are said to have attempted to scale heaven by piling a near-by mountain, Ossa (and Olympus) on Pelion. " It was their ambition," says Homer (in Rieu's translation) " to pile Mount Ossa on Olympus and wooded Pelion on Ossa, so as to make a stairway up to heaven."

As he leaps into his sister's grave, Laertes says :
" Now pile your dust upon the
    quick and dead,
Till of this flat a mountain you
    have made,
To o'ertop old Pelion, or the
    skyish head
Of blue Olympus " ;
and thirty lines further on Hamlet refuses to be outfaced by Laertes :
" Be buried quick with her, and
    so will I.
And if thou prate of mountains,
    let them throw
Millions of acres on us, till our
    ground,
Singeing his pate against the
    burning zone,
Make Ossa like a wart ! "

Pĕlŏponnē'sus, i.e. the island of Pelops, the mythical king expelled from Phrygia who settled in the peninsula. It is connected with Hellas proper by the isthmus of Corinth. Its chief provinces were Achaia in the north, Elis in the west, Laconia in the south and east, and Arcadia in the centre.

The modern name of the peninsula is the Morea, a name given to it in the middle ages because it was thought to resemble a mulberry leaf in shape.

(Greek moron = black mulberry).

Pĕ'lops, son of Tantalus and so grandson of Zeus. He was driven from his Kingdom of Phrygia and migrated with his great wealth to Elis. Here he married Hippodami'a, daughter of the King of Elis whom he defeated in a chariot-race before he could marry her. (Cf. the story of the Arcadian maiden, Atalanta). My'rtĭlus, the king's charioteer whom Pelops had bribed to help him, with his dying breath cursed Pelops and all his race—a curse which was fulfilled in the misfortunes that befell his sons A'treūs and Thye'stĕs and his grandsons Agamemnon and Menelaus. Pelops now became King of Elis and proceeded to conquer all S. Greece which he called ' Peloponnesus ', i.e. Pelops' island.

One of the most interesting legends about Pelops is that relating to his ivory shoulder. Tantalus, the favourite of the gods, once invited them to a repast. He killed his own son, boiled him and set the flesh before the gods that they might eat it. But the immortal gods, knowing what it was, did not touch it. Dēmē'ter alone, absorbed by grief for her lost daughter, consumed the shoulder of Pelops. Thereupon the gods ordered Hermes to put the limbs of Pelops into a cauldron and thereby restore him to life. When this was done, Clotho took him out of the cauldron, and as the shoulder consumed by Demeter was wanting, the goddess supplied its place by one made of ivory. His descendants, the Pelopidae, as a mark of their origin, were believed to have one shoulder as white as ivory.

Penā'tĕs, the deities of the interior of the Roman house, the household gods, the guardian spirits of the store-cupboard. The images of these gods stood in the central part of the house.

Closely linked with the Penates were other household gods, e.g. the Lā'rēs, regarded as the spirits of ancestors, who watched over the household. The ideas of

Penates and Lares were as intimately connected as ours of 'hearth and home.'

Pēnĕ'lŏpē, wife of Odysseus, King of Ithaca. Their only child was Tĕlĕmăchus who was an infant when Odysseus sailed against Troy. During the long absence of her husband she was beset by suitors, whom she deceived by declaring that she must finish a shroud she was making for her aged father-in-law before she could make up her mind. During the daytime she accordingly worked at the

Penelope's loom, from a vase from Chiusi.

robe, and in the night she undid the work of the day.

A 'Penelope' is a faithful wife. This is what Valeria implies when she says to the wife of Coriolanus : " You would be another Penelope ; yet, they say, all the yarn she spun in Ulysses' absence did but fill Ithaca full of holes."

Penny. The penny of the N.T. (*Matt.* 18²⁸, 20² ; *Mark* 6³⁷, 12¹⁵ ; *Luke* 10³⁵, etc.) is the denarius, a Roman silver coin equivalent in value to an Attic drachma—or what our grandfathers would have called

a franc. From the parable of " The Labourers in the Vineyard " (*Matt.* 20¹⁻¹⁶) it would seem that a denarius was in Christ's time the ordinary wages for a labourer's day.

From the first letter of ' denarius ' we have the ' d ' in ' £. s. d.'

Pentecost. See **Whitsunday.**

Pentĕ'lĭcus, a mountain in Attica, not far from Athens. It was famous for its creamy-white marble used in building the temples on the Acropolis.

Penthĕsĭlĕ'a, daughter of Ares and Queen of the Amazons. After the death of Hector she came to help the Trojans, but was slain by Achilles who mourned over her on account of her beauty, youth and valour.

Maria, the sagacious but diminutive waiting-maid of the Countess Olivia in *Twelfth Night*, is humorously addressed by Sir Toby as Penthesilea, queen of the female-warrior race of Amazons. He is on surer ground two lines later when he says : " She's a beagle ", i.e. a small type of dog used in hare-hunting. Viola had previously, in irony, mixed with admiration, referred to her as " your giant, sweet lady."

Pe'nthēus succeeded his father-in-law Cadmus as King of Thebes. He resisted the introduction of the worship of Dionȳ'sus into his kingdom, was driven mad by the god and was torn to pieces by his own mother and her two sisters who, in their Bacchic frenzy, believed him to be a wild beast. So says Greek legend.

Pe'rdix. Ovid's story is that Perdix (or Tālus) was the nephew of Daedalus and the inventor of the saw and compasses. In envy

Daedalus threw him headlong from the sacred citadel of Minerva ; but the goddess, " who favours the quick of wit," caught him up and changed him into a partridge (*Perdix* is the Greek for partridge). " Remembering that old fall, the partridge is ever fearful of lofty places. She does not lift her body high in flight nor build her nest on trees or on high points of rock ; but she flutters along near the ground and lays her eggs in hedge-rows." A pretty explanation of the bird's habits, surely.

It was probably a misinterpreta-tion of the legend which gave Perdix the *nephew* of Daedalus the same story as that of Tālus. Perdix was the sister of Daedalus and mother of Talus.

Pe'riclēs (c. 500–429 B.C.), the greatest of Athenian statesmen and a distinguished general. He de-voted large sums of money to the erection of magnificent temples and public buildings which made Athens the admiration of Greece. In particular, he was responsible for the building of the Propylae'a and the Pa'rthenon. Pericles was a man of the highest integrity. On his death-bed he claimed as his greatest merit that no Athenian through his means had been made to put on mourning. At his death he was found not to have added a single drachma to his hereditary property. Pericles' noble funeral oration over those who fell in the retreat from Syracuse is to be found, though not in the orator's own words, in the second book of Thucydides' " History of the Pelo-ponnesian War."

Perse'phonē, called **Proser'pĭna** by the Romans, was daughter of Zeus and Dēmē'ter. Homer describes her as the wife of Hades, the dread queen of the Shades who along with her husband rules over the souls of the dead. For the story of her being carried off by Pluto see **Demeter.**

Pe'rseūs, son of Zeus and Danaë, grandson of Acri'sius, King of Argos. [See **Danaë**]. Polyde'ctēs, King of Serīphos, wishing to be rid of Perseus, sent him to fetch the head of **Medū'sa.** Perseus used Medusa's head to turn the giant Atlas into the mountain that bears his name. Proceeding to Aethiopia, he saved and married **Andro'meda.** Returning to Seriphos he found that his mother and Dictys had taken refuge in a temple from the violence of Dictys' brother Poly-dectes, so he went to the palace and changed the king and all his guests into stone. Dictys was made king. Perseus now restored to the gods the arms they had lent him to overcome the Gorgons, and he gave Medusa's head to Athene who placed it in the middle of her aegis or shield. On his way home he stopped at Larissa to take part in the public games, during which he accidentally hit the foot of Acrisius with a quoit and so killed him. Thus he fulfilled the oracle which had told Acrisius that he would die by the hands of Danae's son.

Louis MacNiece's poem " Per-seus " is apposite :

" Borrowed wings on his ankles
  Carrying a stone death
The hero entered the hall,
All in the hall looked up
  Their breath frozen on them
And there was no more shuffle
  or clatter in the hall at all."

Peter, originally called Simon, was the son of Jonas (hence Simon Bar-Jonas, *Matt.* 16[17]) and brother of Andrew. The brothers were fishermen in partnership with Zebedee's sons. They lived first at

Bethsaida (*John* 1⁴⁴) and afterwards at Capernaum (*Matt.* 8⁵,¹⁴), owned fishing boats and had hired servants. Peter was first called by Christ to a temporary companionship : his second call, to definite discipleship, came while the four partners were engaged in their work on the Sea of Tiberias (*Matt.* 4¹⁸). When the twelve apostles were chosen Peter seems to have ranked from the very first as their leader : his name stands first in all the lists. The strong and the weak points of his character are brought out in the gospel narrative. He was loyal, affectionate and enthusiastic, but he was rash, boastful and presumptuous. With James and John he witnessed the Transfiguration ; with Andrew and Zebedee's sons he listened to the predictions of the Second Advent (*Mark* 13³). After the Last Supper he made those protestations of fidelity, so quickly falsified by his threefold denial. On the morning of the Resurrection Peter was the first to enter the tomb, and to him, first of the apostles, the risen Lord appeared. From the time of the Ascension his leadership is clearly recognised by the Church. He advises the appointment of a successor to Judas (*Acts* 1¹⁵··) ; he heals the lame man at the door of the Temple called ' Beautiful ' (3¹··) ; he deals with Ananias and Sapphira (5¹··), with Simon Magus (8²⁰··), with Aeneas (9³²··), with Tabitha (9³⁶), with Cornelius the centurion (10, 11). He was imprisoned by Herod the King and rescued by an angel (12³··), and took an important part in the Conference of Jerusalem (15⁷··). Most probably he suffered martyrdom in Rome shortly after Paul's death there.

To Peter's confession : " Thou art the Christ, the Son of the Living God," our Lord replied :

" Thou art Peter and upon this rock I will build my church " (*Matt.* 16¹⁸). Christ is playing on the words ' Petros ' or Peter and ' petra ' = a rock (or in Aramaic ' Cephas '—See *John* 1⁴²—and ' cepha ' = a rock). Whether the rock is St. Peter himself or the Christian creed he has just uttered need not be argued here.

Peter's Denials. The vivid details of Peter's three-fold denials of Christ can have been supplied only by himself. Sitting by the fire-side in the court-yard of the High Priest's house, during the trial of Christ, Peter was challenged by a maidservant. He denied that he was a disciple, went outside and the cock crew. He returned to the court-yard and was again challenged by a maid. Again he denied, this time with an oath. Then he was recognised by a man who noted his Galilean accent. Peter began to curse and to swear : " I know not the man." Immediately the cock crew for the third time. Christ turned and looked upon Peter who at once remembered how Christ had foretold his denials. He went out and wept bitterly.

Phă'ĕthōn, i.e. ' the shining ', son of Hĕ'lĭos the god of the Sun. He was presumptuous enough to beg his father to allow him for one day to drive the chariot of the sun across the heavens. Helios consented, but the youth being too weak to check the horses, they rushed out of their usual track and came so near the earth as almost to set it on fire. Thereupon Zeus killed him with a flash of lightning.

From his name is derived our ' phaeton ', an open four-wheeled carriage (or car), drawn by two horses, which came into being towards the middle of the eighteenth century.

Phalē'ron, the most easterly of the harbours of Athens. Liners would rather ride in the roadstead of Phaleron Bay than use the more westerly port, the Pīrae'us.

Pharaoh, (i.e. 'Great House'), the Biblical title of the native kings of Egypt, similar in meaning to that of the 'Sublime Porte', i.e. the Turkish Government. This latter title is taken from the chief gate (the Porta Sublima) of the Old Seraglio, the Sultan's principal palace in Constantinople.

Pharisees, one of the two chief Jewish sects in the time of our Lord. They regarded themselves as superior to other men and therefore they would have no dealings with other sects. When for any outward reason they did associate with the Sadducees (or even the Herodians), the real reason for the unholy alliance was strong hostility to Christ Himself. Our Lord severely condemned the Pharisees (and the Scribes, not all of whom were Pharisees) for their hypocrisy in holding to the letter of the law rather than to the spirit. Not that he condemned their attention to detail except when such attention led to neglect of main principles, for, of course, not all Pharisees were hypocrites. See *St. Matthew* 23$^{1-36}$ for Christ's seven-fold condemnation of their hair-splitting tenets.

Phǎ'ros, a small island off the N. coast of Egypt which Alexander united to the coast by a mole. The island was famous for the tower of white marble built on it by Ptolemy II as a lighthouse— one of the Seven Wonders of the Ancient World. The name *pharos*

was applied to any similar light-house or beacon.

Phā'sis, a river of Colchis flowing into the Euxine (Black Sea). It has given its name to the pheasant (in Latin Phāsiāna (avis), i.e. bird of the Phasis).

Phei'dïas. Like Praxi'telēs, a native of Athens and a great sculptor. Pericles entrusted him with the sculptures and a general superintendence of the works of art he was building in Athens. The chief of these were the Propy-lae'a, the great porch leading to the Acropolis, and the temple of Athene called the Parthenon, both of which were built entirely of marble. Within that magnificent shrine was enclosed Pheidias' colossal statue of Athene, made of ivory and gold. Completing his work in Athens Pheidias went to Olympia where he executed his statue of the Olympian Zeus, the greatest of all his works. Later, he returned to Athens where he was accused first of peculation and then of impiety. He was thrown into prison where he died of disease in 432 B.C.

Pheidi'ppidēs, a courier sent by the Athenians to Sparta in 490 B.C. to ask for aid against the Persians. The two cities are 150 miles apart and Pheidippides arrived on the second day from his leaving Athens. Later in the year he ran from Marathon to Athens, a distance of 26 miles, to announce the victory of the Athenians over the Persians, and (according to Browning) fell dead from exhaustion as soon as he had delivered his message. This feat of the Athenian courier is commemorated by the 'Marathon Race', instituted at the revival of the Olympic Games in 1896.

'Pheidippides' ("Spare the

horses ") is probably a joke of Aristophanes. Modern texts read ' Philippides '. If Philippides ever did the run (Lucian is the sole authority for it and Browning gave it its English currency. Browning's version of the courier's death is probably borrowed from the story of another athlete) he would probably have taken the longer, but easier, run of 26 plus miles which skirts the fringe of Mt. Pentelicus.

See Robert Browning's narrative poem *Pheidippides* :

" And thee, best runner of
   Greece,
Whose limbs did duty indeed,—
   what gift is promised thyself ?
. . . Pan spoke thus : ' For what
   thou hast done
Count on a worthy reward ! Hence-
   forth be allowed thee release
From the racer's toil, no vulgar
   reward in praise or in pelf ! ''
The promised reward was the glorious death of a hero.

Philē'mōn, husband of Baucis. Zeus and Hermes once assumed the appearance of ordinary mortals and visited Phrygia ; but no one was willing to receive them until the hospitable hut of Philemon and Baucis was opened to them. Zeus rewarded the good old couple by taking them to a hill, while all the neighbouring district was flooded. Here Zeus appointed them the guardians of his temple, and allowed them both to die at the same moment and then changed them into trees.

See Swift's narrative, *Baucis and Philemon*, in octosyllabic verse.

Phi'lippi, the first city in Macedonia in which the apostle Paul preached the Gospel in Europe (*Acts* 16$^{12-40}$).

Here Octavius and Antony defeated Brutus and Cassius in 42 B.C. See the closing few words of iv, 3

(and v) of Shakespeare's *Julius Caesar*. The ghost of the murdered Caesar, in reality the offended spirit of history itself, utters very few words indeed to Brutus, but " they pass sentence of death on Caesar's murderers."

Brutus : Speak to me what thou
   art.
Ghost : Thy evil spirit, Brutus.
Brutus : Why com'st thou ?
Ghost : To tell thee thou shalt
   see me at Philippi.
Brutus : Well, then I shall see
   thee again ?
Ghost : Ay, at Philippi.
Brutus : Why, I will see thee at
   Philippi, then.
         [*Exit* Ghost.
Retribution could not have been more poignantly expressed.

Phili'ppic. Demosthenes (383–322 B.C.), the famous Athenian orator and statesman, delivered three speeches against Philip of Macedon, who was attempting to subjugate Greece, urging his countrymen (like a classical Lord Roberts or a Mr. Winston Churchill) to arm for their liberty against Philip. These speeches are known as " Philippics."

Cicero (106–43 B.C.), much as he admired the man, hated the tyrant in C. Julius Caesar, and after his murder the orator joined in the fight for liberty against Marcus Antonius. He delivered (or published) fourteen speeches against Antony, the man who had tried to make Caesar King. These speeches, too, have the title ' Philippics '.

Hence a ' philippic ' is a passionately aggressive speech, a savage invective, a diatribe.

Philistines, a tribe of warlike invaders who inhabited the S. seacoast of Palestine. They first became a danger to Israel in the time of Samson and remained her constant rivals throughout most

O.T. history. They lived in five cities and ruled a country that was wonderfully fertile. Their cities were wellnigh impregnable. They were well armed, having both chariots and armour. They were probably skilled at smiths' work. They fought to secure tribute and trade-routes. They worshipped Baalzebub, Ashteroth and Dagon. They carried their gods into battle and had a reputation as diviners. This persistent people never seem to have lost their warlike spirit in the midst of luxury, and they were probably never more than a garrison in the midst of a subject people. There is a tradition that they came from Crete after the destruction of the sea-empire of Minos. See *Gen.* 10¹⁴, *Deut.* 2²³, I *Chron.* 1¹². All these references concern the Philistines, who are said to have come from Caphtor, i.e. (most probably) Crete.

From the seventeenth century, non-students were regarded by German university students as unenlightened and uncultured persons, and to them the term ' Philister ' was given. In his essay on Heine Matthew Arnold adapted this term and applied it to the middle-class manufacturers of the country whose interests were almost exclusively materialistic. Carlyle called this lack of culture " gigmanity " : as though the possession of a gig was a mark of respectability which distinguished the " respectable " man from his less well-to-do fellows.

Philocte′tēs, the best archer in the Trojan war. At his death Heracles bequeathed him his poisoned arrows. On his voyage to Troy he was left behind by his men in the island of Lemnos because he was disabled by an evil-smelling snake-bite. He remained in this island till the tenth year of

the Trojan war, when Odysseus and Diomē′dēs came to fetch him; for an oracle had declared that the city could not be taken without the arrows of Heracles. He accompanied these heroes to Troy where his wound was cured. He afterwards slew Paris, whereupon Troy fell into the hands of the Greeks.

Philomē′la. See **Pandion.**

Phi′neūs, a soothsayer King of Thrace, blinded because he had revealed the counsels of Zeus. He had blinded his own sons on a false accusation made against them, and in consequence was tormented by the Harpies. Whenever a meal was placed before him, the Harpies darted down from the air and carried it off. He was delivered from them by the two sons of Cleopatra, his first wife, who were numbered with the heroes of the *Argo*. In return, Phineus explained to the Argonauts how they should reach Colchis, and in particular shewed them how to pass between the Clashing Rocks at the entrance to the Euxine.

Phlĕ′gĕthōn, i.e. the ' flaming ', the river of the nether world whose waters were flames.

Phoe′bē, the moon goddess. See **Artemis ; Diana.**
" To-morrow night, when Phoebe doth behold
Her silver visage in the watery glass." (*M.N.D.* 1, 1, 209)

Phoe′bus, the sun-god. See **Apollo.**
Milton has ' drouth of Phoebus ' i.e. thirst caused by the hot sun (*Comus* 66), and Shakespeare writes ' in the eye of Phoebus ', i.e. exposed to the heat of the sun (*Henry V*).

Phoe′nix, a mythical bird of
Arabia, said to live five hundred
years and then to build for himself
a funeral pile of spices and aromatic
wood, to settle upon it and die.
From the ashes a new phoenix at
once arose.

So in *Samson Agonistes* Milton
compares Virtue with the Phoenix :
" Like that self-begotten bird
In the Arabian woods embost
    (i.e. hidden),
That no second knows nor third ;
And, though her body die, her
    fame survives,
A secular bird (i.e. one that lives
    for centuries), ages of lives."
Figuratively, a ' phoenix ' is a
matchless person, a unique speci-
men, e.g.
" She is alone the Arabian bird "
    (Iachimo of Imogen,
       in *Cymbeline*).

Cf. La Fontaine's "Le Corbeau et
le Renard ' :
" Vous êtes le phénix des hôtes
    de ces bois,"
and George Darley's
" O Blest unfabled Incense Tree,"
    (No. 126 in Bridge's *Spirit of
Man* and 39 in the *Oxford Book of
Victorian Verse*).

Phri′xus. Phrixus and He′llē
were the children of A′thamas, a
King of Thessaly, and Nĕ′phĕlē.
When Athamas later married Īnō
she ill-treated her step-children.
As Ino was on the point of sacrificing them to Zeus, Nephele rescued
them and they were enabled to
ride away through the air on the
ram with the golden fleece, the
gift of Hermes. Helle fell off into
the sea as the ram was crossing the
strait into Europe and the sea into
which she fell was called after her
the Hellespont (the Sea of Helle).
Phrixus reached Colchis in safety,
sacrificed the ram to Zeus and gave
its fleece to King Aeëtēs who
fastened it to an oak-tree in the

*Phrixus riding on a ram across the
Hellespont, with Helle, fallen into the
sea. (Pompeian painting).*

Grove of Ares. For its capture by
Jason see **Argonauts.**

Pictī, a people inhabiting the
northern part of Britain. It is
supposed that the name (= the
' tattooed men ') was given to them
by the Romans because they
painted their bodies. Their name
frequently appears in later Roman
writers in connection with that of
the Scōtī—the ' Picts and Scots '
that we read of in our school
history books.
See Stevenson's *Heather Ale* for an
interesting legend about the Picts.

Pī′cus, a Latin prophetic divinity.
Virgil writes :
    " Latinus, aged king,
Son of Marica, the Laurentian
    nymph,
And Faunus, son of Picus, who
    for sire

Claims Saturn, first fount of this royal blood."

Legend says that Circe was in love with him and changed him into a woodpecker (Latin *picus* = woodpecker). This bird was sacred to Mars, so Picus is sometimes represented as a warlike king of Italy.

Pĭĕ′rĭa, a narrow slip of country on the S.E. coast of Macedonia. It was one of the earliest seats of the worship of the Muses.

Pope speaks of the fountain Hĭ′ppocrē′nē (i.e. Horse-spring) as ' the Pierian spring '.

Pĭ′ndar, c. 522–442 B.C., was regarded by the ancients as the greatest lyric poet of Greece. His extant poems, divided into four books, are all odes written in honour of victors in the Greek national games.

Gray calls his Odes *The Progress of Poesy* and *The Bard* " Pindaric Odes ". They are an imitation in structure and form of Pindar's triumphal odes. When warned that such austere poetry would never win popularity, Gray replied : " My taste for praise is not like that of children for fruit. If there were nothing but medlars and black-berries in the world, I could be very well content to go without any at all." In other words, nothing but the best would suffice for the fastidious Gray.

In one of his sonnets Milton asks the Royalist commander to spare the house in Aldersgate Street in which he was living, just as Alexander the Great, when he sacked Pindar's native Thebes in the course of his conquest of Greece, had spared the house of the Greek poet :

" Lift not thy spear against the Muses' bower :

The great Emathian conqueror bid spare
The house of Pindarus, when temple and tower
Went to the ground."

Pīrae′us, the most important harbour of Athens, about five miles S.W. of the city. In early days Piraeus used to be connected with Athens by two long walls, built at the instigation of Themistocles, some few remains of which are still standing. To-day an electric railway connects Athens with its harbour.

Pīrī′thŏus, son of Ixīŏn and king of the mythical Lăpĭthae in Thessaly. When he was celebrating his marriage with Hippodami′a, a Centaur carried her off, and this act occasioned the fight between the Centaurs and the Lapithae in which the Centaurs were defeated. His friendship with Theseus, the Athenian king, was proverbial. The two friends resolved to carry off Persĕ′phŏnē, queen of the lower world. They were seized by Pluto and chained to a rock. Heracles freed Theseus, but Pirithous was left bound on the wheel on which his father had suffered.

Plă′to (428–347 B.C.), the Greek philosopher. In his twentieth year he is said to have become a pupil of Socrates and one of his most ardent admirers. After Socrates' death in 399 he went to Megara and later visited Sicily. There is a story that the elder Dionysius disliked Plato's freedom of speech so much that he had him sold as a slave. On his return to Athens he taught (without fee) in the gymnasium of the Academy and in his own garden at Colō′nus. The writings of Plato are in the form of dialogue, Socrates being represented as the leader of the discussions. Plato's method of teaching is called the ' Socratic ' method. It elicits truth by question and answer. His dialogues number 35. One of the most famous is the *Phae'do* which gives an account of the trial and death of Socrates and includes a discussion on the immortality of the soul.

Plau'tus, the most celebrated comic poet of Rome. In his younger days he was desperately poor and was obliged to seek work from a baker who employed him in turning a handmill. When he was about thirty years of age he began to write comedies and continued to write them for forty years. Twenty of his plays are extant. He has been imitated by many modern poets. One of his plays, the *Menae'chmi,* turns on the comic situations arising from the likeness between a merchant's twin sons. It gave Shakespeare the main ideas for his extravagant farce, the *Comedy of Errors,* a story of two pairs of brothers so exactly alike that no one can tell them apart.

Pliny (*a*) The Elder. He was an intimate friend of the Emperor Vespasian. He perished in the eruption of Vesuvius which overwhelmed Herculā'nĕum and Pompēii in A.D. 79. The only work of his which has come down to us is his *Natural History* in 37 books.
(*b*) The Younger, nephew of the above. He was a rich, kind-hearted man with poor health. Ten books of his carefully written letters survive, and from them we learn many interesting facts in the life of his contemporaries. One of his letters gives an account of the eruption of Vesuvius and of his uncle's death. He wrote this letter to his friend Tacitus, the historian, who wanted a first-hand account of the eruption so that he might hand it down accurately to posterity.

Plū'tarch, the Greek biographer whose *Parallel Lives* of forty-six Greeks and Romans has immortalised his name. The Lives are arranged in pairs. Each pair contains the Life of a Greek and of a Roman and is followed by a comparison of the two men. The biographer gives a real portrait of the man and of the times in which he lived. The *Lives* was translated by a great Elizabethan, Sir Thomas North, not direct from the Greek but from the French of Bishop Amyot's version. Shakespeare read and studied North and turned some of his splendid prose into immortal verse : frequently he retained the very words of North's racy English. A study of *Julius Caesar, Coriolanus* or *Antony and Cleopatra,* together with relevant extracts from North's *Plutarch,* will show how deeply indebted the dramatist was to the illustrious translator of the Greek biographies.

Plū'to, a surname of Hades, the God of the Nether World.
See **Hades.**

Plū'tus, the personification of wealth, son of Dēmē'ter. That Wealth should be the son of the Earth-goddess expresses the idea that riches come from the earth—primarily from agriculture, but also from metals.

Plu'vius, a surname of Jupiter worshipped as the giver of rain.
A policy insuring the holder against the risk of a wet holiday is known as a " Jupiter Pluvius," or simply a " Pluvius " policy.

Po'llux. See **Dioscuri.**

Polyde'ctēs, King of Serīphos. See **Perseus.**

Polyhy′mnia, the Muse of Sublime Hymn. See **Muses.**

Polyphē′mus, one of the Cyclōpes. He is represented as a gigantic monster, having only one eye in the centre of his forehead. He dwelt in a cave near Mt. Aetna. When Odysseus was driven upon Sicily he would have been eaten by the Cyclops if he had not put out the eye of the monster while in a drunken sleep. Odysseus then escaped by concealing himself under the belly of one of the sheep of Polyphemus as they were driven out of the cave to feed.

Poly′xĕna, daughter of Priam and Hecuba, beloved by Achilles. When the Greeks, on their voyage home, were still lingering on the coast of Thrace, the shade of Achilles appeared to them, demanding that Polyxena should be sacrificed to him. Nĕopt′olĕmus, Achilles' son, accordingly sacrificed her on his father's tomb.

Pōmō′na, the Italian goddess of the fruit of trees. She is represented by the poets as beloved by several of the rustic divinities, such as Silvanus. (Lat. *Poma* = apples).

Pompē′ii, a city of Campania at the foot of Mt. Vesuvius. It was overwhelmed in A.D. 79, with Herculā′neum and Stăbĭae, by the great eruption of Vesuvius. The lava did not reach Pompeii, but the town was covered with successive layers of ashes. Thus a great part of it has been preserved with its market-places, theatres, baths, temples and private houses, and the excavation of these has thrown much light upon all subjects connected with the private life of the ancient Romans.

For an interesting account of Roman life at the time of the eruption see Bulwer Lytton's *The Last Days of Pompeii.*

Pompey (106–48 B.C.), a successful Roman general. He received the surname of ' Great ' on his return to Rome victorious over the Numidians. After service in Spain he was given the task of ridding the Mediterranean of pirates : in forty days he cleared the western sea and restored communication between Spain, Africa and Italy. Next year (66) he defeated Mithridā′tes. Altogether he had three triumphs—for his victories in Africa, in Europe and in Asia. But he was no statesman. In 60 he joined Caesar and Crassus in the first triumvirate, and married Caesar's daughter Julia ; but it gradually became clear to him that a struggle must take place sooner or later between him and Caesar. Civil war broke out between them and Pompey was heavily defeated in 48 at Pharsālus. He escaped to Egypt, but as he was landing he was stabbed in the back by one of his former centurions.

For Caesar's " triumph over Pompey's blood " see the speech of the tribune Marullus in *Julius Caesar* i, i, 36–56.

Pontius Pilate, procurator (or Roman Governor) of Judaea from A.D. 26 to 36. The Jews regarded him as an obstinate and savagely cruel man. His conduct was responsible for insurrection at Jerusalem and in Samaria. In N.T. our interest is fixed on his conduct at the trial of our Lord. Mark's account (15^{1-15}) is concise. Jesus, condemned by the Sanhedrin for blasphemy, is brought bound to Pilate. Pilate begins his examination by asking : " Art thou the King of the Jews ? " and Jesus answers : " Thou sayest "—an answer which it is difficult to understand as anything less than an admission of the truth of the charge. Yet no formal sentence follows, only a prolonged accusation which is met with such resolute silence on the part of the Prisoner as to astonish the judge. The advent of the people to claim the release of a convict causes a diversion. Pilate endeavours to secure the escape of Jesus from the malice of the chief priests by a popular vote, and henceforth the matter is one between him and the people. They choose Barabbas, and repeatedly demand the crucifixion of Jesus, and prevail.

Matthew adds the account of Pilate's wife's dream and of the washing of Pilate's hands before the multitude. Luke explains how the religious charge, on which our Lord had been condemned by the Sanhedrin, was transformed into the political charge on which he was tried by Pilate. Luke also brings out strongly the efforts Pilate made to secure the release of his Prisoner. To Pilate the situation was merely one of rivalry between religious teachers. But if he did not yield to the popular clamour there might be an outburst, and as a Roman official he must avoid uproar at any cost. To him the risk of riot far outweighed possible lack of justice to an obscure Jew.

The tradition that Pilate was buried on Mt. Pilatus near Lucerne, or that he committed suicide there, cannot possibly have any foundation.

Po'rsen(n)a, King of the Etruscan town of Clusium. He marched against Rome at the head of a vast army to restore Tarquinius Superbus to the throne. He took possession of the hill Jānĭ'cŭlum, and would have entered the city by the bridge, the Pons Sublĭ'cĭus (i.e. the bridge on piles), which connected Rome with the Janiculum, had it not been for the prowess of Horatius Coclēs who kept the whole Etruscan army at bay while his comrades broke down the bridge behind him. Such was the tale by which Roman vanity concealed one of the earliest and greatest disasters of the city.

Macaulay tells the story in his spirited poem "Horatius", the best known of his *Lays of Ancient Rome*.

See **Cocles**.

Portland Vase, The. One of Keats's most marvellous poems, even among his marvellous odes, is that "On a Grecian Urn." The poet had been to the British Museum where he had seen and obviously handled some Grecian vases. His keen poetic imagination then seems to have made an amalgam of their varied beauty, and the result is a "flowery tale"

The Portland Vase. (*British Museum*). *The material used consists of a ground of dark blue glass, and an upper layer of opaque white glass, in which the design was engraved.*

as exquisite as the Greek sculptures themselves.

One of these artistic gems is the Portland Vase, bought in 1786 by the Duke of Portland. "The material of the vase was composed of two layers of glass, white over dark blue, and then the white was ground away by hand, so as to leave the design in white upon the blue background, a scheme of decoration imitated with great success by the Wedgwood artists. . . . This priceless treasure was smashed to pieces by an insane visitor. It has, however, been repaired with great skill." (Stobart : *The Glory that was Greece.*)

Among the priceless objects of art in Holland House, Kensington, is the vase known as the ' Holland House Urn.' It " exhibits a sacrifice, twelve human figures and two animals, a hog and a bull. In the midst stands an altar with fruit upon it, upon which the priest is apparently laying a cake. A person stands above it playing a pipe. Another raises the axe to slay the sacrifice. There are other attendant figures and two trees depicted on the part of the urn forming the etching " (A. C. Downer : *The Odes of Keats*). A comparison between the poem and this description of the urn would seem to settle the main source of Keats's inspiration for his Ode.

Posei′dōn, called Neptūnus by the Romans, was the god of the sea. His brothers were Zeus and Hades. He was the implacable foe of the Trojans because Lāo′medon refused to give him (and Apollo) the reward stipulated for their building the walls of Troy for him. He was hostile to Odysseus, who had blinded his son Polyphē′mus, and prevented him from returning home. Altogether he is a violent and ill-tempered deity, a blend of the

god of the earthquake or the wind with a sea-deity of the country that the Greeks came to occupy. His wife was the Nē′rĕid Amphi-

Poseidon. (*From a medal*). *The god of the sea is a standing figure (as usual in art) with the trident. He has a cloak thrown over his left arm.*

trī′tē and their son the merman Trīton. The symbol of Poseidon's power was the trident, very like that held by the figure of Britannia on our copper coins.

Potiphar, an officer of Pharaoh's household and the captain of the guard, possibly an Egyptian who had risen to a high position under the foreign dynasty of the " Shepherd " Kings. He seems to have been a wealthy man with a considerable establishment the direction of which he gave to Joseph. Potiphar's wife tempted Joseph and made a false accusation against him. He was thrown into prison where he gained further favour, especially as an interpreter of dreams.

Praxī′tĕles, a native of Athens, and one of the greatest Greek sculptors. His most beautiful work, in the estimation of ancient writers, was his marble statue of Aphrodī′tē of which the Venus de' Medici is an imitation. His skill in delineating beauty of form can best be seen in his statue of Apollo, bearing the infant Dionysus on his left arm and holding up (probably) a bunch of grapes in his right hand. This statue was found in 1877 and is now in the museum at Olympia.

Pri'am, son of Lāo'medon, husband of He'cuba, and King of Troy at the time of the Trojan war. When the Greeks landed on the Trojan coast Priam was already advanced in years and took no active part in the war. After Hector's death, accompanied by Hermes he went to Achilles' tent to ransom his son's body for burial and obtained it. After the fall of Troy the aged King put on his armour and was on the point of rushing against the enemy; but he was persuaded by Hecuba to take refuge with her as a suppliant at the altar of Zeus. But his son Pŏli'tes, pursued by Pyrrhus, rushed into the temple and died at his father's feet; whereupon Priam, overcome with indignation, hurled his spear with feeble hand against Pyrrhus and was killed by him.

Pricks, to kick against the. In the course of his defence before King Agrippa at Caesarea, Paul gave an account of his conversion. He said he had heard a voice from heaven saying : " Saul, Saul, why persecutest thou me ? It is hard for thee to kick against the pricks (R.V. the goad) " (*Acts* 26[14]).

The ordinary ox-goad in Palestine is a long stick with a pointed iron shoe.

The proverb is of Greek and Latin origin and means ' to resist to one's own hurt ', as an ox would if he were to kick against his master's goad.

See the third section of R. L. Stevenson's *Travels with a Donkey*

for an eloquent defence of the use of the goad.

Pri'scian, Roman grammarian of the sixth century.

" To break Priscian's head " is to violate a grammatical rule. Holofernes, the schoolmaster in *Love's Labour's Lost*, criticizes the Latin of Sir Nathaniel the Curate, saying "Priscian ! a little scratched : 'twill serve ", i.e. " Your Latin is somewhat mutilated "—' false Latin ', as he calls it a few lines later.

"Some free from rhyme or reason, rule or check,
Break Priscian's head and Pegasus's neck."
Pope : *The Dunciad*.

Pro'cnē, see **Pandion**.

Procru'stēs, i.e. ' The Stretcher ', a mythical robber who used to tie upon a bed all travellers who fell into his hands. If they were shorter than the bed, he stretched their limbs until they were of the same length. If they were longer than the bed, he made them of the same length by cutting off part of their limbs. He was slain by Theseus.

The ' bed of Procrustes ' has become proverbial = complete uniformity. The adjective ' Procrustean ' (reducing to a uniform standard by violent means) most aptly applies to the products, both human and material, of our present-age mass-produced civilization.

Prodigal Son, a reckless squanderer who returns home repentant. See *Luke* 15[11-32].

Among Shakespearean references to the parable are :

(i) In *As You Like It* Orlando makes this retort to his brother Oliver : " Shall I keep your hogs

and eat husks with them ? What prodigal portion have I spent that I should come to such penury ? " and (ii) in 1 *Henry IV* Falstaff refers to his pressed men as " fattened prodigals lately come from some swine-keeping, from eating draff (i.e. offal) and husks."
See **The Fatted Calf.**

Prōmē′thēus (i.e. Forethought), a Titan, brother of Atlas and Epimē′thēus (i.e. Afterthought). He made man out of clay, and when Zeus oppressed mankind he stole fire from heaven for their benefit. Displeased at being outwitted by the cunning Prometheus Zeus caused Hēphae′stus to fashion a woman out of clay [see **Pandora**] and gave her, not to Prometheus who foresaw the trouble she would cause, but to his brother Epimetheus. In her box she brought all kinds of diseases and sufferings which were unleashed on mankind when it was opened. Further, Zeus chained Prometheus to a rock on Mt. Caucasus where a vulture in the daytime fed on his liver which grew again each succeeding night. Heracles killed the vulture and so freed Prometheus.

Elizabethan dramatists freely talk of ' Promethean fire ' and Shakespeare makes Othello say to Desdemona just before he stifles her :
" Once put out thy light,
I know not where is that Promethean heat
That can thy light relume "
(*Othello*, v, 2, 10-12).
The *Prometheus Bound* of Aeschylus makes magnificent reading in Gilbert Murray's verse translation. Shelley's lyrical drama *Prometheus Unbound* is more difficult. Charles Kingsley puts the story of the two brothers into the mouth of Mother Carey in the penultimate chapter of his delightful *Water Babies*.

Prŏpo′ntis, the small sea between the Hellespont and the Bosporus, now called the sea of Marmora.

Proser′pina. See **Persephone.**

Prōtesilā′us. See **Laodamia.**

Prō′tēus, the prophetic old man of the sea, is described in the earliest legends as a subject of Posei′don, whose flocks (the seals) he tended. Virgil places his dwelling in the island of Cār′păthos, between Crete and Rhodes. (Hence Milton calls Proteus " the Carpathian wizard.") At midday Proteus would rise from the sea and sleep in the shadow of the rocks. Anyone wishing to learn the future from him was obliged to catch hold of him at that time. As soon as he was seized, he assumed every possible shape (" a bristly boar, a deadly tiger, a scaly serpent or a lioness with tawny neck : . . . the fierce roar of flame . . . fleeting water " (Virgil's fourth *Georgic*). But whenever he saw that his endeavours were of no avail, he resumed his usual form and told the truth.

The adjective protean = changeable, shifting, even versatile.

Psȳ′chē was the youngest of three daughters of a king, and by her beauty excited the jealousy of Venus. Cupid fell in love with her and visited her every night, unseen and unknown, and left her as soon as day began to dawn. Her jealous sisters made her believe that he was a hideous monster. So, one night, while Cupid was asleep, she drew near to him with a lamp. A drop of hot oil fell from her lamp upon his shoulder. This awoke Cupid who fled. Psyche wandered about from temple to temple, inquiring after her lover, and at length came to the palace of Venus. There her real sufferings began, for Venus treated her as a slave and imposed the most impossible tasks on her. Cupid invisibly assisted her and at length she overcame the jealousy of Venus. At Cupid's request Jupiter made her immortal : she was carried to heaven where she was united to Cupid for ever.

This may be regarded as an allegory in which Psyche is the human soul, purified by misfortunes and thereby prepared for the enjoyment of true and pure happiness.

Wm. Morris re-tells the story in the *Earthly Paradise.* See also Robert Bridge's *Eros and Psyche.*

Punic Faith, i.e. faithlessness. The Carthaginians were of Phoenician origin and in consequence Roman writers commonly called them ' Poeni '. The Romans regarded them as proverbially unreliable, without the slightest idea of what they themselves meant by *fides,* or loyalty.

Cf. the similar exchange of charges of bad faith made by French and English : e.g. ' to take French leave ' = ' filer à l' anglais(e) '

Pygmā'lion, a legendary King of Cyprus who is said to have fallen in love with the ivory image of a maiden which he himself had made. At his request Aphrodī'tē breathed life into it and " graced with her presence the marriage she had made."

William Morris tells the story in his *Earthly Paradise.* Gilbert calls his comedy *Pygmalion and Galatea* " an original mythological comedy." When Bernard Shaw wrote a play about a flower-girl being trained by a Professor of Phonetics to pass for a Duchess, he gave it the title *Pygmalion.*

Pygmies. The Greek *pygmē* is a measure of length, the distance from the elbow to the knuckles, just over 13 inches. The Pygmies were fabulous people of this height, first mentioned by Homer as dwelling on the shores of Ocean and attacked by cranes in springtime. Legend represents them as cutting down individual ears of corn with hatchets, and going out to battle against the cranes, mounted on tiny goats and lambs. They are said to have attacked Heracles in much the same way as the Lilliputians attacked the sleeping Gulliver, and to have climbed up his goblet by means of tiny ladders. They were, indeed, the legendary forebears of Swift's resourceful manikins.

Explorers of Africa between the Congo and the Upper Nile have discovered dwarfish races ; but these are races in which the average male stature does not exceed 4 feet 9 inches—veritable giants compared with the pygmies of classical legend.

Pȳ'ladēs. See **Orestes.**

Pȳ'los, the legendary home of Nestor, on the W. coast of the Peloponnesus.

Py'ramus. See **Thisbe.**

Py'rrha. See **Deucalion.**

Py'rrhus. See **Neoptolemus.**

Pȳtha'goras, philosopher and mathematician of Samos in the 6th century B.C. He is said to have evolved the doctrine of the " music of the spheres " which he believed to be unheard by men. This doctrine is frequently referred to by Shakespeare and by Milton, e.g. *The Merchant of Venice,* v, 1, 60–65 ; *The Nativity Ode,* 125–132. Pythagoras taught the doctrine of the transmigration of souls from one man, at his death, into another man and into animals, and from animals to men. In *Twelfth Night*, as though to test the sanity of the Puritan Malvolvio, the Clown asks him :

Clown : What is the opinion of Pythagoras concerning wild fowl ?

Mal. : That the soul of our grandam might haply inhabit a bird.

Malvolvio's Puritanism is deeply offended at such a pagan question, and he " no way approves his opinion." See also *A.Y.L.I.*, iii, 2, 157. Young students will remember Pythagoras best from his mathematical discovery that " the square on the hypotenuse of a right-angled triangle is equal to the sum of the squares on the other two sides "—Euclid I, 47, to our grandfathers.

Py'thia, the priestess of Apollo at Delphi.
See **Delphi.**

Py'thŏn, the serpent which was produced from the mud left on the earth after the deluge of Deucalion. He lived in the caves of Mt. Parnassus, and was slain by Apollo who founded the Pythian Games in commemoration of his victory.

Rachel, Jacob's wife and mother of Joseph and Benjamin. The incidents of her life are to be found in *Gen.* 29–33, 35. Her death in giving birth to Benjamin and Jacob's deep grief and ever-living regret all help to make up a touching story which has kept her memory alive. *Jeremiah* 31^{15} describes Rachel in her tomb in the cave of Machpelah weeping over the fate of her descendants who are about to be carried off into captivity by the Chaldeans : " A voice was

heard in Ramah, lamentation and bitter weeping : Rachel weeping for her children refused to be comforted for her children, because they were not." *Matthew* (2$^{17-18}$) goes further and applies God's promised purpose for his chosen, Rachel's descendants, to the lamentation of the mothers of Israel over the slaughter of the Innocents by Herod.

Charles Lamb describes the well-to-do mothers of many young children, clandestinely abducted from their homes to be turned into chimney-sweeps, as " many noble Rachels mourning for their children."

Ravens. Elijah was fed by Ravens.
See **Widow's Cruse, The.**

Regil'lus, Lake, memorable for the victory gained on its banks by the Romans over the Latins, 498 B.C. Legend has it that the twin gods, Castor and Pollux, rode in front of the Roman cavalry as they charged. That same day at evening they appeared in the Forum and, after washing the foam from the backs of their horses, announced to the waiting crowds that the Romans were the victors.

See Macaulay's spirited lay " The Battle of the Lake Regillus." This is how the poet describes the strange horsemen :

" He [Aulus the Dictator] was
 aware of a princely pair
 That rode at his right hand.
So like they were, no mortal
 Might one from other know :
White as snow their armour was :
 Their steeds were white as
  snow..
Never on earthly anvil
 Did such rare armour gleam ;
And never did such gallant
 steeds
  Drink of an earthly stream."

Rĕ'mus. See **Rōmulus.**

Rhădăma'nthus, son of Zeus and Europa and brother of King Minos of Crete. In fear of his brother he fled into Boeotia where he married Alcmēne. According to Homer, he lived in Elysium ; but later tradition makes him one of the judges of the dead, because he had in life been notable for wisdom and justice.

Rhe'a, a Greek nature-goddess, later identified with the Phrygian goddess Cy'belē, the ' Great

Rhea, or Cybele. (From a Roman lamp). As giver of wealth, Rhea became recognised in the great cities ; hence her crown of walled cities. She is enthroned, with cymbals in her hand and lions at her feet.

Mother '. She is represented as the (sister and) wife of Cronos, and the mother of Dēmē'ter, Hera, Hades, Posei'don and Zeus.

Rhē'a Si'lvia, the mother of Rō'mulus and Rēmus, the legendary founders of Rome. Amū'lius, the last of the traditional Alban kings, ousted his elder brother, Nu'mitor, the rightful king, whose

daughter, Rhēa Silvia, he prevented from marrying by making her a Vestal Virgin. But she gave birth to the twin sons, whose father according to the legend was Mars himself. In his fear and anger Amulius ordered the mother to be imprisoned for ever, and the baby boys to be thrown into the Tiber.
See **Romulus.**

Rhē'nus, the Latin name for the river we call the Rhine.

Rhē'sus, a Thracian king who assisted the Trojans. An oracle had declared that Troy would never be taken if the snow-white horses of Rhesus should once drink the water of the Xanthus and feed upon the grass of the Trojan plain. But as soon as Rhesus had reached the Trojan territory and had pitched his tents late at night, Odysseus and Diomē'dēs penetrated his camp, slew Rhesus and carried off his horses.

The story is told in Book X of *The Iliad,* and in *Rhesus,* an early play by Euripides.

Rhŏ'dănus, the Latin name for the river we call the Rhone.

Rhodes, the most easterly island of the Aegean Sea. At the entrance to the harbour of the city of Rhodes was the famous statue of the Sungod, the Colossus, the work of the native sculptor Charēs, which was overthrown by an earthquake.

Rivers of Hades.
Milton catalogues them in *Paradise Lost :*
" Four infernal rivers, that
disgorge
Into the burning lake their
baleful streams—
Abhorréd Styx, the flood of
deadly hate ;

Sad Acheron of sorrow, black
    and deep ;
Cocytus, named of lamentation
    loud
Heard on the rueful stream ;
    fierce Phlegethon,
Whose waves of torrent fire
    inflame with rage.
                    Bk. ii, 575–81.

In *Doctor Faustus,* Faust swears
    " by the kingdoms of infernal
    rule,
Of Styx, of Acheron, and the
    fiery lake
Of ever-burning Phlegethon."

Rod. In the East the rod or
staff was the symbol of travel. A
typical instance of this is to be
found in the instructions given for
the rite of the Passover (*Ex.* 12[11]) :
" Thus shall ye eat it : with your
loins girded, your shoes on your
feet, and your staff in your hand ;
and ye shall eat it in haste." The
shepherd of the Bible carries both
rod and staff : " thy rod and thy
staff they comfort me " (*Ps.* 23[4]).
Here the rod is a club or mace
with a rounded head, a weapon of
defence against robbers or wild
beasts ; the staff is a pole, like
an alpenstock, for aid in climbing,
for clearing a way through under-
growth, or for dealing with refrac-
tory animals. The staff is sometimes a symbol of authority, e.g.
the staff in the hand of the Angel
of the Lord (*Judges* 6[21]). A shepherd counted his sheep by passing
them " under the rod " as they
entered the fold (see *Lev.* 27[32]).
According to legend Joseph of
Arimathaea came to England and
planted his rod at Glastonbury in
Somersetshire, since when it has
been miraculously preserved and
blossoms every Christmas.

Rome. It is often said that Rome
is built on seven hills. It is true
that on the left bank of the Tiber
there is a group of low hills which
rise somewhat steeply from the
river and which afforded useful
means of defence to early settlers.
These eminences are of volcanic
origin and have been carved out
by erosion. Three have thus
become isolated hills—the Palatine,
the Aventine and the Capitoline—
all defensible positions. The other
four are hills only when seen from
the river-valley. Ancient Rome
centred round these ' Seven Hills '
—hence the ' City of the Seven
Hills '.

Rome. For various topics, see
under the following :

(*a*) *Legendary history :* **Rhea
Silvia ; Romulus.**

(*b*) *Early history :* **Lars Porsena ;
Horatius, Coriolanus.**

(*c*) *Fora,* i.e. open spaces of
ground, paved with stones, surrounded by buildings and used as
market-places or for the transac-
tion of public business : **Forum.**

(*d*) *Campi,* i.e. open spaces, or
plains : **Campus Martius.**

(*e*) *Temples :* **Janus, Pantheon.**

(*f*) *Circuses :* **Circus Maximus.**

(*g*) *Amphitheatres :* **Colosseum.**

(*h*) *Gardens :* the *horti Caesaris*
on the right bank of the Tiber
which Caesar bequeathed to the
people (see *Julius Caesar* iii, 2, 252) :
" Moreover, he hath left you all
    his walks,
His private arbours and new-
    planted orchards,
On this side Tiber : he hath left
    them you,
And to your heirs for ever—
    common pleasures,
To walk abroad and recreate
    yourselves."

(*i*) *Roads leading out of Rome :*
Appian Way.

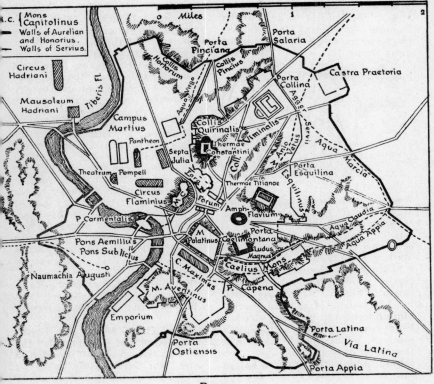

Rome.

Rŏ′mulus, traditional founder of Rome. For the birth of Romulus and his twin Remus see **Rhea Silvia.** The children were discovered in a she-wolf's den by the King's shepherd, Faustulus, who handed them over to the care of his wife. When they grew up, they discovered their parentage, slew Amū′lius the king and placed their grandfather Nu′mitōr on the throne. They themselves determined to found a city on the banks of the Tiber. They quarrelled about the place where the new city should be built and the quarrel was decided by augury in favour of Romulus, who proceeded to mark out his city and to build its wall. Remus leapt over the wall in scorn and was slain by his brother. As soon as his city was built, Romulus found his people too few, so he set apart a sanctuary on the Capitoline hill in which homicides and runaway slaves might take refuge. The city thus became filled with men, but they needed women. Romulus therefore invited his neighbours, the Latins and Sabines, to a festival during which the Roman youths rushed upon their guests and carried off the maidens (Rape of the Sabine

Women). Ultimately the Romans and Sabines agreed to unite under Romulus as king. After reigning thirty-seven years he was taken away from the world. He was

Romulus and Remus suckled by the Wolf. (From the Etruscan bronze statue in the Capitol).

reviewing his people in the Campus Martius when the sun was suddenly eclipsed and a dreadful storm dispersed them. When daylight returned, Romulus had disappeared, for his father, Mars, had carried him up to heaven in a fiery chariot. From heaven he sent his people a message, telling them that it was the wish of the gods that they should become the greatest nation on earth provided they devoted themselves to the arts of war.

Rose of Sharon.

" I am the rose of Sharon and the lily of the valleys " (Solomon). The eastern flower has not been identified, but Hebrew scholars have decided that the " rose " must be a bulbous flower, possibly Autumn crocus (i.e. colchicum), asphodel or narcissus. The narcissus abounds in the plain of Sharon.

Rosetta Stone,

a ' stēlē ' or pillar, so called because found (by Napoleon's troops) in 1798 near Rosetta in the Nile delta. It is now in the British Museum. On it is inscribed an Egyptian decree in Egyptian hieroglyphics (as well as in demotic or popular characters), with a version in Greek underneath. The importance of the discovery is the fact that the stone furnished the key with which scholars have been enabled to decipher the hieroglyphics of Ancient Egypt and thereby to unravel many secrets of the Bible.

Ru'bicon,

a small Italian river falling into the Adriatic and forming the boundary in the republican period between the province of Cisalpine Gaul and Italy proper. By crossing it at the head of his army in 49 B.C. Caesar passed beyond the limits of his own province and so declared war against the republic. *Jacta alea esto* (let the die be cast) he is alleged to have said as he came to his decision.

Figuratively, ' to cross the Rubicon ' is to adopt a measure from which it is not possible to recede.

Rule, The Golden.

Our Lord's summary of the teaching of " the law and the prophets " is referred to as " the Golden Rule " :

" All things whatsoever ye would that men should do unto you, do ye even so unto them " (*Matt.* 7¹²).

Ruth.

The story of Ruth is told in a prose idyll of great beauty. Famine in Judah had compelled Elimelech of Bethlehem to go to the land of Moab with his wife Naomi and his two sons. One son married Ruth and the other Orpah, both Moabite women. The sons died and on Elimelech's death Naomi, after ten years in Moab, resolved to return to Judah where there was again plenty. Ruth went with her, but Orpah was induced to remain in Moab. When Naomi and Ruth reached Bethlehem at the beginning of the barley harvest,

Ruth went out to glean in the field of Boaz, a wealthy man and a near kinsman of Elimelech. Upon hearing who Ruth was and of her kindness to her mother-in-law, Boaz treated her with the utmost consideration and helped Naomi to regain her lost inheritance. Ultimately he married Ruth. Their son Obed was father of Jesse, King David's father.

In his " Ode to a Nightingale " Keats suggests that the nightingale's song may have cheered the young Moabite widow :
" Perhaps the selfsame song that
found a path
Through the sad heart of Ruth,
when, sick for home,
She stood in tears amid the
alien corn."
But Ruth was not " sick for home," nor did she weep. Indeed the main part of the Biblical narrative emphasises her choice to stay with Naomi in Bethlehem. Moreover, nightingales were never to be found in Judea.

Sabbath's Day's Journey.

The Law of Moses forbad Jews to travel on the Sabbath further than the distance between the Ark and the extreme limit of the camp—about two-thirds of a mile, i.e. they were not allowed to leave the camp on the Sabbath day. Later, when they had emerged from the wilderness and began to live in cities, the law was extended : they were then not allowed to leave the precincts of the city.

" The mount called Olivet, which is nigh unto Jerusalem, a sabbath day's journey off." (*Acts* 1¹²).
Hence a ' Sabbath day's journey ' means a short and easy one, and is so used by Milton in *Samson Agonistes*, " no journey of a sabbath day."

Sadducees, a sect or school among the Jews at the time of Christ, much more prominently political than religious. Their Hebrew name means ' the just ', ' the righteous ', and they claimed to be the " true righteous ones " as opposed to the Pharisees. Their distinctive religious doctrines consisted mainly of negations. They denied that the Israelites possessed an oral law transmitted to them by Moses. They denied immortality and the resurrection of the dead. They denied the existence of angel or spirit. They rapidly disappeared from history after the first century, and thereafter among the Jews the opinions of the Pharisees exclusively predominated. It is worth noting how sects like the Pharisees and the Sadducees, opposed to each other both in religious and in political beliefs, were united in their hostility to the teaching of Christ. See, for example, *Matt.* 16¹⁻⁴, how they combined in tempting Him to shew them a sign from heaven.

Sa'lamis, an island off the coast of Attica, from which it is separated by a narrow channel. Here in 480 B.C. a great battle was fought in which the Persian fleet of Xerxes was defeated by the Greeks. Xerxes himself witnessed the battle from a spur of Mount Aegä'leos, opposite the island.

" A king sate on the rocky brow
Which looks o'er sea-born
Salamis ;
And ships, by thousands, lay
below,
And men in nations ;—all were
his !
He counted them at break of
day—
And when the sun set, where
were they ?
Byron : *Don Juan, III,* lxxxvi.

Sallust (Gaius Sallustius Crispus) 86–34 B.C., the Roman historian. His surviving works are :

(i) The *Catilīna*, a history of the conspiracy of Catiline during the consulship of Cicero, 63, B.C.

(ii) The *Jugurtha*, a history of the war the Romans waged against Jugurtha, King of Numidia (111–106 B.C.).

Salt. As a preservative salt became the emblem of constancy. Hence a ' covenant of salt ' (e.g. *Lev.* 2¹³) was binding. Salt was a symbol of life and vigour (*Matt.* 5¹³) : " Ye are the salt of the earth : but if the salt have lost his savour wherewith shall it be salted ? " Salt earth produced nothing, for the salt is not " fit for the land." Hence the sites of cities when destroyed were sown with salt (*Judges* 9⁴⁵). Cf. the state of the island of Walcheren when the dykes had been bombed to let in the sea-water during the German occupation.

Sa′mos, one of the principal islands of the Aegean Sea. It was the birthplace of the philosopher Pȳtha′goras. The capital city, also called Samos, had many splendid buildings, especially the Temple of Hera.

Samothrā′ce, a small island midway between Troas and Neapolis (*Acts* 16¹¹). A famous statue, called " The Winged Victory of Samothrace," was found on the island some seventy years ago. It is now in the Louvre.

See **Victory, Statues of.**

Samson, Judge of Israel for twenty years. For his life teeming with exploits see *Judges* cc. 13–16. " From first to last his story is

that of an utterly selfish and unscrupulous adventurer. . . . It is only redeemed from the staleness and vulgarity of commonplace rascality by the elements of supernatural strength, headlong valour, and a certain grim humour . . . the grotesque figure of this swaggering, hectoring bully . . . a sort of Hebrew Rob Roy whose choleric temper, dauntless courage and prodigious bodily strength marked him out as a champion of Israel in many a wild foray across the border into the rich lowlands of Philistia " (Frazer : *Folklore of the Old Testament*).

Milton's *Samson Agonistes* is a drama on classical lines of the last twenty-four hours of its hero's life, the day of vengeance when, in the words of Mark Pattison, " the idolatrous crew should be smitten with a swift destruction in the midst of their insolent revelry."

Statue of Winged Victory from Samothrace. (*Paris*).

Sanhedrin. The Great Sanhedrin was a body of 71 priests, elders and scribes, presided over by the " prince " or " partiarch " with an assessor as vice-president. This supreme Jewish Tribunal decided questions religious, criminal and civil. It was in session daily except Sabbaths and festivals, between the hours of morning and evening sacrifice.

Sappho (pronounced Saf'fo), a native of Lesbos, was a lyric poetess who wrote love poems in a great variety of metres. The ' Sapphic stanza ', which she is supposed to have invented, was used by Horace in many of his odes. In English light verse, use is sometimes made of a similar four-line stanza, the fourth line being a short one. Thus, from the " Knife-Grinder " of George Canning and J. H. Frere :

" Story ! God bless you ! I have
none to tell, sir,
Only last night a-drinking at the
Chequers,
This poor old hat and breeches,
as you see, were
Torn in a scuffle."

In a notable poem in which he says in effect that Greek poetry is famous everywhere—except in Greece, Byron maintains that the poems of Sappho, along with Homer's epics and Anacreon's love-songs, no longer find favour in the Isles of Greece.

In *South Wind* Mr. Norman Douglas refers to an eccentric French lady, a lyric poetess, who built a house for herself near a precipice which she thought " might come in handy," for " she craved to die like Sappho, her ideal." But " she died, at a patriarchal age, in her bed, after writing a scholarly pamphlet to prove that the tale of Sappho's leap over the famous silvery crag was a myth."

Sarpē'don, a Lycian prince. In the Trojan war he was an ally of the Trojans, and was slain by Patro'clus. By command of Zeus Apollo cleansed Sarpedon's body from blood and dust, covered it with ambrosia, and gave it to Sleep and Death to carry into Lycia, there to be honourably buried.

Satan, the name of the principal evil spirit. The word signifies *adversary,* or *accuser.* Thus Satan is he who calumniates God to man and man to God with the object of setting them at variance.

Cf. **Devil.**

Sa'turn, an old Italian god of agriculture, especially connected with seed-time and harvest. Popular tradition made him a king of Italy who introduced agriculture and consequently the arts of civilized life into his country. He is represented as wedded to Ops, the goddess of plenty and fertility. Later, he became identified with the Greek Cronus who in one of his aspects was a harvest god. His reign is the " golden age " of Italy, the time of universal peace, innocence and prosperity—the ideal state of society.

His festival, the Saturnalia, was held towards the end of December as a sort of harvest-home. During the festival no public business could be transacted, the law-courts and schools were closed and special indulgences were granted to slaves. They were relieved of all ordinary work, were granted freedom of speech and partook of a banquet, attired in the clothes of their masters who waited upon them at table.

Satyrs, nature-deities of mountain forests and streams. They represented the vital powers of nature, with their bristly hair, nose broad and somewhat turned up, the ears pointed at the top like those of animals, small horns growing out of the top of the forehead and a tail like that of a horse or of a goat. The Roman poets confound the Satyrs with the Italian Fauni.

Scae'vŏla, a legendary hero of Rome in her early days. C. Mūcius, a young patrician, resolved to murder Porsena who was blockading Rome. He was captured and when threatened with death he thrust his right hand into a fire and held it there without flinching. Porsena in admiration freed him and evacuated Roman territory. Mucius received the name of Scaevola, or left-handed, from the loss of his right hand in the fire.

Scaman'der, the celebrated river of the Troad. The story of the struggle between Achilles and the River is told in *Iliad* xxi. Despite aid from Poseidon and Athene, Achilles would have been overwhelmed if Hera had not urged her son Hēphae'stus to drive the river back with his " unwearying fire."

Scapegoat. On the day of atonement two goats were brought to the High Priest. By casting lots he chose one of them " for the Lord " and the other " for Azazel." The first goat was at once sacrificed; the second, the ' scapegoat ', was led off alive into the wilderness, bearing symbolically the sins of the Priest and of the people which the Priest by confession had transferred to it.

The phrase " for Azazel " is difficult. In the A.V. it is translated ' scape-goat '; but it is probable that ' Azazel ' is a proper name denoting an evil spirit inhabiting remote and desolate places.

A ' scape (i.e. escape) goat ' is a person who takes the blame for another's offence. A government minister is sometimes made the scapegoat for the errors of the Cabinet as a whole. Cf. the ' whipping-boy ' of the Stuart days who was educated with a prince and who took all the punishment that the prince should have had.

Sylvia Townsend Warner takes an unusual view of a scapegoat in her poem of that name which begins :
" See the scapegoat, happy beast,
    From every personal sin released,
    And in the desert hidden apart,
    Dancing with a careless heart."

Sci'pio, a celebrated Roman family, the most famous members of which were two who conquered the Carthaginians :
(i) Scipio Africānus major, in the Second Punic War, in which he gained a decisive victory over Hannibal in the battle of Zama, 202 B.C.
(ii) Scipio Africānus minor, in the Third Punic War, in which he destroyed Carthage in 146 B.C.

Scī'rōn, a legendary robber of Attica who compelled his victims on the Scironian rock to wash his feet and then kicked them into the sea. He was slain by Theseus.

Scribes. In the O.T. the term ' scribe ' has a very wide use. It includes any minor official—judicial, civil, military or industrial. Later, after the Captivity, it always denotes a professional student of Holy Scripture, an interpreter of the Law, especially of the Law of Moses. The N.T. equivalents are ' scribe ', ' lawyer ', ' doctor of the law'. They had two main functions : (i) to interpret and develop the law ; (ii) to train students of the law. Under (i) they added to the law by declaring a prevailing custom or tradition to be binding. Traditions so added were numerous, intricate, puerile and burdensome. The 'traditions of the elders and scribes' became more exacting than the original laws. Under (ii) the scribes assembled young men whom they trained in the oral and the written law. The teacher sat on a raised platform and the pupils sat on the ground at his feet. (See what Paul has to say in his defence (*Acts* 22³): " . . . brought up in this city (i.e. Jerusalem) at the feet of Gamaliel, and taught according to the perfect manner of the law of the fathers.") The teaching was in theory gratuitous, the teacher maintaining himself by some trade, but substantial fees were often exacted. The chief qualification of a pupil was a retentive memory. He was to be " like a well lined with cement, which loses not one drop." The scribe recited the exact words of his own teacher and his pupils repeated them after him until they knew them by heart. Our Lord's attitude to the scribes was unfavourable. See *Matt.* 5³⁰, 15, 23. It is remarked that Christ 'spoke with authority ', i.e. without bolstering up His arguments by quoting the opinions of learned predecessors, as the scribes did.

Scy′lla and Chăry′bdis. Scylla was a fearful monster, barking like a dog, with twelve feet and six long necks and heads each of which contained three rows of sharp teeth. She dwelt in a cave on the Italian rock (now called Promontory Scyllaeum). On the Sicilian side of the strait lived Charybdis who thrice every day swallowed down the waters of the sea and thrice threw them up again. They were a genuine terror to seamen of old who frequently fell into the clutches of the one

while trying to avoid the other. Neither, of course, presents any trouble to sailors of to-day. " To be between Scylla and Charybdis " is, therefore, to be between two extremes, either of which is difficult to avoid without falling foul of the other.

Scylla. (*From a coin of Agrigentum*). *Her barking voice was improved by later myths into dogs surrounding her lower limbs.*

Homer's story, as outlined above, may profitably be read in E. V. Rieu's translation of the *Odyssey* (Penguin), Book 12, especially lines 85–110. Failing this, Kingsley's *The Heroes* (Pt. v of " The Argonauts ") gives a succinct account.

Milton seems to have believed that these monsters could be charmed by the song of the Sirens :

Scylla wept,
And chid her barking waves into attention,
And fell Charybdis murmured soft applause.
(*Comus*, 257–9).

Scythians, a nomad people, shepherds or herdsmen, who had no fixed habitation but roamed over a vast tract of country at their pleasure and according to the wants of their cattle. They lived in a kind of covered wagons which a Greek poet describes as " lofty houses of wicker-work, on well-wheeled chariots." Some of their tribes had become more civilized : they learnt agriculture and, in the region now called Ukraine, they became a great corn-exporting country. The name ' Scythian ' is applied in Roman literature to the people and places N. of the Euxine, i.e. what we call to-day the Steppes of Southern Russia in Europe.

Secrecy. " When thou doest alms, let not thy left hand know what thy right hand doeth." This in-junction on almsgiving, from the Sermon on the Mount, has become proverbial for secrecy. Almsgiving, without the correct motive, is destitute of merit.

Selē'nē, called Lūna by the Romans, was the goddess of the moon, i.e. the moon personified as a divine being. She was a daughter of Hȳpe'rion and sister of Hē'lios and E'ōs. Like Helios, she drove across the heavens in a chariot drawn by two white horses. In later myths she was identified with A'rtemis or Diana.

See **Endymion.**

Sĕ'mĕlē, the mother of Dionȳ'sus (or Bacchus).

See **Dionysus.**

Se'neca (died A.D. 65), philo-sopher and author of twelve dia-logues, many letters and nine tragedies. He was tutor to the youthful Domitius (afterwards the emperor Nero) and became one of his chief advisers, exerting all his influence to check Nero's vices. He was accused of plotting against Nero. His wealth and gardens (superior to those of the emperor) and his disparagement of Nero's skill in driving and singing were all urged against him. Nero ordered him to take his own life, which he did with stoical if somewhat theatri-cal courage.

Seneca's prose appealed to the essayists Montaigne and Bacon. The titles of some of his so-called Dialogues are : On Anger, On Leisure, on Shortness of Life ; and his short, incisive sentences might well have been Bacon's model.

Septuagint, a Greek version of the O.T. made, according to legend, by 72 Jewish scholars (6 from each of the twelve tribes) in 72 days in a building specially erected on the island of Pharos off Alexandria.

Sepulchre, Whited. " Woe unto you, Scribes and Pharisees, hypo-crites, for ye are like unto sepul-chres, which outwardly appear beautiful, but inwardly are full of dead men's bones and of all un-cleanness " (*Matt.* 23²⁷). Jewish tombs were whitewashed so that passers-by might not unconsciously incur ceremonial defilement by coming in contact with them. Jewish law (*Num.* 19¹⁶) ordained : " Whosoever toucheth . . . a dead body, or a bone of a man, or a grave shall be unclean seven days."

In general, ' whited sepulchre ' is a term applied to a person who, under a fair exterior, conceals a foul mind, a hypocrite. When Morocco reads in the written scroll " Gilded tombs do worms infold " (*M.V.* 2, 7, 69). and when we read in Sonnet cɪ :

" it lies in thee
To make him much outlive a gilded tomb,"
we may well have Shakespeare's version of what the Jews of old meant by " whited sepulchres."

Sē'quănă, the Latin name for the river Seine.

Sē'rĭca, a country in the extreme E. of Asia (probably China) famous as the native region of the silkworm. The adjective *sēricus* gives us ' silken '.

Seven. In the Hebrew mind a mystical significance was attached in a peculiar degree to the number ' seven '. Its origin is probably to be found in the number of the days of the week, the fourth part of the lunar month being a convenient division of time. The seventh day, the sabbath, had an ever-increasing sanctity and hence gave to the number ' seven ' the mystical significance of holiness, perfection and completeness which it came to possess, as is seen from its usage in the Bible. Thus the number ' seven ' continually occurs in the O.T. regulations for worship (e.g. *Lev.* 4⁶). In his dreams Pharaoh saw ' seven well-favoured kine '' and '' seven other kine, ill-favoured '' ; '' seven ears of corn in one stalk, full and good '' and '' seven ears withered, thin and blasted with the east wind.'' While besieging Jericho Joshua said : '' Let seven priests bear seven trumpets of rams' horns before the ark of the Lord.'' In the early days of the Church the apostles appointed the office of deaconship to seven chosen men (*Acts* 6³). But frequently the sacred association of ' seven ' is dropped. In reply to Peter's question : '' How oft shall my brother sin against me, and I forgive him ? till seven times ? '' our Lord replied : '' I say not unto thee, Until seven times : but, Until seventy times seven '' (*Matt.* 18²¹,²²).

Sheep and goats. Speaking of the Final Judgement, St. Matthew says (25³²,³) : '' The Son of Man shall separate [all the nations] one from another, as the shepherd separateth the sheep from the goats : and he shall set the sheep on his right hand, but the goats on the left.'' By the ' sheep ' and the ' goats ' the evangelist means the ' good ' and the ' bad '. Similarly (13³⁸⁻⁹) Christ explains the ' wheat ' and the ' tares ' as '' the sons of the kingdom '' and '' the sons of the evil one.''

Shepherd. In the patriarchal age the Hebrews were nomads and practically every man was a shepherd. Flocks were tended not only by the sons of wealthy chiefs (e.g. Joseph's brethren, *Gen.* 37¹²), but even by their daughters (e.g. Rachel, *Gen.* 29⁶). The solitary and responsible nature of a shepherd's work tended to produce a strong, simple and devout type of character such as we see in David. His life was one of hardship and danger. He was exposed to the extremes of heat and cold (*Gen.* 31⁴⁰) ; he had to encounter the attacks of wild beasts (1 *Sam.* 17³⁴) and robbers (*Gen.* 31¹⁹). His equipment was simple : a mantle of sheep-skin ; a scrip or wallet containing a small quantity of food ; a sling and a staff. He supplied the flock with water, either at a running stream or at troughs attached to wells or cisterns (*Gen.* 29⁸). At evening he brought them back to the fold and counted them by passing them '' under the rod '' as they entered. Finally, he or a deputy (the ' hireling ' of *John* 10¹²) watched the entrance of the fold throughout the night (*John* 10³).

The word ' shepherd ' is often used metaphorically in the Bible. The ruler or prince came to be called '' the shepherd of his people.'' Our Lord appropriates the title pre-eminently to Himself : '' I am the good shepherd and know my sheep and am known of mine.''

Shewbread. Twelve cakes of unleavened bread, placed on the Table of Shewbread in two rows or piles, as a memorial offered to Jehovah. The cakes remained seven days and were changed every sabbath when the stale ones were eaten by the priests. Though the stale cakes might be eaten only by the priests, they were in an extreme case on the sabbath given by the priest at Nob to David and his young men (*1 Sam.* 21⁴⁻⁶). Christ answered the Pharisees who were grumbling at His disciples plucking and eating ears of corn on the sabbath day by referring them to this relaxation of the old Mosaic law in a case of necessity (*Matt.* 12³'⁴). If the priest of Nob was correct in what he did, how in similar circumstances could Christ's disciples be wrong ?

The Table of Shewbread was two cubits long, one broad and one and a half high. It was made of acacia wood overlaid with pure gold. Read *Exodus* 25²³⁻⁸.

Shibboleth, the test-word used by Jephthah to detect the fleeing Ephraimites at the fords of the Jordan. The dialect of Ephraim was evidently different from that of the pursuing Gileadites, and they unintentionally divulged their tribe by pronouncing the word ' sibboleth ' (*Judges* 12¹⁻¹⁶).

The word is now used to mean the watch-word of, e.g., a political party.

See *Samson Agonistes* 277–289 :
" . . . so many died
Without reprieve, adjudged to
death
For want of well pronouncing
Shibboleth."

Sibyls, The, prophetic women of Greek and Roman mythology. The earliest and most famous is the Cumaean Sibyl, who was consulted by Aeneas before he descended into the Lower World on his errand to see Anchises' shade.

The Sibylline Books were collections of oracles, probably written in Greek hexameters, which were consulted in time of national trouble. Legend says that the Cumaean Sybil offered nine volumes of these oracles to Tarqinius Superbus for 300 pieces of gold. When he refused to buy them she destroyed three and then offered him the remaining six at the same high price. Again Tarquin refused to buy and she destroyed a further three and again offered him the remainder at her original price. Tarquin then paid the gold for the three volumes. The books were kept in the temple of the Capitoline Jupiter and were destroyed when the temple was burnt in 82 B.C.

Sĭlē′nus, originally a Lydian deity (cf. the story of Midas), the god of springs and running water. Hence,

Silenus on a wine-skin. (*From a bronze statue at Naples*). *He is represented as an oldish man with shaggy hair and beard, seated astride on his wine-skin.*

like nymphs and other nature-deities, he had prophetic powers. In Greek poetry he is represented as the satyr-like attendant of Diony̆'sus. In art he is represented as an oldish man with shaggy hair and beard, crowned with ivy; sometimes he is seated astride on his wine-skin.

Silvā'nus, an Italian deity of the country. Woods and trees were his especial province, but he also presided over flocks and herds, from which he drove off wolves. A bronze tablet inscribed to the god Silvanus was unearthed at Colchester in Essex in September, 1946.

Simo'is, a river of the Troad. It joins the Scămă'nder in the Plain of Troy and then flows N. into the Hellespont.

Simony. Working independently but in some measure under the supervision of the Apostles in Jerusalem, Philip founded a church in Samaria and by his preaching and the working of miracles he was able to turn many of the heathen to Christianity. Among his converts was Simon who had ' amazed (i.e. bewildered) the Samaritans with his sorceries.' The East was (and is) full of magicians and sorcerers, most of whom were (and are) impostors; but we cannot reckon Simon as a charlatan. Later, Peter and John were sent from Jerusalem to consolidate Philip's good work, and when Simon saw that the gift of the Holy Ghost was bestowed ' by the laying on of the Apostles' hands ' he asked in all sincerity that he might buy this power. Peter severely rebuked him: " Thy money perish with thee because thou hast thought that the gift of God may be purchased with money. Thou hast neither part nor lot in this matter." The story leaves Simon praying against the consequences of his unconscious presumption (*Acts* 8⁹⁻²⁵).

Simony is traffic in sacred offices, the buying and selling of church appointments.

Si'nis, a robber who frequented the isthmus of Corinth and killed the travellers whom he captured by fastening them to the top of a fir-tree, which he bent down and then let spring up again. He himself was killed in this manner by Theseus.

Si'rens, fabulous sea-nymphs who had the power of charming by their songs all who heard them. When Odysseus, forewarned by Ci'rcē, came near their island, he stuffed the ears of his companions with wax and tied himself to the mast of his vessel until he was so far off that he could no longer hear their song. The Sirens are also connected with the legend of the Argonauts. When the Argonauts sailed by their island the Sirens began to sing, but in vain, for O'rpheus surpassed them. As it had been decreed that they should live only till someone hearing their song should pass by unmoved, they threw themselves into the sea and were changed into rocks.

In general, a *siren* is a dangerously fascinating temptress; but it seems rough luck on her and her class that the warning wail of the acoustic instrument we all came to loathe in the war should have been called a ' siren '.

Si'rius, the dog-star, which is at the height of its power in July and August. The " dog-days," the time when dogs were popularly believed to be most likely to go mad, became proverbial with the Romans as they are with us.

Odysseus and the Sirens. *(From a vase in the British Museum).* *Odysseus had himself fastened to the mast and filled the ears of his companions with wax so that they might not be attracted by the sirens' song.*

Milton calls Sirius " the swart star ", probably because during the dog-days people's complexions become ' swarthy ' under the influence of the sun.

Si'syphus. Some accounts make Sisyphus a son of Autolycus and the father of Odysseus and of Sinon—a lineage which would explain the cunning of these last two. As King of Corinth (which he is said to have founded) he promoted commerce, but he was fraudulent, avaricious, deceitful. Whatever his offences on earth— whether he betrayed the designs of the gods or contrived to chain Death whom Zeus had sent to fetch him—his punishment in the lower world was a hard one. His task was to roll uphill a huge stone which, as soon as it reached the top, " came bounding down again to level ground."

The adjective ' Sisyphean ' (= eternally laborious) is in use.

Sock, the soccus, the low shoe which did not fit closely and was not fastened. Shoes of this description were for use in the house

A comic actor wearing Socci. Cf. Cothurnus.

by both men and women. They were worn by comic actors.

' Sock ' and ' buskin ' are often used for ' Comedy ' and ' Tragedy '. Speaking of L'Allegro's pleasure in comedies, Milton refers to Jonson's ' learned sock ', i.e. the display of classical learning in his comedies. Il Penseroso's delight, on the other hand, was in ' the buskin'd stage ', i.e. in tragic drama.

See **Buskin**.

So'crates, the greatest of Athenian philosophers, 469–399 B.C. His physical constitution was robust : he went barefoot in all seasons of the year and the same homely clothing sufficed for him in winter as well as in summer. His wife was Xanthi'ppē, by repute a peevish, quarrelsome woman. Socrates believed that he had a religious mission, and thought that he constantly heard a prophetic or supernatural voice, interfering at times when he was about to do anything, not telling him what to do but only what to avoid. This guidance, like the voice of conscience, he always followed. It was spoken of by later writers as the Daemon or Genius of Socrates. He never wrote anything, but he made oral instruction the business of his life, and that without any pay for his teaching. He frequented the market-place and the gymnasia and the public walks, conversing with young and old, rich and poor, with all, in short, who felt any desire for his instruction. What we know of his methods of teaching we have learned from the writings of his pupils : Xe'nophon in his *Memorabilia* and Plato in his *Dialogues*. The method of teaching that he used, the Socratic method, consisted of eliciting truth by question and answer. He would begin his work by professing ignorance and by skilful questions would prove that those who said they knew in reality knew nothing.

This profession of ignorance is known as ' Socratic Irony.'
" Well didst thou speak, Athena's wisest son !
' All that we know is, nothing can be known '."
(Byron : *Childe Harold*).
In 399 he was accused of impiety and of corrupting youth. He was condemned to die by drinking hemlock. Plato in the *Phaedo* describes the philosopher's last hours discussing with his friends the question of the immortality of the soul.

Sol, in Roman mythology the sun-god. See **Helios**.

Sŏli or **Sŏloi,** an Athenian settlement on the coast of Cilicia in Asia Minor. Its inhabitants were so remote from the culture of Athens that their speech degenerated and their manners became uncouth.
A ' solecism ' is a violation of the grammatical laws of a language either spoken or written, tactless awkward manners, a breach of good behaviour generally.

Solomon, second son of Bathsheba and David. When born he was called Solomon, or ' Peaceful ', but Nathan with prophetic insight named him Jedidiah, or ' Beloved of Jehovah '. His reign of forty years was remarkable for the erection of the Temple, preparations for which had been made on a most extensive scale by David. Jehovah had not allowed David to build the Temple because he was a " man of war." At Gibeon, Solomon was bidden by God in a vision to choose a gift and wisely chose " an understanding heart " rather than riches and a long life : these were " added unto him " as a reward for his wise choice. The visit of the Queen of Sheba (1 *Kings*

10^{1-13}) was no doubt only one of similar royal visits made by monarchs to behold the glory and hear the wisdom of Solomon. According to legend the child of Solomon and the Queen of Sheba succeeded to the throne of Abyssinia, and from a mistranslation of the name of a ring given him by Solomon fable created the name ' Prester John ' —a mythical and mysterious Christian king in Africa who reappears at intervals over a long period of legendary history.

Solomon's wisdom in ordinary events is excellently illustrated by the story of the two women who came before him for judgement (1 *Kings* 3^{16-28}).

Only one book in O.T. is genuine Solomonic : " The Proverbs of Solomon, the son of David, King of Israel."

So'lon (c. 638–c. 558), a famous Athenian legislator, reckoned as one of the Seven Sages of Greece. He reformed the constitution, first repealing all the laws of Drā'co except those relating to murder [See **Draco**]. His laws were inscribed on wooden rollers and triangular tablets and were set up first in the Acropolis and later in the Agora for all to read. Later he travelled extensively, visiting Egypt and Cyprus. For his famous interview with Croesus in Lydia see **Croesus.** When he returned to Athens ten years or so later, he found that his Constitution had been overthrown and that the supreme power had been seized by his former friend Peisi'istrătus.

Somnus (Gk. Hypnos), the personification and god of sleep, is described as a brother of Death and as a son of Night. In works of art Sleep and Death are represented alike as two youths, sleeping or holding inverted torches in their hands.

So'phoclēs, 495–406 B.C., the most famous of Athenian tragedians. His contemporaries agree that he was the greatest of the three great tragic poets of classical Greece. He was thirty years younger than Ae'schylus and fifteen years older than Euri'pidēs. Altogether he wrote 130 plays, only seven of which are extant, including the famous trilogy on the Theban legend—*Oedipus Rex* (taken by Aristotle as a model of dramatic construction and placed by critics at the very summit of Greek tragic art), *Oedipus at Colonus* and *Antigone*.

Spar'tacus, a Thracian who was successively a shepherd, a soldier and a chief of banditti. He was taken prisoner and sold to a trainer of gladiators. He persuaded his fellow-prisoners to make an attempt to gain their freedom. He became the chosen leader of about seventy of them who were joined by large numbers of runaway slaves, and for two years defeated one Roman army after another and laid waste the entire country. He was finally defeated and slain in a decisive battle near the river Sī'lărus in lower Italy.

The story is told in the historical novel *Spartacus* by J. Leslie Mitchell.

Spartans, the inhabitants of Sparta (or Lăcĕdae'mōn), the capital city of Laconia in the Peloponnesus. Prior to the seventh century they had a reputation for lyric poetry and music and were notorious for their luxury and individual freedom. Later (traditionally at the instigation of the poet Tyrt'ǣus) they effected a complete revolution in their way of living and became renowned for the hardiness of their upbringing. Endurance and frugality were their characteristic qualities. Their new-born children were washed in the ice-cold streams that flowed from the snow-capped mountains and no deformed child was allowed to live. When a boy was seven years old he was taken from his home and his military training began. He wore the scantiest of clothing all the year round, ate frugally and was severely trained in gymnastics and the use of arms. Spartan girls, too, were trained to gymnastics. To the Spartans war was the only trade. They showed supreme courage in battle : no mother mourned the loss of her son in battle so long as his wounds were " in front." Their speech was brief and very much to the point. " *Laconic* " is our epithet for such speech.

Shakespeare refers to a special breed of bloodhounds reared by the Spartans. In *A Midsummer Night's Dream* Hippolyta tells Theseus :

" I was with Hercules and Cadmus once,

When in a wood of Crete they bay'd the bear

With hounds of Sparta : never did I hear

such gallant chiding."

The famous epitaph of Sīmo'nides on Leō'nidas and his Three Hundred is translated by Canon Rawlinson :

" Go, stranger, and to Lacedaemon tell

That here, obeying her behests, we fell."

Sphinx, i.e. the strangler, a she-monster with a woman's head, a dog's body, a serpent's tail, a bird's wings, a lion's paws and a human voice. This monster had been sent by Hera against the Thebans. She lay on the top of a rock by the highway and proposed a riddle to passers-by. Those who failed to solve the riddle she devoured. Oe'dipus (*quem v.*) heard that the Thebans would make their deliverer from the

Sphinx their King, so he determined to slay her. As he approached the Sphinx chanted her riddle : " What is the wonderful creature that in the morning goes on four legs, at noon on two, and in the evening on three ? " After thought, Oedipus replied : " Man in childhood crawls on hands and feet ; in his manhood he walks upright, and in his old age he is supported by a stick. The wonderful creature is Man." Immediately on hearing this reply, the Sphinx threw herself from the rock and fell dead.

The legend of the Sphinx almost certainly came to Greece from Egypt ; but the Egyptian sphinx is the figure of a lion without wings, and a human head, and was male. The largest figure of the Egyptian Sphinx is at Gizeh near Memphis on the lower Nile, the ancient capital of Egypt. For a description of the Gizeh sphinx read Kinglake's *Eothen*, c. 20.

The modern use of ' sphinx ' = an enigmatical person, a facial expression that is inscrutable and puzzling—all this summed up in a ' Sphinx-like expression '.

Spŏr'ădes, groups of ' scattered ' islands in the Aegean Sea, off Crete and the west coast of Asia Minor.

Sta'gĭra, a town in Macedonia, the birthplace of Aristotle. In consequence, the philosopher is sometimes called the ' Stagirite '.

Ste'ntŏr, herald of the Greeks in the Trojan war, famous for his loud voice. " [Hera] shouted in the likeness of great-hearted Stentor, with a voice of bronze, whose cry was loud as the cry of fifty other men " (*Iliad*).

Hence, *Stentorian*.

Stra'bo, a native of Asia Minor. He wrote, in Greek, a most interesting work on Geography (in seventeen books) which has come down to us entire, with the exception of one book. It is the most important ancient work on geography to be preserved.

Strȳmon, a river in Macedonia, the banks of which were a favourite haunt of cranes.

Styx, the principal river of the lower world round which it flowed seven times. The river was the divinity by whom the most solemn oaths were sworn :
" the Stygian marsh
Whose sanctity the gods revere
in oaths."
(Aen. vi.).

" Fate bars them (i.e. the sad souls of suicides), bound by the unlovely marsh
Of gloomy waters, ninefold
Stygian coils."
(Virgil *Aen.* vi, tr. Richards).

In 2 *Henry IV* 2, 4, 137 Pistol, bombastic as usual, calls the Styx " Pluto's damned lake."

We apply the adjective *Stygian,* e.g. to night, darkness. Cf. ' Egyptian Darkness.'

Suetō′nius, Roman historian whose chief work is his *Lives of the Twelve Caesars.* These lives make pleasant interesting reading, especially perhaps in Philemon Holland's quaint Elizabethan prose. Judge Clements, in his anthology of Tudor Translations, says : " [Holland] translated Suetonius into language so entertaining and malicious that we can see the Emperors in dressing-gowns and night-caps, we can be at their elbow when they dine, we can wander along the corridors of royal palaces and peep behind the curtains."

Sū′nium, a cape forming the S. extremity of Attica, with a town of the same name upon it. On its highest point was a splendid temple of Athene, fully 300 feet above the sea. Eleven columns of the temple still remain standing. They have given the modern name, C. Colonni, to the cape.

Byron several times refers to Sunium, e.g.
" Place me on Sunium's marbled steep,
Where nothing, save the waves and I,
May hear our mutual murmurs sweep."
Don Juan III.

Swords into Plowshares, to beat, i.e. cease fighting and turn to the activities of peace.

Foretelling the time when wars should cease, Isaiah (2⁴) says : " they shall beat their swords into plowshares and their spears into pruning hooks : nation shall not lift up sword against nation, neither shall they learn war any more." Joel speaks of the reverse idea. Foretelling God's judgements against the enemies of His people, he says : " Proclaim ye this among the Gentiles : Prepare war . . . beat your plowshares into swords and your pruning-hooks into spears " (*Joel* 3⁹,¹⁰).

Sȳ′baris, a Greek town in Lucania in the South of Italy the inhabitants of which became notorious for their love of luxury and pleasure.

Hence a *sybarite* is a person too fond of his physical well-being, a voluptuary.

The adjective is sybaritic, applied to such nouns as ' comfort ', ' luxury '.

Sȳ′racuse, the wealthiest and most populous town in Sicily, founded in 743 B.C. as a Greek colony under Archias of Corinth. The Athenians in vain besieged it in 414; but in 212, after a two years' siege, it was captured by the Romans despite the various engines of war devised by Archimēdēs to assist his fellow-citizens. From this time Syracuse became a town of the Roman province of Sicily.

See **Archimedes.**

Sȳ′rinx, an Arcadian nymph who, being pursued by Pan, jumped into the river Ladon where she was changed into a reed. Pan then made his flute of the reed.

See **Pan.**

Sy′rtēs, the Greek name for the two great gulfs, the modern gulfs of Sidra and Gabes, in the N. African coast. They were proverbially dangerous by reason of their sand-banks.

Tabernacle, a large tent, 30 by 10 cubits. The framework was formed of boards of acacia, overlaid on both sides with thin plates of gold, and the ceiling of ten curtains of fine twisted linen. The tent was divided by a curtain of similar material into the Most Holy or Holy of Holies (a cube of 10 cubits) and the Holy Place (20 by 10 by 10). The Ark of the Covenant, containing the tables of the ten Commandments, rested in the Most Holy. The Holy Place contained the Altar of Incense, the Golden Candlestick and the Table of Shewbread. The Tabernacle stood in an open space, 100 by 50, called the Court, where stood the Altar of Burnt-offerings and the Laver of brass in which the priests performed their religious ablutions.

The Tabernacle was a temporary erection, the plan of which was revealed by God himself to Moses on the Mount (*Ex.* 26³⁰). It accompanied the Israelites in their wanderings until it was set up in Shiloh (*Jos.* 18¹) where it remained throughout the period of the Judges. When the Temple was finished the Tabernacle was taken to Jerusalem and probably preserved, as

South-east view of the Tabernacle. (*As restored by Fergusson*).

a sacred relic, in one of the chambers of the Temple.

See **Shewbread ; Ark of the Covenant.**

Ta'citus, Cornēlius, the historian, son-in-law of Julius Agricola (Governor of Britain A.D. 78–85), and friend of the younger Pliny. For acuteness of thought and insight into character, he is among the greatest of historians. For power of description in a few telling words he is unrivalled. His style is terse and highly polished. His works include (i) the *Life of Agricola*, an admirable biography, especially interesting to us for its history of the conquest of Britain ;

(ii) *Germania*, a treatise describing the Germanic nations, religion and habits ;

(iii) *Histories*, covering the years 68 to 96. Only the first four books survive in their entirety ;

(iv) *Annals*, covering the years 14 to 68. Books 1–4 and 7–10 have come down to us complete, as have parts of the other books. Tacitus died c. 117.

Tae'nărum, modern Cape Matapan, the southerly point of the Peloponnesus. On this promontory was a cave, one of the supposed entrances to the underworld (probably so considered because of the stern and gloomy character of its rocks), through which Heracles is said to have dragged Cerberus to the upper world.

Talent. Read the parable of the Talents (*Matt.* 25[14-30]). The talent is a large sum of money, possibly not less than £250 in our currency. For purposes of trade one servant receives five talents, another two and a third, one, in accordance with their lord's estimate of the servant's

ability. Two make good and are encouraged to seek wider responsibility. The third is too lazy to attempt to increase his talent and is condemned. " To him that hath shall be given ; whosoever hath not, from him shall be taken away even that which he hath."

In general, ' talent ' has the figurative sense of aptitude for something, whether physical, mental or moral. We even use the participial ' talented ' to mean ' gifted ', e.g. a talented musician. Milton's " one talent " (Sonnet *on his Blindness*) was his power of writing. Unlike the third servant of the parable, the poet continued to use his ' one talent ', for his great poems, *Paradise Lost, Paradise Regained* and *Samson Agonistes* were written after he became totally blind at the age of 44.

Talmud, the name given to the great mass of the learning of Israel's sagas and legends collected from age to age, and at length reduced to writing in a final form ; the body of Jewish traditional law.

Tālos or **Tālus.**
(i) Son of Perdix, the sister of Dae'dalus. For the confusion in the stories of Talus and Perdix see **Perdix.**

(ii) A man of brass, the work of Hēphae'stus. He watched the island of Crete by walking round it thrice every day. Whenever he saw strangers approaching he made himself red-hot in fire, and then embraced the strangers when they landed. In the Argonaut story Talus receives the voyagers with a shower of stones. He had a vein running down to his foot, where the blood was stopped by a nail. By her magic Medea made this nail fall out, and Talus bled to death. The story of Talus burning strangers by his embrace may well have arisen from the practice of offering human sacrifices to an image of Moloch.

Tăm′ĕsis, the Latin name for the river Thames.

Ta′ntalus, a wealthy King, perhaps of Lydia. His father was Zeus himself and he was a favourite among the gods until he offended them. Greek poets regard him as the type of extreme prosperity followed by a sudden and fearful downfall. The causes of his punishment after death are differently stated. Homer says he had divulged secrets entrusted to him at table by Zeus. He was punished in the lower world by being afflicted with a raging thirst, and at the same time placed in the midst of a lake the waters of which always receded from him as soon as he attempted to drink them. Over his head, moreover, hung branches of fruit which receded in like manner when he stretched out his hand to reach them. His punishment became proverbial.

We have the verb ' to tantalize ' = to provoke a person by holding out to him hopes that can never be fulfilled. A locked stand for spirit-decanters which are in full view but which cannot be reached without the key is known as a ' tantalus '—a late nineteenth century use of the noun.

Tarpē′ia, daughter of the Governor of the Roman citadel on the Capitoline Hill. According to legend she was tempted by the gold on the Sabine bracelets and collars to open a gate of the fortress to Tatius and his Sabines. As they entered they threw their shields upon her and so crushed her to death. In consequence part of the Capitoline was called the ' Tarpeian Rock '. From it

criminals, condemned to death for treason, were cast headlong down.

The " noble " tribunes, " the people's mouths," were determined that Coriolanus was a traitor. The cruel Sicinius gave orders to the Aediles :

" Therefore lay hold of him ;
Bear him to the rock Tarpeian,
    and from thence
Into destruction cast him."
        (*Cor*. iii, 1, 212).

Tarquin, the name of two legendary kings of Rome.

(i) Tarquinius Priscus, the fifth king, whose reign was distinguished by great exploits in war and by great works in peace. He defeated the Latins and the Sabines. He built vast sewers by which the lower parts of Rome were drained. He was murdered after reigning 38 years.

(ii) Tarquinius Superbus, the seventh king, grandson of Priscus. His cruelty and tyranny obtained for him the surname of *Superbus* (i.e. the Proud). He purchased the Sibylline books [see **Sibyls**]. Unable to take the city of Gabii by storm, he had recourse to stratagem. His son, Sextus, pretending to be ill-treated by his father, fled to Gabii the inhabitants of which entrusted him with the command of their troops. Sextus thereupon sent a messenger to his father to enquire how he should deliver the city into his hands. The king, who was walking in his garden when the message arrived, made no reply, but kept striking off the heads of the tallest poppies with his stick. Sextus took the hint. He put to death or banished all the leading men of the place and then had no difficulty in compelling it to submit. Tarquin and his family were expelled from Rome by the insurrection that followed the outrage offered to Lucrētia by Sextus,

510 B.C. After reigning 24 years Superbus died at Cumae.

The great Temple of Jupiter was said to have been built on the Capitoline Hill by Superbus. Legend has it that when men were digging the foundations of the Temple they found a severed head, still bleeding, deep in the earth. Hence the name ' Capitoline ', i.e. the hill of the ' caput ' or head.

Tarsus, the chief city of Cilicia, a district in S.E. Asia Minor. Antony made it a ' free city ' (i.e. one enjoying a certain amount of local self-government) as a reward for taking Caesar's part in the Civil War. It was the birthplace of St. Paul.

See **Tartessus.**

Ta′rtarus, the part of Hades divided from the rest of the underworld by the blazing Pўriphlĕ′gĕthon and reserved for the punishment of the enemies of the gods, such as Ixīon and Tantalus. But frequently ' Tartarus ' is merely synonymous with Hades.

Sir Toby (*Twelfth Night* ii, 5, *ad fin.*) will follow Maria " to the gates of Tartar." The same Elizabethan form is used in *Henry V* ii, 2, 123, where the king couples a ' traitor ' with ' vasty Tartar.'

Tarte′ssus, a district on both sides of the river Baetis (modern Guadalquivir) in the lower part of its course, rich in metals, iron, tin, lead, silver and, to some extent, gold. For long it was regarded as the Tarshish of Scripture.

Tarshish is mentioned in *Gen.* 10⁴ with countries in and near Asia Minor (see 1 *Chron.* 1⁷). The navy of Tarshish visited Palestine every third year in Solomon's time (1 *Kings* 10²²). The imports of " ivory, apes and peacocks " are not found in Spain, but they may easily have been brought overland from India to Tarsus in Cilicia. There are still silver mines near Tarsus and iron mines in the same region. Jeremiah (10⁹) notices silver from Tarshish and Ezekiel (27¹²) mentions silver, iron, tin and lead brought in its ships to Tyre. Josephus definitely places Tarshish at Tarsus. There would seem, therefore, no difficulty in accepting the Jewish opinion that Tarsus was Tarshish.

Tāў′gĕtus, a massive mountain range separating Lacō′nia and Messē′nia and terminating in Cape Tae′nărum.

Tĕ′lămōn, father of Ajax the Great. He was one of the Calydonian hunters and one of the Argonauts.

In architecture a ' telamon ' is a large sculptured male figure used as a supporting column. Cf. the corresponding *căryă′tid* or sculptured female figure, similarly used.

Tēlĕ′gŏnus, son of Odysseus and Circē. After Odysseus had returned to Ithaca, Circe sent out Telegonus in search of his father. A storm cast his ship on the coast of Ithaca. Being pressed for hunger, Telegonus began to plunder the fields. Odysseus and Tēlĕ′măchus, being informed of the ravages caused by the stranger, went out to fight against him. Telegonus unwittingly killed his father by running him through with a spear which he had received from his mother.

Tēlĕ′măchus, son of Odysseus and Pēne′lopē. He was still an infant when the Trojan war began. When his father had been absent from home nearly twenty years, Telemachus, accompanied by Athene in the guise of Mentor, went to Pylos and Sparta to gather information about him. He was hospitably received by Nestor who sent his own son to conduct Telemachus to Sparta. Menelā'us, too, received him kindly. Then he returned home ; and on his arrival he found his father whom he aided in slaying Penelope's suitors.

In *Ulysses* Tennyson represents the aged father saying of his son :
" This is my son, mine own
       Telemachus,
To whom I leave the sceptre and
       the isle . . .
Most blameless is he, centred in
       the sphere
Of common duties, decent not
       to fail
In offices of tenderness, and pay
Meet adoration to my household
       gods,
When I am gone."

Te'lephus, a king of Mȳ'sia in Asia Minor. He attempted to prevent the Greeks from landing on the coast of Mysia. Dionȳ'sus, however, caused him to stumble over a vine, whereupon he was wounded by Achilles. Being informed by an oracle that the wound could be cured only by ' the wounder ', Telephus went to the Grecian camp. As the Greeks had likewise learnt from an oracle that without the aid of Telephus they could not reach Troy, Achilles cured Telephus by means of the rust of the spear by which he had been wounded. Telephus in return pointed out to the Greeks the road they had to take.

Euripides is constantly attacked by Aristophanes for disgracing the dignity of tragedy by bringing Telephus on to the stage (in his lost play of that name) in rags and squalor.

Te'llus, in Roman mythology goddess of the Earth, corresponding with the Greek Gē or Gae'a.

Tempē, a beautiful romantic valley in the N. of Thessaly, between Mts. Olympus and Ossa. So celebrated was the scenery of Tempe that its name was given to any beautiful valley.

Tĕnĕdos, a small island of the Aegean, off the coast of Troas, about 12 miles from the mouth of the Hellespont. In the Trojan war it was the station to which the Greeks withdrew their fleet in order to induce the Trojans to think they had departed, and so to admit the wooden horse into Troy.

Terence (Publius Terentius Afer), second century, B.C., the Latin comic poet. He was born at Carthage, and at an early age came to Rome where he became the slave of a Roman senator, Publius Terentius Lucanus. He was freed by his master and, as usual in such circumstances, took his patron's name (Terentius). Six comedies have come down to us and they are probably all that Terence produced.

Tē'reūs. See **Pandīon.**

Terpsi'chorē, the Muse of Choral Dance and Song. See **Muses.**

Tē'thys, daughter of Ū'ranus, wife of Ōce'anus and mother of the Oceanides and of the numerous river-gods.

Teu'cer. (i) the legendary first king of Troy. Hence the Trojans are often called *Teucri.*
(ii) the half-brother of Ajax and the best archer among the Greeks at Troy.

Tha'latta ! Tha'latta ! (i.e. The Sea ! the Sea !). The cry of joy uttered by the 10,000 Greeks when on their retreat from Persia they reached a point from which they could see the waters of the Euxine (Black Sea).

Tha'lēs of Mīlē'tus, one of the Seven Sages of Greece. He was mathematician and astronomer.

Thalī'a, the Muse of Comedy. See **Muses.**

Thă'nătos, called **Mors** by the Romans, the god of death, is described as the brother of Sleep. In art Death was sometimes represented as a slumbering youth, sometimes as a winged deity with an inverted torch.

Thebes, the chief city in Boeotia. Its acropolis was called Cadmēa because it was said to have been founded by the Phoenician Cadmus. Theban legends said that the fortifications were constructed by Amph'īon and his brother Zē'thus. When Amphion played his lyre the stones moved of their own accord and formed the wall. Thebes was the reputed birthplace of Dionȳ'sus and of Heracles. It was the scene of the tragedy of Lā'ius and Oedipus. When the city was taken by Alexander in 336 it was entirely destroyed with the exception of the temples and the house of the poet Pindar.

See **Cadmus ; Amphion ; Oedipus ; Pindar.**

Thĕ'mis, daughter of Ūrănus and Gē (and so a Titaness), mother of the Seasons and of the Fates. She is the personification of law, custom and equity : so she is described as reigning in the assemblies of men and as convening, by the command of Zeus, the assembly of the gods. She is represented on coins with a figure like that of Athē'nē, holding a cornucopia and a pair of scales.

Themi'stocles (c. 514–459 B.C.), the great Athenian statesman and commander who fortified Athens and its main port, the Piraeus, persuaded the Athenians to employ the produce of the silver mines of Laurium in building ships and thereby laid the foundation of his ultimate success against the Persians in the naval battle of Salamis, 480. This battle, in which the greater part of Xerxes' fleet was destroyed, established not merely the reputation of Themistocles among his fellow countrymen, but the supremacy of Greece. Later, Themistocles was ostracised from Athens and went into retirement. He was without doubt the builder of Athenian greatness as a sea-power.

Theŏ'crĭtus, the Greek pastoral poet, was a native of Syracuse or of Cōs. He was the father of bucolic poetry. Virgil (in Latin) and Spenser and Milton are all influenced by him. His *Idylls* are *pictures* (Gk. *eidullia* = little pictures) of the ordinary life of the common people of Sicily. We venture to print C. S. Calverley's version of the short nineteenth idyll :

Love Stealing Honey

――――――

" Once thievish Love the honeyed
    hives would rob,
When a bee stung him : soon
    he felt a throb
Through all his finger-tips, and,
    wild with pain,
Blew on his hands and stamped
    and jumped in vain.
To Aphrodite then he told his
    woe :
' How can a thing so tiny hurt
    one so ? '
She smiled and said : ' Why,
    thou'rt a tiny thing,
As is the bee ; yet sorely thou
    canst sting.'

Compare with this Herrick's delicious translation of the Anacreontic version of the story :

" Cupid, as he lay among
Roses, by a bee was stung ;
Whereupon in anger flying
To his mother, said, thus
crying :
' Help ! O help ! your boy's
a-dying .'
' And why, my pretty lad ? '
said she.
Then blubbering, replied he :
' A winged snake has bitten me,
Which country people call a
bee.'
At which she smiled, then with
her hairs
And kisses drying up his tears,
' Alas ! ' said she, ' my wag, if
this
Such a pernicious torment is,
Come, tell me then how great's
the smart
Of those thou woundest with
thy dart ! ' "

Thermŏ′pўlae, i.e. the *Hot Gates*, a celebrated pass leading from Thessaly into Locris. It was the only pass by which an enemy could penetrate from N. into S. Greece : whence its great importance in Grecian history.
See **Leonidas.**

Thersī′tēs, an officer in the Greek army at Troy.
" Much store had he of scurrilous
words,
Idle and scurrilous words, to
hurl at kings.
Bow-legged he was and halted
on one foot :
His shoulders, hunched, en-
croached upon his chest ;
And bore a peaked head—scant
hairs grew thereon."
(*Iliad* ii, translated by
C. S. Calverley).
His querulous, railing outlook was on a par with his physical deformities. Exasperated at his jeering remarks over Achilles' grief for the death of Penthesilē′a, Achilles killed him.

Shakespeare introduces him (in *Troilus and Cressida*) as " a deformed and scurrilous Grecian." See the angry scene between him, Ajax, Achilles and Patroclus (II, 1).

Thē′sēus, the great legendary hero of Attica, son (according to Attic tradition) of Ae′gēus, King of Athens. He was brought up in his mother's native Troe′zēn. When he reached maturity he took by his mother's directions the sword and sandals (the tokens which had been left by Aegeus) and proceeded to Athens. As he went he emulated Heracles by destroying robbers and monsters that infested the country [see **Sinis ; Sciron ; Procrustes**]. He was acknowledged by Aegeus and declared his successor. Theseus then went of his own accord as one of the seven youths whom the Athenians were obliged to send every year, with seven maidens, to Crete to be devoured by the Minotaur. [See **Ariadne**]. When Aegeus perished in the sea, Theseus became King of Athens. He again emulated Heracles by assailing the Amazons and carrying off their queen Antī′opē. The Amazons then invaded Attica and Theseus defeated them in a battle fought in the midst of the city. For his friendship and co-operation with Pīri′thŏus, see **Pirithous.** Theseus was finally driven from Athens by his rebellious subjects. He retired to Scȳ′ros where he was probably murdered.

According to Plutarch (whose *Lives*, translated by Sir Thomas North, Shakespeare knew well and frequently used as sources for dramatic material) Theseus married either Antiope or her sister Hippo′lyta, Queen of the Amazons.

Theseus is King of Athens in *A Midsummer Night's Dream* and marries Hippolyta ; but, unfortunately perhaps, Shakespeare gives this great man of action very little to do in the play. The hunting-scene in the middle of iv, 1 is noteworthy.

Thessaloni'ca (modern Salonica), the chief city in Macedonia with an important harbour. It lay on the Egnatian Road which led from the W. shores of Greece to Byzantium and the East. It was visited by St. Paul (*Acts* 17$^{1-15}$) about A.D. 53, and two years afterwards he addressed from Corinth two epistles to his converts in Thessalonica.

Thessaly, the largest division of Greece. Thessaly proper is a vast plain shut in on every side by mountain barriers, broken only at the N.E. corner by the valley of Tempē which separates Mt. Ossa from Mt. Olympus. Two other districts were included under the general name of Thessaly: Magnē'sia, a long narrow strip of country in the E., and Mālis in the S. Thessaly was the legendary home of the Centaurs and the Lapithae. The Argonautic expedition started from Io'lchos (modern Volo) in Magnesia.

The'tis, wife of Pēleus and mother of Achilles.
See **Peleus** ; **Apple** (i) ; **Achilles**.

Thirty pieces of silver is the price of a person's treachery. Judas received thirty shekels of silver (the amount fixed by the law of Moses for the loss of an ox) for betraying Christ. (*Matt.* 26^{16}).

Thisbē, a Babylonian maiden, beloved by Pyramus. The lovers living in adjoining houses often secretly conversed with each other through an opening in the wall, as their parents would not sanction their marriage. Once, they agreed to meet at the tomb of Ninus. Thisbe arrived first. While she was waiting for Pyramus she saw a lioness which had just torn an ox to pieces, so she fled. In her haste she dropped her garment which the lioness soiled with blood. In the meantime Pyramus arrived and imagined that she had been murdered. He killed himself under a mulberry tree, the fruit of which henceforth was as red as blood. When Thisbe found the body of her lover, she, too, stabbed herself.

Shakespeare closes *A Midsummer Night's Dream* with the ridiculous interlude of " Pyramus and Thisbe," based on Golding's translation of the story as given in Ovid's *Metamorphoses.* The story was immensely popular in Elizabethan times, so Shakespeare's burlesque of it would be certain of the approval of the ' groundlings '.

Thomas, one of the Twelve, called Didymus (i.e. twin). A week after the Resurrection, all the Apostles except Thomas were gathered together for worship and conference when Jesus appeared to them, and showed them His hands and His side. They were " glad when they saw the Lord." They then told Thomas of His appearance, but even the emphatic testimony of ten competent witnesses failed to convince him that Jesus had risen. " Except I shall see in His hands the print of the nails, and put my finger into the print of the nails, and thrust my hand into his side, I will not believe " (*St. John,* 20^{25}).

According to tradition Thomas was the missionary who introduced Christianity into India.

A " doubting Thomas " is simply a person who will not believe except on the evidence of his own sight and touch.

Thrace, a vast space of country in S.E. Europe. The historical account of the Thracians is of a savage people, but brave and war-like. They despised agriculture, drank deep, and quarrelled notoriously over their wine-cups. On the other hand the earlier, legendary account of the Thracians is of a civilized people, cultivators of the vine, among whom were born poets like Orpheus.

Milton and Shakespeare refer to Orpheus as the ' Thracian bard ', the ' Thracian singer ', torn to pieces by the Thracian women in their Bacchanalian frenzy.

Thra′sō, a boastful character in Terence's comedy *Eunū′chus.*

Rosalind in *As You Like It* uses ' thrasonical ' = boastful : " Caesar's thrasonical brag of—' I came, saw and overcame '." A reference to Caesar's announcement to the Senate of his victory near Zela, 47 B.C.

Thūcy′didēs (c. 460–c. 400 B.C.), the critical historian of the Peloponnesian War. He was scrupulously careful in ascertaining facts and his narrative is brief and concise— bare facts expressed in the fewest possible words. Yet his power to produce pathos is unsurpassed by any prose writer, as can be seen in his account of the plague in Athens (given in seven chapters of the Second Book).

Thū′lē, an island in the N. part of the German Ocean, regarded by the ancients as the most northerly point in the whole earth. Pȳthĕas, a Greek navigator contemporary with Aristotle, says Thule was a six days' sail from Britain, and the day and night there were each six months long. Therefore Thule lay within the Arctic Circle. The real Thule was probably Norway ; but there is confusion with Mainland, the largest isle of the Shetlands.

Hence the expression ' Ultima Thule ', used figuratively, means ' any far-away unknown region ' (C.O.D.), ' the uttermost point attainable ' (Harvey).

Tiber (in Latin, Tĭbĕris or Tĭbĕrī′nus), the chief river in central Italy on which, 16 miles by land from its mouth at Ostia, stood the city of Rome. The waters of the river are muddy and yellowish, whence it is frequently called by the Roman poets *flāvus Tiberis* (yellow Tiber). The Tiber was worshipped as a river-god under its deified personification Tiberīnus : thus, in Macaulay's " Horatius "

(i) " But by the yellow Tiber
    Was tumult and affright."
(ii) " Oh, Tiber ! father Tiber !
    To whom the Romans pray."

Tiberias, the capital of the tetrarchy of Herod Antipas, who built the city and named it in honour of Tiberius, Emperor of Rome. It was thus a great city in our Lord's time, but was regarded as unclean because built over ancient tombs. Our Lord does not seem ever to have entered Tiberias, which is only once noticed (*John* 6[23]). From this city the Sea of Galilee was called the Sea of Tiberias.

Tīmōn, the Athenian Misanthrope, lived in the time of the Peloponnesian war. So long as his riches lasted, he entertained his friends (and parasites) until he was ruined. He was then refused aid even by the richest of his former ' friends ' : his nature completely changed and he lived in a cave as far from the haunts of men as possible. He admitted no one to his company save the exiled Alcibī'adēs.

Shakespeare's *Timon of Athens* is a play of no great dramatic value. The key to it is Timon's own words : " I am a *misanthrope* and hate mankind."

Tīrĕ'sĭas, a celebrated soothsayer of Thebes. He was blind from his seventh year, possibly as a punishment for revealing to men things which they ought not to have known, possibly because he had seen Athene bathing in the fountain Hi'ppocrēnē. His mother prayed to Athene to restore his sight, but as the goddess could not do this, she gave him the power of understanding the voices of birds and a staff, with the help of which he could walk as safely as if he had his eyesight. He lived to be a very old man : some say he outlived seven generations of men.

He forms the subject of one of Tennyson's classical poems. In this poem Tiresias laments the coming fate of Thebes :

" the great God Ares . . .

. . . Stood out before a darkness, crying ' Thebes,

Thy Thebes shall fall and perish, for I loathe

The seed of Cadmus'."

Ti'ryns, one of the most ancient fortresses in all Greece, in the plain of Argolis, at the head of the Gulf of Nauplia. The walls of the citadel were built of huge ' Cyclopean ' stones—colossal roughly-hewn blocks from fifteen to over fifty feet thick.

See **Mycenae**.

Tīsi'phonē. See **Eumenides**.

Tī'tans, The, sons (and daughters, see **Themis**) of Ū'ranus (Heaven) and Gē or Gae'a (Earth). It is said that Uranus threw his hundred-handed sons and the Cyclopes into Tartarus. Ge, in indignation, produced iron, persuaded the Titans to rise against their father and gave the Titan Crŏ'nus an iron sickle. Cronus mutilated his father with the sickle, the Titans deposed him, liberated their brothers from Tartarus and raised Cronus to the throne. Cronus then hurled the Cyclopes back into Tartarus, married his sister Rhea and, warned by his parents that he would be dethroned by one of his own children, swallowed them successively at birth. But Rhea saved her sixth son Zeus who, when grown up, united with his brothers and sisters against Cronus and the ruling Titans. This conflict with the Titans lasted ten years till at length Ge promised Zeus victory if he would deliver the Cyclopes from Tartarus. Zeus now revolted against Cronus and overcame the Titans with the aid of thunderbolts forged by the Cyclopes. (N.B. The Fight of the Titans is sometimes confused by ancient writers with the Fight of the Giants).

The name ' Titans ' is also given to those divine or semi-divine beings who were descended from the Titans, e.g. Prome'theus and especially Hē'lios and Selē'nē. Shakespeare refers to the Sun as Titan : e.g.

" And Titan, tired in the mid-day heat,

With burning eye did hotly overlook them " ;

(*Venus and Adonis*)

and describes Falstaff sweating until he resembles a dish of melted butter : " Did'st thou never see Titan kiss a dish of butter ? pitiful-hearted [Titan], that melted at the sweet tale of the sun's ! If thou did'st, behold that compound," i.e. the perspiring Falstaff.

(1 *Henry IV*, ii, 4, 120).

Tithō′nus, in Greek mythology, brother of Priam. By the prayers of Eōs (Aurora), who loved him, he obtained the gift of immortality, but not eternal youth. In consequence he became withered and shrunken in his old age. As he could not die Eos changed him into a cicada or tree-cricket.

In one of his classical poems, ' Tithonus ', Tennyson makes " this grey shadow, once a man " lament his fate, i.e. the " cruel immortality " that consumes him.

Ti′tўus, a giant who was killed by Artemis and Apollo because he had insulted their mother Lēto. He was cast into Tartarus where Odysseus saw him " prone on the ground and covering nine roods as he lay." Describing Tartarus and its inhabitants to Aeneas, the Sibyl gives this picture :

" Tityos, too, son of All-Mother Earth,
Could there be seen : through nine whole roods his bulk
Lies stretching, and his deathless liver and flesh
Teeming with torments the huge vulture crops
With hooked beak."

(Richards' trans. *Aen.* vi, 595–9).

Tomī, a town of Thrace (modern Kustenji or Constanta), the place of Ovid's banishment. The poet's grim picture of the climate of Tomi is not overdrawn. " Snow lies all winter, the Danube and the sea are frozen hard, even wine freezes in the jar and is served in pieces ! The hair of the barbarians tinkles with ice " (Prof. A. L. Wheeler).

Trā′jan, Roman Emperor A.D. 98–117, of Spanish blood. He was a great soldier and an equally great administrator. He reduced Dacia (in Central Europe) to the form of a Roman province and conquered

the greater part of the Parthian empire (S.E. of the Caspian). He made the road over the Pontine Marshes (25 miles S.E. of Rome) ; improved the harbour at Ostia ; built the aqueduct at Rome called Trāj′āna after him, and, above all, constructed the Forum Trājānum with its law-court and libraries and the Column of Trajan, celebrating his Dacian victories, set between the law-court and the libraries.

Tres Tabernae, or Three Taverns, on the Appian Way about 30 miles from Rome. Here " the brethren came (from Rome) to meet " Paul and his friends " (*Acts* 28[15]).

Trīna′cria (= with three promontories), a name for the island of Sicily.

Trī′tōn, son of Poseidon and Amphitrī′tē, who dwelt with his father and mother in a golden palace in the bottom of the sea. Later writers describe him as riding over the sea on sea-horses or other monsters. Sometimes we

Triton. (From a Roman Lamp).
The Tritons were supposed to have the human figure in the upper part of their bodies and that of a fish in the lower part. They blow a shell-trumpet as they follow in the train of Poseidon.

M

find mention of Tritons in the plural. They were supposed to have the human figure in the upper part of their bodies and that of a fish in the lower part. They blow a shell-trumpet (*concha*) as they follow in the train of Poseidon to calm the sea at his command : they are his heralds.

In *Lycidas* Milton refers to Triton as " the herald of the sea," and in *Comus* he has " scaly Triton's winding shell " i.e. the concha. See also Wordsworth's sonnet " The World is too much with us."

" Hear you this Triton of the minnows ? " asks Coriolanus about the detested tribune Sicinius. The implication is that the tribune was as important a personage among the smaller people, the citizens, as Triton was among the smaller fish, the minnows.

Trō′ad, the region about Troy. It is for the most part mountainous, being intersected by Mt. Ida and its branches. The chief river of the plain is the Scamander with its affluent Simois.

Trojan. ' To fight like a Trojan ' figuratively means ' to fight with supreme courage ', as the Trojans did against the Greeks.

Shakespeare uses ' Trojan ' more than once as a cant term for robber, a dissolute (or at any rate, a very jovial) fellow. So in 1 *Henry IV* Gadshill tells the chamber-attendant at Rochester, " Tut ! there are other Trojans that thou dreamest not of, the which for sport sake are content to do the profession (i.e. that of highway robbery) some grace." ' Corinthian ' (1 *Henry IV*, 2, 4, 12) and ' Ephesian ' (2 *Henry IV*, 2, 2, 144) are similarly used.

Trōs, see **Troy.**

Troy (Trōja or Īlium or Pergama), the chief city of the Troad in the Homeric age, and the capital of the dominion ruled over by Priam. The mythical account of the Kingdom of Troy is briefly as follows. Teucer, the first King, had a daughter who married Da′rdanus, the chieftain of the country N.E. of the Troad. Dardanus had two sons, Īlus and Erichthŏnīus, and the latter was the father of Trōs from whom the country and people derived the names of Trōas and Trōës. Tros was the father of Īlus who founded the city, called after him Īlium and also, after his father, Trōja. The next King was Lāo′mĕdon, and after him Priam. In his reign the city was taken and destroyed by the confederated Greeks, after a ten years' siege.

Thus the Trojans are known as *Teucri* (after Teucer) ; *Trŏës* or *Trojani* (after Trōs) ; *Dardanidae,* i.e. descendants of Dardanus.

Tu′llĭus, Se′rvĭus, a man of humble origin who according to legend was the sixth king of Rome. He had two daughters, both named Tullia. One of them he married to Tarquinius Superbus and the other to Tarquin's gentle brother Aruns. Tarquin's wife was a sweet, kindly woman ; the other Tullia was hard and ambitious. Aruns and Tarquin's Tullia mysteriously died : then Tarquin married Aruns' widow. She was his undoing, for when Servius Tullius was murdered by Tarquin's men she is said to have driven the chariot over her father's dead body. From that day the scene of the horror was known as *Vīcus Scelerātus,* or Wicked Street.

Tu′llus Hosti′lius, legendary third King of Rome. His reign was full of wars, especially between Rome and Alba. Three brothers of the

Horātia gens (an ancient patrician family) fought with three brothers from Alba, the Curiā'tii, to determine whether Rome or Alba was to exercise the supremacy. The battle was long undecided. Two of the Horatii fell ; but the three Curiatii, though alive, were severely wounded. Seeing this, the surviving Horatius, still unhurt, pretended to flee, and vanquished his wounded opponents separately. He returned in triumph, bearing his threefold spoils. As he approached the city gate his sister, Horatia, met him and recognised the mantle of her betrothed lover, one of the Curiatii, on his shoulder. Her grief drew on her the wrath of Horatius who stabbed her, exclaiming : ' So perish every Roman woman who bewails a foe.' For this murder he was sentenced to be scourged and hanged, but he appealed to the burghers who prescribed a nominal punishment. With veiled head, led by his father, Horatius passed under a gibbet—' sister's gibbet ', as it was called.

Tu'rnus, King of the Rutulians at the time of the arrival of Aeneas in Italy. He fought against Aeneas because the King of Latium had given to the Trojan hero his daughter Lāvī'nia already promised to Turnus. He appears in the *Aeneid* as a brave spirited warrior. In the end he was killed by Aeneas.

Tȳ'phōn or Tȳphō'ēus, a 100-headed monster of the primitive world, the embodiment in myth of volcanoes and earthquakes. Hence he is represented sometimes as a fire-breathing giant, sometimes as a hurricane. In some accounts he is the father of Cerberus, the Hydra of Lerna and the Chimaera, as well as of the evil winds and the Harpies. He aimed at the sovereignty over gods and men, but was killed by Zeus by a thunderbolt. He was buried under Mt. Aetna, the workshop of Hephaestus.

Aeschylus describes Typhon as living in a " Cilician den." Milton follows him and speaks (in *Paradise Lost*) of

"Typhon, whom the den
By ancient Tarsus held."

(Greek tȳphōn = whirlwind).

Uli'xēs or Uly'ssēs. See **Odysseus**.

Upper Room. This was a sort of parlour, a room in a Jewish house used for interviews ; such a " summer chamber " as that in which Ehud, the left-handed Benjaminite, killed Eglon King of Moab (*Judg.* 3^{20-25}). It was probably in such an ' upper room ' in the house of Mary (John Mark's mother) that, " on the night that he was betrayed " our Lord held the Last Supper (*Luke* 22^{12-38}). In this room, too, the Eleven waited with the Holy Women for the coming of the Holy Ghost (*Acts* 1^{13}). Mary's house subsequently became the headquarters of the early Church in Jerusalem (*Acts* $12^{12...}$).

In legend Joseph of Arimathaea brought the cup used at the Last Supper to Britain with some of Christ's blood in it. This cup was known as the Holy Grail, and is an important feature in the story of King Arthur. See Malory's *Le Morte D'Arthur* and Tennyson's symbolical *The Holy Grail*, the eighth poem in the series known as the *Idylls of the King*.

Ura'nia, the Muse of Astronomy. See **Muses**.

Ū'rănus, the personification of the heavens, the son (and husband) of Gae'a or Gē, the father of the Titans, of the Cyclopes and of Bria'reōs, Cottus and Gȳēs (the hundred-handed giants). He was dethroned by Cronus at the instigation of Gaea.

Urim and Thummim, possibly two sacred jewels, ornaments in the High Priest's breastplate of Judgement. As the words are plural (meaning ' Decisions ' and ' oracles ', or, as some think ' Light ' and ' Truth ') they may have been a set of rods of different lengths. It appears, however, from 1 *Sam.* 14⁴⁰⁻⁴² that they could only answer ' yes ' or ' no ', and so it took a very long time to get the answer to a complicated question : see *Josh.* 7¹⁶⁻¹⁸ ; and in 1 *Sam.* 14¹⁹ Saul cannot wait for the answer. Some authorities think they are not two things, but two names for one and the same thing. If this is correct, the two sides of the jewel were known respectively as Urim and Thummim, one being engraved with the " Ineffable name ", the other being plain. When " inquiring of the Lord ", the priest put his hand in the breastplate and drew out the stone (see 1 *Sam.* 14¹⁹), the verdict being according to which side was uppermost. In this way Eleazer divines for Joshua (*Numb.* 27²¹), Ahiah for Saul (1 *Sam.* 14¹⁸) and Abiathar for David (1 *Sam.* 23⁹). It is a sign of Saul's official degradation that the Lord answered him not by Urim (1 *Sam.* 28⁶). This method of high-priestly divination apparently disappeared with the deposition of Abiathar at the beginning of the reign of Solomon.

Milton (*P.L.* vi, 760, 1) speaks of the Son of God as

" in celestial panoply all arm'd

Of radiant Urim, work divinely wrought,"

(based on the description of Aaron's breastplate, *Ex.* 28³⁰⁻³⁵). So, too, Tennyson (*Coming of Arthur* 298) of Arthur's sword Excalibur,

" rich,with jewels, elfin Urim." i.e. fairy jewellery of awe-inspiring significance.

Van'dals : a confederacy of Gothic peoples who dwelt originally on the N. coast of Germany. In the 4th and 5th centuries A.D., they passed through Germany and Gaul and invaded Spain where they established a powerful kingdom, the name of which still survives in (V)Andalusia. In 429 they crossed into Africa under their King Genseric, the most terrible of all the barbarian invaders. In 535 Belisā'rius, General of Justinian, destroyed the Vandal Kingdom in Africa.

In their conquests the Vandals destroyed vast numbers of books and works of art, especially in Italy. So a ' vandal ' is a term of opprobrium, a barbarian, one opposed to culture in any form. Cf. Goth, Hun.

Va'rius Rū'fus, companion and friend of Virgil and Horace. Virgil made him one of his literary executors.

Va'rrō, Terentius, ' the most learned of the Romans,' was a man of vast and varied erudition and a most voluminous author. Only two of his works survive, one treating of agriculture and the other a grammatical treatise. His greatest work, his *Antiquities*, would have given us valuable information on Roman customs, politics and religion had it survived. He died 28 B.C. at the age of 89.

Věnus, the Roman goddess of gardens and spring flowers, identified later with Aphrodītē as the goddess of love.

The famous statue, the Venus of Milo (or Melos, an island in the

Cyclades group), was found in 1820 near the ruins of the capital of the island. It is housed in the Louvre in Paris.

See **Aphrodite** ; **Praxiteles**.

Verulā'mium (St. Albans), chief town of Cassivellaunus. It was destroyed by the Britons under Boudicca (Boadicea) in their insurrection against the Romans, but was rebuilt and continued to be an important place.

Francis Bacon was first **Baron Verulam** and Viscount **St. Albans**.

Ve'sta, Italian goddess of the blazing hearth, corresponding to the Greek He'stia. The hearth-fire in every home was guarded by the daughters of the household. Vesta's Temple, in the Forum, contained the Sacred Fire which Aeneas was thought to have brought from Troy, the State hearth on which the safety and well-being of the state depended. The Sacred Fire, representing the continuous life of the city, was guarded by Virgin priestesses, the Vestal Virgins, four (or later, six) in number, who were regarded as representing the daughters of the King's household in the same way as the Temple represented his home. If a Vestal was proved guilty of unfaithfulness she was buried alive in a vault in the *Campus Scelerātus* (the " Field of Pollution "), within the city walls. The germ of the cult of Vesta is to be found in the great difficulty experienced by primitive man in obtaining fire and in the consequent veneration with which he regarded it. Let any doubter try to raise fire by the friction of two pieces of wood !

Vesu'vius, the volcano inland from the Bay of Naples. In A.D. 79 there was a most violent eruption from the mountain which over-whelmed Hercula'neum, Pompē'ii and Stăbii. Pliny the younger describes the eruption in a letter to his friend Tacitus. The elder Pliny perished in the disaster.

Victory, statues of.
The early Greeks were realists and regarded the attachment of wings to human figures as something unnatural. Indeed the gem-like Temple of Athene Nī'kē on the Acropolis was called the Temple of Nike Apteros or Wingless Victory. It commemorated the victories of the Greeks over their Persian invaders. In later days a balustrade was placed round the shrine and on it figures of winged Victories were sculptured. These graceful figures are now housed in the Museum on the Acropolis. According to Aristophanes Achernos, a sculptor of the middle sixth century, B.C., was the first to represent Nike with wings. An early statue from the island of Delos, possibly the work of Achernos, is that of a winged female figure kneeling sideways on the left knee, thereby representing rapid sideways motion. The wings on the winged statues would appear to symbolize the headlong rout and the pursuit of a beaten foe, Victory descending from heaven in rushing motion to start the rout.

The two most famous Winged Victories known to us are those found on the island of Samothrace and at Olympia. The former, known as the Winged Victory of Samothrace is now in the Louvre. It represents a figure in rapid motion. The latter, the Nike of Paeō'nius (a fifth century sculptor of Me'ndē in Thrace), is housed in the museum at Olympia. It is a statue of Nike on a high pedestal, the goddess being represented as floating down to earth, trailing all her draperies behind her.

Vine. The vine is frequently referred to in the Bible. Vines of Palestine were (and are) celebrated for their luxuriant growth and their immense clusters of grapes (see *Numb.* 13²³). The vine is a frequent subject of metaphor in Holy Scripture. 'To dwell under one's own vine and fig-tree' is a sign of domestic happiness and peace. Our Lord selected a vine to show the mutual love between Himself and His members. " I am the true vine," He said (*John* 15¹⁻⁶). The vintage season was one of general festivity when the people lived among the vineyards in lodges and tents, somewhat as Kentish ' hoppers' have long done and still do to-day. The grapes were carried in baskets to the wine-press on the head and shoulders or slung upon a yoke. The vineyard was generally on a hill, surrounded by a wall or hedge to keep out wild boars, jackals and foxes. Within the vineyard were towers of stone in

Egyptian Wine-press. Similar wine-presses are still to be seen in Palestine.

which the vine-dressers lived. The wine-presses consisted of two vats, usually hewn out of the solid rock, and were placed at different elevations. In the upper vat the grapes

were trodden, and the lower one received the expressed juice.

See the Parable of the Wicked Husbandmen (*Matt.* 21³³⁻⁴⁶).

Vi′rgil (Publius Vergilius Marō) 70–19 B.C. His father had a small estate and kept bees. After finishing his education Virgil retired to his farm, largely on account of his health. This farm was twice confiscated, once after the battle of Philippi and again later when the poet himself barely escaped being killed. Maecē′nas, a patron of literature and learning and a friend of the Emperor Augustus, helped him to get back his land and encouraged his work as a poet. But Virgil continued to have bad health. He died in his 51st year at Brundisium on his way back from Greece in the company of the Emperor. His chief works were :

(i) *Bucolics* (Herdsmen's Songs) or *Eclogues* (Selections), ten short poems based on the *Idylls* of Theo′critus ;

(ii) *Georgics* or ' Agricultural Poem ', in four books. This poem is generally regarded as Virgil's masterpiece. It was dedicated to his patron Maecenas ;

(iii) *Ae′neid*, an epic in 12 books, on the model of the great Homeric poems. Its real object is to set forth the glories of Rome and, less directly, of the reigning house of Augustus. It is said that Virgil was not satisfied with the poem and in his last illness wished to burn it ; but his friends Varius and Tucca preserved it and published it.

As a boy Tennyson loved Virgil, and in his lines " To Virgil ", written at the request of the Mantuans for the nineteenth centenary of the poet's death, he acknowledges his love :

" I salute thee, Mantovano,

    I that loved thee since my
        day began,

Wielder of the stateliest
measure
ever moulded by the lips of
man."
Let lovers of Virgil either in the
original or in the second-hand read
Tennyson's complete poem which
recalls
(a) the *Aeneid* :
" Roman Virgil, thou that singest
Ilion's lofty temples robed in
fire,
Ilion falling, Rome arising,
wars, and filial faith and
Dido's pyre " ;
(b) the *Georgics* :
" Thou that singest wheat and
woodland,
tilth and vineyard, hive and
horse and herd."

Virgi'nia, daughter of a centurion,
whose beauty urged the decemvir
Appius Claudius to get one of his
clients to claim her as his slave.
" Where'er ye shed the honey, the
buzzing flies will crowd ;
Where'er ye fling the carrion, the
raven's croak is loud ;
Where'er down Tiber garbage
floats, the greedy pike ye see ;
And whereso'er such lord is found,
such client still will be."
Appius himself was the judge !
When her father saw that all hope
for his daughter's safety was gone
he stabbed her, exclaiming : " There
is no way but this to keep thee
free." As a result of this tragedy
the decemvirs were deprived of
their power, Virginia's father was
elected tribune and by his orders
Appius was dragged off to prison
where he put an end to his life.
Macaulay tells the story in one
of his less popular lays, " Virginia."

Vitrū'vius, author of a treatise on
Architecture. It deals with a vast
variety of such interesting things as
sun-dials and water-clocks, but it
is of no great literary value.

Volu'mnia, the proud, aristo-
cratic mother of Coriolanus.

Vu'lcan, the Italian god of fire,
i.e. of destructive fire and not of
the kindly hearth-fire. In literature
he is entirely identified with Hephaestus.
See **Hephaestus.**

Vulgate, the Latin version of the
Bible prepared in the fourth century by St. Jerome. A later edition,
published under Clement VIII in
1593, is still the official version of
the Roman Catholic Church. It
may claim to have exercised a
wider influence on the Christian
Church than any other version, or
even than the original Greek and
Hebrew.
A new authorised translation of
the Vulgate, of which the New
Testament appeared in 1946, is in
process of being made by Monseig-
neur Knox.

Watches, of the Night. A division
of time, probably of military origin.
(a) In O.T. times the night was
divided into three watches : (i)
from sunset till about 10 o'clock ;
(ii) the " middle watch " (*Judges*
7[19]), till about 2 a.m. ; (iii) the
" morning watch " (1 *Sam.* 11[11]),
till sunrise.
(b) In the Greek and Roman
periods there were four watches,
and this was the division of the
night in our Lord's time : (i) *Even*,
6–9 p.m. (cf. *Mark* 11[11]) ; (ii) *Mid-
night*, 9–12 ; (iii) *Cockcrowing*, 12–3
a.m. ; (iv) *Morning*, 3–6 a.m. (cf.
John 18[27]).
See *Mark* 13[35] where the four
night watches are mentioned in
order.

Wedding-garment. See the
Parable of the Wedding Feast
(*Matt.* 22[1-14]), and in particular
the last three verses. The parable

shows the unworthiness of the Jewish leaders to share in the joys of the Advent of the King.

Charles Lamb, in "The Praise of Chimney-Sweepers," refers to "one unfortunate wight who, relying upon his dusky suit, had intruded himself into our party [a solemn supper to the master-sweeps in and about London], but by tokens was providentially discovered in time to be no chimney-sweep, was quoited out of the presence . . . as not having on the wedding-garment," i.e. because he did not wear the sweep's garb.

Weighed in the Balance.
See **Writing on the Wall**.

Whitsunday, i.e. White Sunday, the 7th Sunday after Easter. Possibly it was "so called from the white garments worn at baptisms usually celebrated at this time" (Weekly). The Jewish feast of Pentecost (Greek = 50th) was held on the 50th day after the Passover. In the Christian Church the significance of Pentecost was enhanced by the outpouring of the Holy Ghost upon the disciples (*Acts*, 2). We read : " there appeared to them tongues parting asunder, like as of fire, and it sat upon each of them . . . and they began to speak with other tongues, as the spirit gave them utterance." The Pentecostal gift of tongues is difficult to explain because it is not clearly defined. Greek and Aramaic would have been understood by almost all Jews present, no matter whence they came. Bystanders, in accusing the disciples of drunkenness, showed that the speech was not of an intelligible nature, and the Apostles possessed no permanent gift of speaking foreign languages. The gift probably implied the ability to overcome the roughness of Galilean speech and to utter ecstatic prayers to and praises of God while in a state of high spiritual tension.

Widow's Cruse, The. In a time of famine and drought Elijah was fed at the brook Cherith night and morning by ravens. When the brook dried up God told Elijah to go to Zarephath where a widow woman would sustain him. She had only " an handful of meal in a barrel and a little oil in a cruse." Elijah rewarded her by promising : " The meal shall not waste neither shall the cruse of oil fail until the day that the Lord sendeth rain upon the earth." (1 *Kings* 17).

Metaphorically, a " widow's cruse of oil " is an unfailing supply. Cf. the medieval romance of the beggar Fortunatus and his inexhaustible purse.

Wilderness.

(*a*) Moses stated in *Numb.* 14^{32} and elsewhere : " Your children shall wander in the wilderness forty years." Nowadays, " to wander in the wilderness " refers politically to a party out of office and seeking to regain power.

(*b*) In the Wilderness of Judaea John the Baptist preached repentance : " The voice of one crying in the wilderness " (from *Isaiah* 40^{3-5}). Metaphorically, " a voice in the wilderness " is an unheeded reformer or advocate of a new course of action. Mr. Churchill spoke of himself as " a voice crying in the wilderness " when his warnings about the growing might of Germany went unheeded for years.

Winds (Lat. *Ventī*). The ruler of all the winds is Ae'olus who resides in the island Aeolia ; but the other gods also, especially Zeus, exercise a power over them. Homer mentions by name Bŏrĕas (N. wind),

Eurus (E.), Nŏtus (or Auster, S. wind), and Zĕphўrus (or Favŏnius), W. wind. St. Luke mentions the Euraquilo, (A.V. Euroclydon) a stormy NE. wind (*Acts* 27[14]). In Athens there is a remarkable monument representing the winds, the so-called " Tower of the Winds." It is an octagonal tower, each of its sides representing one of the eight principal winds in a flying attitude. A bronze Triton mounted on the top acted as a weather-cock, a wand in his hand pointing to the direction of the wind blowing at the time.

Wolf in Sheep's Clothing, one who deliberately disguises his rapacity in order the easier to deceive the innocent. Christ uses the figure (*Matt.* 7[15]) of " false prophets " who could disguise their real nature by adopting the accepted dress of the genuine prophet.

Wonders, Seven, of the Ancient World.
The Pyramids of Egypt.
The Hanging Gardens of Nebuchadnezzar at Babylon.
The Temple of Diana at Ephesus.
Pheidias' Statue of Olympian Zeus at Olympia.
The Mausoleum at Halicarnassus.
The Colossus of Rhodes.
The Pharos Lighthouse off Alexandria.

Writing on the Wall. *Daniel* v tells the story of Belshazzar's impious feast. Belshazzar, the last native King of Babylon, entertained his wives and friends on the night in which Darius the Median took Babylon, when " they brought the golden vessels that were taken out of the temple of the House of God which was in Jerusalem, and they drank in them." All at once a mysterious hand appeared writing, apparently in Aramaic characters, on the palace wall. The astrologers could not read the writing, so Belshazzar in his frenzy promised that the interpreter of the words should be the third ruler in his kingdom. At the queen's request Daniel was brought in " to shew the interpretation " of the words. He explained one of the three mysterious words, TEKEL, as " thou art weighed in the balance and art found wanting."
Read Byron's " Vision of Belshazzar " and his " Ode to Napoleon Buonaparte," ll. 100, 101 :
" Weigh'd in the balance, hero dust
   Is vile as vulgar clay."
In general, the " writing on the wall " is a clear warning that retribution is on the way. Cf. *Punch's* magnificent cartoon of the hand tracing " Bikini " on the wall, just before the American test of the atom bomb in the Pacific atoll (1946).

Xanthi′ppē, the proverbially peevish and quarrelsome wife of the Greek philosopher Socrates.
" Be she
As old as Sibyl and as curst and
   shrewd
As Socrates' Xantippe,"
the heiress Katharina, despite " her scolding tongue ", would be welcomed by Petruchio as his wife. (*The Taming of the Shrew.*)

Xa′nthus (i) Homer's name (i.e. Yellow River, probably from the silt it carried down) for the river Scamander of the Troad.
(ii) One of Achilles' horses (the other was Balius = piebald, dappled).
" Auto′medon the charioteer put to the pair of horses, Chestnut and Bay, whose sire was the West Wind, and their dam the Harpy Quickfoot " (Rouse : *Achilles*). Xanthus had the power of human speech and prophesied his master's death :

" Your day of death is near. It is no fault of ours, but the will of God and of Fate." So spoke Xanthus (or Chestnut) to Achilles as he was going out with Agamemnon and the other Achaean leaders to battle against the Trojans.

Xe'nophon (c. 430–c. 355 B.C.), an Athenian, a pupil of Socrates and an historian. He joined the expedition of Cyrus the Younger against the Persian King Artaxerxes. The Greeks were left alone on the wide plains between the Tigris and the Euphrates and some of their commanders had been treacherously murdered by the Persian satrap (or viceroy) Tissaphe'rnēs when Xenophon took charge and led them in their memorable retreat along the Tigris to Trapezus (Trebizond) on the Black Sea. Xenophon was greatly embittered by the execution of his old master Socrates, so he joined the Spartans in their fight against the Persians and later against Athens. As a result he was exiled from Athens and settled in Elis near Olympia. Here he spent twenty years hunting, writing his books and entertaining his friends. When he was expelled by the Eleans he is said to have retired to Corinth where he died. His principal works were :

(i) The *Ana'basis*, his simple, candid account of the Greek retreat;

(ii) The *Hellē'nica*, a valuable but baldly expressed continuation of the history of Thucydides ;

(iii) The *Memorābi'lia*, in defence of Socrates ;

(iv) The *Cȳ'ropoedī'a*, a sort of political romance based on the history of Cyrus the Younger.

Xe'rxes. King of Persia 485–465 B.C. In his attacks on Greece he crossed the Hellespont by a bridge of boats, marched through Thrace and Macedonia, and is said to have reached Thermŏ'pўlae with an incredible army of well over two and a half million men. At length he reached Athens and his fleet arrived at Phalē'ron. Xerxes witnessed the battle of Salamis from a lofty seat especially erected for him and saw his mighty fleet defeated and dispersed. He fled back to Asia with all speed. He was murdered by Artabā'nus, commander of his own bodyguard, with a view of setting himself on the throne of Persia.

Zē'no, founder of the Stoic philosophy, was a native of Cyprus. After studying twenty years he opened his ' school ' in Athens in the porch called *Sto'a Poikilē* or Painted Colonnade, whence his followers were called Stoics.

Ze'phyrus, the personification of the West wind. He and the Harpy

Zephyrus. (*From the Temple of the Winds at Athens*). *She is carrying spring flowers.*

Podargē (= Quickfoot) were the parents of the two immortal horses of Achilles, Xa'nthus and Ba'lius (= Chestnut and Piebald).

Zeus, the greatest of the Greek gods, primarily the god of the sky. He is the son of Cronus and Rhea, brother of Poseidon, Pluto, Hestia, Demeter and Hera, and is married to his sister Hera. According to the Homeric account Zeus dwelt on Mt. Olympus in Thessaly, which was believed to penetrate with its lofty summit into heaven itself. He is the supreme ruler who with his counsel managed everything. He is armed with thunder and lightning and the shaking of his

Head of the Olympian Zeus. (*From a bust in the Vatican*). *His statue at Olympia was the work of Pheidias.*

aegis (or shield) produces storm and tempest. In his association with mortal women he assumed various disguises : he visited Da′naë in a shower of gold, Leda as a swan, Europa as a bull. At Olympia in Elis was the sacred precinct of Zeus, with the great altar and temple in which stood originally the statue of Olympian Zeus in gold and

ivory by Pheidias. The eagle, the oak and the summits of mountains were sacred to him, and his attributes are the sceptre, the eagle and the thunderbolt. The Roman Jupiter, to whom the Greek myths relating to Zeus were transferred, was identified with him.

See **Jupiter** ; **Titans** ; **Cyclopes** ; **Typhoeus**.

Zeū′xis, native of Heraclēa in S. Italy, a Greek painter of the fifth century B.C. His masterpiece was the picture of Helen, painted for the temple of Hera at Crŏtōn in Magna Graecia. The accurate painting of ' still life ' Zeuxis and his younger rival Parrha′sius appear to have carried almost to perfection. In a contest between the two the picture of Zeuxis represented a bunch of grapes, so naturally painted that the birds flew at the picture to eat the fruit. Thereupon Zeuxis called upon his rival no longer to delay to draw aside the curtain and show his picture. But the picture of Parrhasius was the curtain itself which Zeuxis had mistaken for real drapery. On discovering his error Zeuxis owned himself defeated, saying that he himself had deceived birds but Parrhasius had deceived an artist.

Ziggurats. Temple-towers of Sumeria or Lower Babylonia. See **Babel**.

APPENDIX A.

A SHORT BIBLIOGRAPHY

World's Manuals. O.U.P.
{ Israel before Christ. Blunt
Israel in World History. Blunt
Ancient Greece. Casson
Growth of Rome. Matheson
Greek Art and Architecture. Gardner & Blomfield
The Writers of Greece. Norwood
The Writers of Rome. J. W. Duff

A. W. F. Blunt : The Ancient World and its Legacy to us. O.U.P.
M. A. Hamilton : Greece. O.U.P.
Hamilton and Luce : Rome. O.U.P.
Hamilton and Blunt : An Outline of Ancient History. O.U.P.
Breasted : { Ancient Times. Ginn
Brief Outline of Ancient Times. Ginn
H. B. Cotterill : Ancient Greece (Great Nations). Harrap
Caiger : Bible and Spade. O.U.P.
Hammerton : Universal History of the World (8 vv.). Amalgamated Press
M. R. James : Our Hellenic Heritage. Macmillan
Rice Holmes : Caesar's Conquest of Gaul.
Cary and Warmington : Ancient Explorers. (Methuen, 12/6).
Sir J. G. Frazer : The Golden Bough. (One vol. abridgement.
Macmillan 18/-).

Tenen : The Ancient World. Macmillan
P. C. Sands : Literary Genius of O.T. O.U.P.
Grose-Hodge : Roman Panorama. (Camb. Press)
Rogers and Harley : Roman Home Life and Religion. O.U.P.
Dora Pym : { Readings from the Literature of Ancient Rome. Harrap
Readings from the Literature of Ancient Greece. ,,
Todd : The Ancient World. Hodder & Stoughton
T. R. Glover : The Ancient World. Penguin Books
J. C. Stobart : { The Glory that was Greece. Sidgwick and Jackson
The Grandeur that was Rome. ,, ,,
Gayley : Classical Myths in English Literature. Ginn
Stuart Jones : Roman Empire. (Story of the Nations). Fisher Unwin
Ward Fowler : Caesar. (Heroes of the Nations). Putnams
Rattey : { The Growth and Structure of the Gospel. Oxford
A Short History of the Hebrews. ,,
Allen : A Short Introduction to the Old Testament. ,,
Treble and King : Everyday Life in Rome. ,,
Robinson : Everyday Life in Ancient Greece. ,,
Walker : Introducing the Bible. Dent.

Cambridge Manuals :
    Dr. Brown : The History of the English Bible.
    Dr. Haddon : The Wanderings of Peoples.
    Dr. Sheppard : Greek Tragedy.
    Prof. Macalister : A History of Civilization in Palestine.
Home University Library. Oxford University Press. 3/6 each.
    G. Murray : Euripides and his Age.
    C. M. Bowra : Ancient Greek Literature.
    J. L. Myers : The Dawn of History.
    D. G. Hogarth : The Ancient East.
    Wallis Budge : Egypt.
    W. W. Fowler : Rome.
    F. Moore : The Literature of the Old Testament.
    Bacon : The Making of the New Testament.
    Burkett : Our Forerunners.
    R. Munro : Prehistoric Britain.
Grundy : Classical Atlas. (John Murray).
John Buchan : { Augustus Caesar. (Hodder & Stoughton).
                { Julius Caesar. (Nelson's ' Short Biographies ').
Collingwood : Roman Britain.

APPENDIX B.

SELECT LIST OF TRANSLATIONS THAT ARE THEMSELVES LITERATURE.

Sir Thomas North : Plutarch's Lives, 1559.
Philemon Holland : Livy, 1600. Suetonius, 1603.
William Adlington : Apuleius, 1566 [in Loeb Library].
    { See *Tudor Translations,* an anthology chosen by Judge Clements.
        Blackwell, 1940.
    { W. W. Skeat's *Shakespeare's Plutarch* (Macmillan) or
    { R. H. Carr's *Four Lives from North's Plutarch.* (Oxford Press).
P. B. Shelley : Cyclops.
R. Browning : Balaustion's Adventure.
J. W. Mackail : Odyssey (verse). Aeneid (prose).
W. Morris : Aeneid, Odyssey (both in verse).
Butcher and Lang : Odyssey.
Lang, Leaf and Myers : Iliad.
Ramsey : Tacitus.
B. Jowett : Thucydides. (Oxford Press).
             The Four ' Socratic Dialogues.' (Oxford Press).
J. E. Flecker : Some Catullus and Meleager.
Headlam : Meleager.
Chapman : Elizabethan translation of Homer in rhyming verse, which
             inspired Keats's famous sonnet.
B. B. Rogers : Aristophanes. (3 vv. in Loeb Library).
             (Some of the plays are published in single volumes,
             Bell, 2/-).
C. S. Calverley : Theocritus and some Odes of Horace.
A. Lang : Theocritus, Bion, Moschus (prose). (Macmillan).

F. J. Church : The Trial and Death of Socrates. (Macmillan).
E. C. Wickham : Horace. (Oxford Press).
H. W. and F. G. Fowler : Lucian. (Oxford Press).
Lewis Campbell : Aeschylus, Sophocles (verse). (World's Classics).
J. H. Frere : Aristophanes, four plays. (World's Classics).
Rawlinson : Herodotus. (Everyman).
A. D. Godley : Herodotus (4 vv. in Loeb Library).
A. S. Way : Apollonius' *Argonautica.*
Cornish and Postgate : Catullus and Tibullus (Loeb Library).
Gilbert Murray's Verse Translations of
    (a) Euripides : *Alcestis, Bacchae, Electra, Hippolytus, Iphigenia in Tauris, Medea, Rhesus, Trojan Women.*
    (b) Aeschylus : *Agamemnon, Choephorae, Eumenides, Persae, Prometheus Vinctus, Seven Against Thebes, Suppliant Women.*
    (c) Sophocles : *Oedipus Rex.*
    (d) Aristophanes : *Frogs.* (All Allen and Unwin).
Fairfax Taylor : Virgil (in Spenserian stanzas). (Everyman).
Jebb : Bacchylides (a lyric poet of the 5th century) whose *Odes* were discovered in 1897.
Greek Anthology : Selection, tr. by J. W. Mackail (Longmans).
Rouse : Iliad and Odyssey, tr. into plain English. (Nelson, 7/6 each).

Special reference must be made to two excellent series : (i) The Loeb Classical Library of Translations of Greek and Latin Authors (Heinemann) 12/6 per vol. (ii) Oxford Library of Translations, 5/– per vol.

APPENDIX C.

SOME HISTORICAL NOVELS

[With due acknowledgements to Nield's *Guide to the best Historical Novels and Tales* (Mathews and Marrot)].
A. **Junior.**
    Henty : The Young Carthaginian. (Blackie).
           The Cat of Bubastes. (Blackie).
    Snedeker : The Spartan. (Hodder).
           Theras. (Dent).
    Church : Two Thousand Years Ago. (Blackie).
    Church and Putnam : The Count of the Saxon Shore. (Seeley).
    Kipling : Puck of Pook's Hill. (Macmillan).
    Harraden : Untold Tales of the Past. (Dent).
                    How Phidias Helped the Image Maker.
                    The Garland of Wild Olive.
                    A True Spartan Heart.
                    How Livia Won the Brooch.
                    The Vestal Virgins.
                    The Eve of Caesar's Triumph.

B. **Senior.**

Abbott : Onesimus. (Macmillan).
     Silanus the Christian. (Black).
Lew Wallace : Ben Hur.
Mitchison : The Conquered. (Cape).
Gilkes : Kallistratus. (Longmans).
Stacpoole : The Street of the Flute-Player. (John Murray).
Atherton : The Immortal Marriage. (John Murray).
Snedeker : The Perilous Seat. (Methuen).
Davis : A Victor of Salamis. (Macmillan).
Ebers : An Egyptian Princess. (Sampson Low).
A. J. Baker : Tyrian Purple. (Leng).
Graves : I, Claudius. (Penguin).
     Claudius the God. (Penguin).
Rider Haggard : Moon of Israel. (John Murray).
" R. Eustace " : The Hidden Treasures of Egypt. (Simpkins).
Sienkiewicz : Quo Vadis ? (Dent).
Whyte Melville : The Gladiators. (Ward Lock).
Lytton : The Last Days of Pompeii.
Newman : Callistes. (Longmans).
Mitchell : Spartacus.
Kingsley : Hypatia.
Lister : These Four Shall Die.
Erskine : The Private Life of Helen of Troy. (Nash).
Conan Doyle : The Last Galley. (John Murray).
Glazebrook : Nicanor of Athens. (Camb. Press).